DISCARD

Goethe's Way of Science

SUNY Series in Environmental and Architectural Phenomenology

David Seamon, editor

The SUNY Series in Environmental and Architectural Phenomenology presents authored and edited volumes that emphasize a qualitative, descriptive approach to architectural and environmental experience and behavior. A key concern is scholarship, education, planning, and design that support and enhance natural and built environments that are beautiful, alive, and humane. A clear conceptual stance is integral to informed research and design, and the series gives first priority to phenomenological and hermeneutical approaches to the environment but also sponsors other styles of qualitative, interpretive research.

Volumes in the series include:

- David Seamon, editor, *Dwelling, Seeing, and Designing: Toward a Phenomenological Ecology* (1993).
- Robert Mugerauer, *Interpretations on Behalf of Place: Environmental Displacements and Alternative Responses* (1994).
- Louise Chawla, *In the First Country of Places: Nature, Poetry, and Childhood Memory* (1994).

Goethe's Way of Science

A Phenomenology of Nature

EDITED BY

DAVID SEAMON

ARTHUR ZAJONC

STATE UNIVERSITY OF NEW YORK PRESS

Chapter 8, "Horns, Hooves, Spots, and Stripes: Form and Pattern in Mammals," by Mark Riegner is an extended version of an article by the same title published in *Orion Nature Quarterly* 4, no. 4 (Autumn, 1985):22–35. The article is reprinted with the permission of *Orion Nature Quarterly*. Chapter 8 also includes several illustrations by Fiona A. Reid from *A Field Guide to Mammals Coloring Book* by Peter Alden. Copyright ©1987 by Houghton Mifflin Company. Reprinted by permission of Houghton Mifflin Company. All rights reserved.

Chapter 10, "Flowforms and the Language of Water," by Mark Riegner and John Wilkes, is a revised version of an article, "Art in the Service of Nature: The Story of Flowforms," published in *Orion Nature Quarterly* 7, no. 1 (Winter, 1988):50–57. The article is reprinted with the permission of *Orion Nature Quarterly*.

Chapter 12, "Counterfeit and Authentic Wholes: Finding a Means of Dwelling in Nature," by Henri Bortoft was originally published in *Dwelling, Place and Environment*, edited by D. Seamon and R. Mugerauer (Dordrecht: Martinus Nijhoff, 1985), pp. 281–302. The article is reprinted with the permission of Kluwer Academic Publishers and Martinus Nijhoff Publishers. ©1985 by Martinus Nijhoff Publishers, Dordrecht, the Netherlands.

Chapter 13, "Light and Cognition: Goethean Studies as a Science of the Future," by Arthur Zajonc, is a slightly amended version of an article, "Light and Cognition: The Imperatives of Science," originally published in W. I. Thompson, ed., *Gaia* 2 (Hudson, N.Y.: Lindisfarne Press, 1991), pp. 111–31. The article is used by permission of Lindisfarne Press, Hudson, N.Y. 12534.

Published by
State University of New York Press

©1998 State University of New York

Printed in the United States of America

For information, address the State University of New York Press,
State University Plaza, Albany, NY 12246

Production by David Ford
Marketing by Patrick Durocher

Library of Congress Cataloging-In-Publication Data

Goethe's way of science : a phenomenology of nature / edited by David Seamon, Arthur Zajonc.
   p. cm. — (Suny series in environmental and architectural phenomenology)
   Includes bibliographical references and index.
   ISBN 0-7914-3681-0 (hc : alk. paper). — ISBN 0-7914-3682-9 (pb : alk. paper)
   1. Goethe, Johann Wolfgang von, 1749–1832—Knowledge—Science. 2. Science—History—18th century. 3. Science—History—19th century. 4. Philosophy of nature—History—18th century. 5. Philosophy of nature—History—19th century. 6. Phenomenology--History—18th century. 7. Phenomenology—History—19th century. I. Seamon, David. II. Zajonc, Arthur. III. Series.
   Q143.G53G64   1998
   501—dc21   97-15660
                                                                            CIP

10 9 8 7 6 5 4 3 2 1

CONTENTS

List of Figures   vii

Preface   xi

Goethe, Nature, and Phenomenology: An Introduction   1
David Seamon

1. Goethe and the Science of His Time:
An Historical Introduction   15
Arthur Zajonc

PART I. GOETHEAN SCIENCE: PHILOSOPHICAL FOUNDATIONS

2. The Metamorphosis of the Scientist   33
Frederick Amrine

3. Goethean Science   55
Walter Heitler

4. Goethe, Science, and Sensory Experience   71
Herbert Hensel

5. The Idea in Nature: Rereading Goethe's Organics   83
Ronald H. Brady

PART II. DOING GOETHEAN SCIENCE

6. Transformations in the Foliage Leaves
of the Higher Plants   115
Jochen Bockemühl

7. The Unity of Science and Art:
Goethean Phenomenology as a New Ecological Discipline   129
Nigel Hoffmann

8. Horns, Hooves, Spots, and Stripes:
   Form and Pattern in Mammals   177
   Mark Riegner

9. Seeing the Animal Whole:
   The Example of the Horse and Lion   213
   Craig Holdrege

10. Flowforms and the Language of Water   233
    Mark Riegner and John Wilkes

PART III. THE FUTURE OF GOETHEAN SCIENCE

11. The Resurrection of Thinking and the Redemption of Faust:
    Goethe's New Scientific Attitude   255
    Alan P. Cottrell

12. Counterfeit and Authentic Wholes:
    Finding a Means for Dwelling in Nature   277
    Henri Bortoft

13. Light and Cognition:
    Goethean Studies as a Science of the Future   299
    Arthur Zajonc

Contributors   315

Index   319

LIST OF FIGURES

Fig. 5.1.   What does one see in this figure?

Fig. 5.2.   Leaves taken from the common buttercup (*Ranunculus acris*)

Fig. 5.3.   Two leaves from the sequence of common-buttercup leaves in figure 5.2

Fig. 6.1.   Development of one of the first leaves of Pennsylvania bittercress (*Cardamine hirsuta*)

Fig. 6.2.   Development of one of the first leaves of ground ivy (*Glechoma hederacea*)

Fig. 6.3.   Mature leaf sequence of corn salad (*Valerianella locusta*)

Fig. 6.4.   Mature leaf sequence of Pennsylvania bittercress, from seed leaf to flower

Fig. 6.5.   Mature leaf sequence of alfalfa (*Medicago sativa*)

Fig. 6.6.   Developmental movement of all the leaves of the hedge mustard (*Sisymbrium officinale*)

Fig. 6.7.   Leaf series of nipplewort (*Lapsana communis*)

Fig. 6.8.   The embryonic development of individual leaves for the nipplewort

Fig. 6.9.   Developmental movement of the leaves of nipplewort

Fig. 7.1.   *Kunzea ambigua*—Flowering branch

Fig. 7.2.   *Kunzea ambigua*—"First impression"

Fig. 7.3.   *Kunzea ambigua*—Three aspects of the plant

Fig. 7.4.   *Kunzea ambigua*—Central stem of shrub

Fig. 7.5.   *Kunzea ambigua*—View of branches (not in flower)

Fig. 7.6.   *Kunzea ambigua*—Flower heads showing bunched structure

Fig. 7.7.   *Kunzea ambigua*—General view of shrub (not in flower)

Fig. 7.8.   *Kunzea ambigua*—Metamorphic sequence

Fig. 7.9.   *Kunzea ambigua*—Gesture sketch

Fig. 7.10. *Kunzea ambigua*—Image of flower as plant "theory"

Fig. 7.11. *Banksia integrifolia*—Flowering branch of immature tree

Fig. 7.12. *Banksia integrifolia*—"First impression"

Fig. 7.13. *Banksia integrifolia*—seedling and slightly more advanced plant

Fig. 7.14. *Banksia integrifolia*—Bark of immature tree
Fig. 7.15. *Banksia integrifolia*—Immature tree
Fig. 7.16. *Banksia integrifolia*—Bark of mature tree
Fig. 7.17. *Banksia integrifolia*—General view of mature tree
Fig. 7.18. *Banksia integrifolia*—Leaf configuration of a very young tree
Fig. 7.19. *Banksia integrifolia*—Leaf whorl of immature tree
Fig. 7.20. *Banksia integrifolia*—General view of environment with immature trees
Fig. 7.21. *Banksia integrifolia*—Metamorphic sequence of leaves
Fig. 7.22. *Banksia integrifolia*—Metamorphic sequence
Fig. 7.23. *Banksia integrifolia*—Gesture sketch
Fig. 7.24. *Banksia integrifolia*—Image of flower as plant "theory"
Fig. 8.1. Skulls of human; carnivore; rodent; and ungulate
Fig. 8.2. Representative mammals: harvest mouse—a rodent; bison—an ungulate; leopard—a carnivore
Fig. 8.3. Perissodactyls: African wild ass; white rhinoceros; Brazilian tapir
Fig. 8.4. Nonruminant artiodactyls: white-lipped peccary; hippopotamus; wild boar
Fig. 8.5. Pygmy hippopotamus
Fig. 8.6. Ruminant artiodactyls: guanaco; yak; chevrotain
Fig. 8.7. Bactrian camel
Fig. 8.8. Heads of black rhinoceros; wart hog; and Scottish highland cattle
Fig. 8.9. Giraffe
Fig. 8.10. White-tailed deer fawn; and buck
Fig. 8.11. Moose calf; and bull
Fig. 8.12. Comparison of gazelle with black wildebeest
Fig. 8.13. Pronghorn
Fig. 8.14. Mountain goat; and bighorn sheep
Fig. 8.15. Muskox
Fig. 8.16. Water buffalo
Fig. 8.17. Threefold relationships among ungulates
Fig. 8.18. Beaver
Fig. 8.19. Capybara
Fig. 8.20. Paca
Fig. 8.21. Least weasel
Fig. 8.22. Lion
Fig. 8.23. Steller sea lion
Fig. 8.24 Walrus
Fig. 8.25. Comparison of gorilla with cotton-top marmoset
Fig. 9.1. *Sus babirusa*
Fig. 9.2. Skeleton of the horse

Fig. 9.3. Skeleton of the lion
Fig. 9.4. Forelimb of horse and lion
Fig. 9.5. Detail of the lower forelimb of horse and lion
Fig. 9.6. Skull of horse
Fig. 9.7. Skull of lion
Fig. 9.8. Silhouette of horse and lion
Fig. 10.1. A train of vortices
Fig. 10.2. Leaf metamorphosis in the Small Scabious
Fig. 10.3. Diagram showing the influence of streaming water on a straight channel
Fig. 10.4. Schematic representation
Fig. 10.5. The "Malmö" Flowform
Fig. 10.6. Diagram of water movement in the radial "Ashdown" Flowform
Fig. 10.7. The "Amsterdam" Flowform
Fig. 10.8. The "Rocker" Flowform
Fig. 10.9. The "Akalla" Flowform
Fig. 10.10. A purification system for comparative research
Fig. 10.11. Original concept for a sevenfold Flowform cascade
Fig. 10.12. Diagram of the transformation of the lemniscate
Fig. 10.13. The Sevenfold Flowform Cascade II
Fig. 10.14. Diagram of the Sevenfold Flowform Cascade II at Chalice Well, Glastonbury, England
Fig. 13.1. The "Particle Test"
Fig. 13.2. The "Wave Test"
Fig. 13.3. The "Delayed-choice Experiment"

PREFACE

Relatively few people know that the eminent German poet and playwright Johann Wolfgang von Goethe (1749–1832) also produced a sizable body of scientific work that focused on such topics as plants, color, clouds, weather, and geology. Goethe's way of science is highly unusual because it seeks to draw together the intuitive awareness of art with the rigorous observation and thinking of science. The fourteen essays of this collection, written by major scholars and practitioners of Goethean science today, consider the philosophical foundations of Goethe's approach and apply the method to the real world of nature, including studies of plants, animals, and the movement of water.

The idea for this volume first arose in the late 1970s during a conversation in Ann Arbor, Michigan, among Arthur Zajonc, Alan P. Cottrell, and Frederick Amrine. Zajonc was studying Goethe's *Theory of Color* and had just finished a paper on his methodology. Cottrell was an established scholar with a special interest in the relationship between Goethe's scientific and literary work. Amrine was developing a wide knowledge of the existing literature on Goethean science.

These three men agreed there should be a volume that not only looked retrospectively at the historical significance of Goethe's work, but also examined contemporary and potential contributions. The volume seemed especially warranted in a time when ecological concerns and the reexamination of science and technology were becoming important scholarly issues.

Nearly twenty years have passed since that Ann Arbor conversation. Cottrell died in 1984, shortly after writing his contribution to the envisioned volume. Several additional articles were solicited for the collection, but problems with potential publishers slowed and then stopped progress.

The partial manuscript languished in a file cabinet until 1993 when Zajonc asked David Seamon if he could help in some way to get the manuscript completed. Having briefly studied Goethean science in England with physicist Henri Bortoft in the early 1970s, Seamon was eager to assist because he saw in Goethe's method a way of approaching the natural world phenomenologically. He realized the collection would make an ideal addition to his State University of New York Press monograph series, "Environmental and Architectural Phenomenology."

As a result, Seamon took on the task of helping Zajonc to complete the collection. In the several years since the volume had been envisioned, younger scholars like Mark Riegner, Nigel Hoffmann, and Craig Holdrege had produced innovative Goethean research that the editors felt should be represented in a revised collection. At the same time, the editors realized the importance of including recent work by some of the longer-established researchers and practitioners like Henri Bortoft, Ronald H. Brady, Jochen Bockemühl, and John Wilkes. As a result, the editors kept only four essays from the original manuscript—Zajonc's historical introduction, Cottrell's chapter, and chapters by Walter Heitler, and Herbert Hensel. These latter two essays, both written in the 1960s, were deemed important because they set the stage for a more contemporary engagement with Goethean science as presented in the other, more recent, essays in the collection.

The resulting volume, we hope, is an in-depth picture of the conceptual and applied state of Goethean science today. We have striven to balance classic philosophical treatments of Goethe's work with more recent examples of how his ideas continue to influence science and related areas like the phenomenology of nature and the philosophy of science.

In completing this volume, we are grateful to Danita Deters, who skillfully dealt with keyboarding and reformatting needs. At State University of New York Press, we are grateful for the attentive assistance from Clay Morgan, Lara Stelmaszyk, Katy Leonard, Judy Spevack, and David Ford. Finally, we must thank Aina Barten, who, as Zajonc's personal assistant, has worked as diligently as the editors in making sure this volume would be completed. Aina has copyedited drafts of chapters, reformatted references, and offered steady encouragement for the importance of Goethean science and this book. Without her generosity, thoughtfulness, and faith, the collection would still be unfinished.

As we have worked on this book, our conviction has grown that Goethe's contributions to science will prove crucial for its future development, especially in areas where the qualitative dimensions of the world must be recognized. Goethe developed a method to encounter and understand the natural world more directly, intuitively, and intimately. This approach promises much for strengthening our love of nature and for helping us to better care for the natural environment and earth.

David Seamon and Arthur Zajonc

David Seamon

Goethe, Nature, and Phenomenology

An Introduction

Johann Wolfgang von Goethe (1749–1832) is best known for his poetry and plays, described by many literary critics as some of the most per-ceptive and evocative imaginative literature ever written. Fewer people realize, however, that Goethe also produced a sizable body of scientific work that focused on such diverse topics as plants, color, clouds, weather, morphology, and geology. Goethe believed that these studies, rather than his literary work, would some day be recognized as his greatest contribution to humankind.[1]

In its time, Goethe's way of science was highly unusual because it moved away from a quantitative, materialist approach to things in nature and emphasized, instead, an intimate, firsthand encounter between student and thing studied. Direct experiential contact became the basis for scientific generalization and understanding. Goethe's contemporaries and several following generations, however, largely ignored his writings on nature. These works were seen either as subjective artistic descriptions written by a scientific dilettante or as a form of philosophical idealism that arbitrarily imposed intellectual constructs on the things of nature. Only in the twentieth century, with the philosophical articulation of phenomenology, do we have a conceptual language able to describe Goethe's way of science accurately. Though there are many styles of *phenomenology*, its central aim, in the words of phenomenological founder Edmund Husserl, is "to the things themselves"—in other words, how would the thing studied describe itself if it had the ability to speak?[2]

In this sense, phenomenology is the exploration and description of phenomena, where *phenomena* are the things or experiences as human beings experience them. Phenomenology is a science of beginnings that demands a thorough, in-depth study of the phenomenon, which must be seen and described as clearly as possible. Accurate description is not a phenomenological end, however, but a means by which the phenomenologist locates the phenomenon's deeper, more generalizable patterns, structures, and meanings.[3] Rephrased in phenomenological language, Goethe's way of science is one early example of a phenomenology of the natural world. He sought a way to open himself to the things of nature, to listen to what they said, and to identify their core aspects and qualities.

The present volume is one contribution toward making Goethe's style of phenomenological science better known. Coeditor Arthur Zajonc and I hope the following essays will help to demonstrate the invaluable assistance that a Goethean science might offer today for better understanding and caring for the natural environment. In this introduction, I review the nature of Goethe's way of science and then overview the essays in the collection. Finally, I briefly discuss the link between Goethean science and environmental phenomenology.[4]

DELICATE EMPIRICISM

One phrase that Goethe used to describe his method was *delicate empiricism* (*zarte Empirie*)—the effort to understand a thing's meaning through prolonged empathetic looking and seeing grounded in direct experience.[5] He sought to use firsthand encounter directed in a kindly but rigorous way to know the thing *in itself.* "Natural objects," he wrote, "should be sought and investigated as they are and not to suit observers, but respectfully as if they were divine beings."[6] Goethe believed that, too often, the methods and recording instruments of conventional science separate the student from the thing studied and lead to an arbitrary or inaccurate understanding:

> It is a calamity that the use of experiment has severed nature from man, so that he is content to understand nature merely through what artificial instruments reveal and by so doing even restricts her achievements. . . . Microscopes and telescopes, in actual fact, confuse man's innate clarity of mind.[7]

Rather than remove himself from the thing, Goethe sought to encounter it intimately through the educable powers of human perception: "The human being himself, to the extent that he makes sound use of his senses, is the most exact physical apparatus that can exist."[8] Goethe's aim was to bring this potential perceptual power to bear on a particular phenomenon and thereby better see and understand it. "One instance, he wrote, "is often worth a thousand, bearing all within itself."[9] His way of investigation sought to guide actively these special moments of recognition and thus gradually to gather a more complete understanding of the phenomenon.[10]

Goethe emphasized that perhaps the greatest danger in the transition from seeing to interpreting is the tendency of the mind to impose an intellectual structure that is not really present in the thing itself: "How difficult it is . . . to refrain from replacing the thing with its sign, to keep the object alive before us instead of killing it with the word."[11] The student must proceed carefully when making the transition from experience and seeing to judgment and interpretation, guarding against such dangers as "impatience, precipitancy, self-satisfaction, rigidity, narrow thoughts, presumption, indolence, indiscretion, instability, and whatever else the entire retinue might be called."[12]

Because accurate looking and seeing are crucial in Goethe's way of study, he stresses the importance of training and education. He believed that observers are not all equal in their ability to see. Each person must develop his or her perceptual powers through effort, practice, and perseverance. "Nature speaks upward to the known senses of man," he wrote, "downward to unknown senses of his."[13] If we cannot understand a particular phenomenon, we must learn to make fuller use of our senses and "to bring our intellect into line with what they tell."[14]

Yet, Goethe argued that it is not enough to train only the outer senses and the intellect. He maintained that, as a person's abilities to see outwardly improve, so do his or her *inner* recognitions and perceptions become more sensitive: "Each phenomenon in nature, rightly observed, wakens in us a new organ of inner understanding."[15] As one learns to see more clearly, he or she also learns to see more *deeply*. One becomes more "at home" with the phenomenon, understanding it with greater empathy, concern, and respect.

In time, he believed, this method reveals affective, qualitative meanings as well as empirical, sensual content. "There may be a difference," he claimed, "between seeing and seeing. . . . The eyes of the spirit have to work in perpetual living connexion with those of the body, for one otherwise risks seeing yet seeing past a thing."[16] This kind of understanding does not come readily, but it can be had, Goethe argued, by anyone who immerses himself or herself in systematic training. "Thus, not through an extraordinary spiritual gift, not through momentary inspiration, unexpected and unique, but through consistent work, did I eventually achieve such satisfactory results," he wrote about his own scientific discoveries.[17]

THE *UR-PHENOMENON*

Goethe argued that, in time, out of commitment, practice, and proper efforts, the student would discover the "ur-phenomenon" (*Urphänomen*), the essential pattern or process of a thing. *Ur-* bears the connotation of primordial, basic, elemental, archetypal; the ur-phenomenon may be thought of as the "deep-down phenomenon," the essential core of a thing that makes it what it is and what it becomes.[18] For example, in his botanical work, Goethe saw the ur-phenomenon of the plant as arising out of the interplay between two opposing forces: the "vertical tendency" and "horizontal tendency."[19] The former is the plant's inescapable need to grow upward; the latter, the nourishing, expanding principle that gives solidity to the plant.[20] Only when these two forces are in balance can the plant grow normally.

Goethe believed that the powers of human perception and understanding cannot penetrate beyond the ur-phenomenon. It is "an ultimate which can not itself be explained, which is in fact not in need of explanation, but from which all that we observe can be made intelligible."[21] The key procedural need in discovering the ur-phenomenon, Goethe argued, is maintaining continuous experiential contact with the thing *throughout* the course of investigation—to intellectualize abstractly as little as possible. "Pure experience," he wrote, "should lie at the root of all physical sciences. . . . A theory can be judged worthy only when all experiences are brought under one roof and assist in their subsequent application."[22]

Yet, Goethe saw no inherent conflict between experience and idea or between fact and conception. He believed that genuine understanding entailed a mutual interplay of both fact and theory. Their resolution is to be found in the ur-phenomenon, which marks out the things in the foreground and brings all other phenomena into relation with it.[23] If study is conducted properly, facts and theory can arise smoothly together because each is part and parcel of the other:

> The highest is to understand that all fact is really theory. The blue of the sky reveals to us the basic law of color. Search nothing beyond the phenomena, they themselves are the theory.[24]

THEORY OF COLOR

One of the clearest illustrations of Goethe's way of study is his work on color and light as they are experienced in the everyday world. Skeptical of Newton's theory of color, Goethe began his own studies in the late 1780s and published *Theory of Color* (*Zur Farbenlehre*) in 1810.[25] The crux of his color theory is its experiential source: rather than impose theoretical statements (as he felt Newton had), Goethe sought to allow light and color to be displayed in an ordered series of experiments that readers could experience for themselves. Goethe claimed that if one carefully conducts these experiments with "constant and rigorous effort," he or she will discover from his or her own experiences the underlying processes through which all color appears.[26]

Theory of Color begins with an examination of physiological colors—that is, colors contingent upon the state and activity of the eye, as for example, the orange after-image we see after looking at a blue flame. Goethe first requests the reader to explore the effect of darkness and light in general terms. He asks the student to consider experiences such as the following, to conduct them carefully as experiments: (1) to keep one's eyes open in a totally dark place for a time; (2) to look at a white, strongly illuminated surface, then turn to objects moderately lighted.[27] Goethe explains that, in the first experiment, the eye is "in the utmost relaxation and susceptibility"; it feels "a sense of privation" and strives to perceive outwardly into the darkness.[28] The results of the second experiment are the reverse of the first: the eye, "in an overstrained state and scarcely susceptible at all," is dazzled and for a time cannot see the moderately lighted objects.[29]

For Goethe, simple experiments like these intimate an essential aspect of human seeing: darkness in the world instantaneously produces in the eye an inclination to light; light, an inclination to darkness. The working of the eye indicates an active dialectic between darkness and light: The eye "shows its vital energy, its fitness to receive the impression of the object, precisely by spontaneously tending to an opposite state."[30]

Goethe concluded that this reciprocity between darkness and light points to the ur-phenomenon of color: Color is the resolution of the tension between darkness and light. Thus, darkness weakened by light leads to the darker colors of blue, indigo, and violet, while light dimmed by darkness creates the lighter colors of yellow, orange, and red. Unlike Newton, who theorized that colors are entities that have merely arisen out of light (as, for example, through refraction in a prism), Goethe came to believe that colors are *new* formations that develop through the dialectical action between darkness and light.[31] Darkness is not a total, passive absence of light as Newton had suggested but, rather, an active presence, opposing itself to light and interacting with it. *Theory of Color* presents a way to demonstrate firsthand this dialectical relationship and color as its result.[32]

For Goethe, tension and its reconciliation are prime forces in nature and can be discovered in countless ways. Light and darkness, colors and their complements, colored objects seen and the resulting after-images, seeing and thing seen, person and world—all point toward an instantaneous, living dialectic that joins the parts in a dynamic, interpenetrating whole. This relationship, says the philosopher Eric Heller, is a "a creative conservation between within and without, a kind of dialectical education through which the individual form becomes in actuality what from the very beginning it had been potentially. For what is within and what is without are . . . merely poles of one and the same thing."[33]

THE ESSAYS

The above introduction to Goethe's way of science is only a sketch, and the essays of this collection demonstrate in a much more rounded way the nature of Goethean science and its great potential for understanding the natural world. Physicist Arthur Zajonc's introductory essay reviews Goethe's scientific studies and their historical context, particularly Goethe's relationship with Enlightenment science and Romanticism. In turn, the four essays of part I discuss the philosophical foundations of Goethean science and clarify its epistemology and methodology. In his essay, German scholar Frederick Amrine demonstrates that Goethe's effort to foster a way of knowledge grounded in qualitative description anticipates several developments in the contemporary philosophy of science. In the next two essays of part I, physicist Walter Heitler and physiologist Herbert Hensel examine the goals of Goethean science and illustrate how its method and discoveries compare and contrast with conventional scientific work. Last, philosopher Ronald H. Brady draws on the phenomenological notion of intentionality to clarify Goethe's understanding of growth and metamorphosis in nature.

Though the essays in part I by Walter Heitler and Herbert Hensel were written in the 1960s, Zajonc and I have chosen to include them because they establish an important conceptual base without which more recent Goethean research would not be possible. Heitler was a major physicist of the twentieth century and helped to develop the quantum theory of radiation. Similarly, Hensel was an expert on sensory physiology and eventually became interested in developing what would be called today a "phenomenology of sense experience." During the 1960s, both men gave attention to the relationship between science and the humanities; they envisioned a Goethean science as figuring prominently in the argument. In this sense, both men's essays set the framework from the standpoint of a 1960s science for a more contemporary engagement with the issues as illustrated by Amrine and Brady in this part of the volume and by the other contributors in parts II and III.

The five essays of part II move beyond conceptual discussions of Goethe's science to the question of how it is practiced in the real world of nature. Biologist Jochen Bockemühl considers plant growth from a Goethean standpoint, tracing the changes in leaf form as a plant matures. Drawing on Bockemühl's approach, ecologist Nigel Hoffmann explores the qualitative nature of two specific Australian plants and strikingly demonstrates, through the use of poetry and painting, the importance of an intuitive dimension in Goethe's way of seeing.

The next two essays of Part II illustrate the value of Goethe's approach for understanding animal forms. Drawing on the work of zoologist Wolfgang Schad, ecologist Mark Riegner uses a Goethean approach to explore the form of mammals. By observing such qualities as body shape, tooth formation, coloration, and habitat preference, Riegner presents an innovative way of reading the natures of rodents, ungulates, and carnivores. Biologist Craig Holdrege takes a similar approach in his perceptive effort to present a Goethean phenomenology of the horse and the lion. Both his and Riegner's interpretations demonstrate that, through a Goethean approach, each animal reveals its unique manner of presence in the world. This presence, Holdrege emphasizes, is what the animal is, and any efforts to alter this presence—as with the piecemeal manipulations of genetic engineering—can radically change the whole animal and its relationship with the environment. His example is the rat-sized transgenic mouse made so heavy that it can no longer climb a plant stem to gather the seeds it needs for food.

In the last essay of part II, Mark Riegner and sculptor John Wilkes present Wilkes' efforts to design what he calls "Flowforms"—fountain-like vessels through which water flows in rhythmic motion. In creating Flowforms, Wilkes was greatly affected by the Goethean studies of water done by German hydrologist Theodor Schwenk, who concluded that the essence of water's movement is found in the tension between the linear tug of gravity and water's inherent tendency to draw itself into a sphere. Schwenk demonstrated that water reconciles this tension in three characteristic ways: the meander, the wave, and the vortex.[34]

In his Flowform research, Wilkes asks how these essential patterns of water can be incorporated in built form so that human made channels and vessels can support and enhance the basic movements of water rather than force them into unnatural surroundings as, for example, in channelized rivers with straight banks that interfere with the need of water to meander. Instead of forcing water to do what we human beings want, why not help it to maintain its own natural patterns and move the best it can? Riegner and Wilkes demonstrate that this kind of thinking leads to designed environments that work better both ecologically and aesthetically.

The three essays in part III of the volume discuss the future of Goethean science. German scholar Alan P. Cottrell demonstrates how Goethe's approach moves away from the reductionist thinking of positivist science and facilitates an increasing freedom and self-determination both for the researcher and the thing he or she studies. In turn, physicist Henri Bortoft links Goethean science with the search for authentic wholes and a way to study nature in a deeper, more heartfelt way. Bortoft argues that one of the most important values of Goethe's way of science is to foster *understanding*. To understand, suggests Bortoft, is to see the way things belong together and to see why they are together as they are.[35]

The last essay of the collection, by Arthur Zajonc, sees Goethe's way of understanding as the basis for a science of the future. Zajonc examines how recent experiments in quantum physics call into question the one-track mechanistic model of nature and many of the strictures of classical forms of thought on which that model is based. He believes that we must look toward a new science of nature freed from a mechanistic model that emphasizes measurement and exactitude. As do other contributors to this collection, Zajonc offers, as a prototype, the artist's way of seeing and shows how Goethe's method provides a way to combine intuitive insight and procedural rigor.

GOETHE, PHENOMENOLOGY, AND NATURE

As editor of the State University of New York Press series in Environmental and Architectural Phenomenology, I have sought volumes that offer perceptive interpretations of the natural and built worlds, particularly as they contribute to human well-being. At the same time, I believe that qualitative, descriptive research, because it stimulates a more intimate relationship between student and thing studied, has the power to strengthen individual responsibility and concern toward natural and built environments.

In selecting a book on Goethean science to be included in a series on phenomenology, I am aware that many mainstream scholars, especially philosophers, may be critical or ambivalent for a number of reasons.

First, it may be argued that, historically, Goethe's efforts preceded Husserl's work by over a century and, therefore, cannot be associated with a tradition that came later.[36] A second, more difficult, issue is the question of method: Goethe's emphasis on remaining with the experience of the thing throughout the course of study is a crucial point of contrast with Husserl's style of phenomenology, in which the student begins with experience but then, drawing back, examines it cerebrally through reflection, *epoché*, and other tools of intellect.[37]

On the other hand, some thinkers within the phenomenological movement itself—for example, philosophers Martin Heidegger and Maurice Merleau-Ponty—came to dispute much of Edmund Husserl's method and many of his conclusions. These phenomenological thinkers argued that the invariant, transcendental structures that Husserl sought in the realm of consciousness were questionable because he based their reality on speculative, cerebral reflection rather than on actual human experience taking place within the world of everyday life.[38] Over time, these thinkers' critical emphasis on real-world existence led to a phenomenological style most commonly called today "existential phenomenology" (in contrast to Husserl's "pure" or "transcendental phenomenology"). Clearly, Goethe's method is much closer to this form of phenomenology, since his aim was to begin from and *stay with* experience, which becomes the descriptive basis for generalization and interpretation.[39]

In this sense, existential phenomenologists can find many points of methodological similarity with Goethean science. On the other hand, some existential phenomenologists may feel much less comfortable with Goethe's ontological and metaphysical conclusions, which suggest an interlinkage and harmony among all things of nature, including humankind. As philosopher L. L. Whyte writes, Goethe's central ambition ". . . was nothing less than to see all nature as one, to discover an objective principle of continuity running through the whole, from the geological rocks to the processes of aesthetic creation. Moreover, this discovery of the unity of nature implies the simultaneous self-discovery of man, since man could thereby come to understand himself better."[40]

As an existential phenomenologist, my view about Goethe's holistic vision of nature is that each reader must make up his or her mind as to its truth or error by studying Goethe's scientific works and conducting *personally* the exercises and experiments that he claims brought him to this understanding of nature. For my own part, I have found my encounter with Goethe's work, especially his *Theory of Color*, a rewarding and sometimes revelatory pathway for seeing more sensitively and for feeling a stronger kinship with the natural world.[41]

In our postmodern time of fragmentation and relativity, we must somehow find ways to bring our thoughts, feelings, and actions in harmony both with ourselves and with the world in which we live. I believe strongly that Goethean science provides a rich, intuitive approach to meeting nature and discovering patterns and relationships that are not only stimulating intellectually but also satisfying emotionally and spiritually.[42] Goethe's method teaches a mode of interaction between people and environment that involves reciprocity, wonderment, and gratitude. He wished us to encounter nature respectfully and to discover how all its parts, including ourselves, belong. In this way, perhaps, we come to feel more care for the natural world, which answers back with meaning. May the essays of this volume help the reader to know this experience.

NOTES

1. The most complete set of Goethe's scientific writings in English is J. W. von Goethe, *Goethe: Scientific Studies*, ed. and trans. D. Miller (New York: Suhrkamp, 1988; reprinted by Princeton University Press, 1994); this work includes a selection of Goethe's writings on morphology, botany, zoology, geology, meteorology, and physics as well as several of his writings on "Methodology and General Scientific Topics." Also useful is J. W. von Goethe, *Goethe's Botanical Writings*, trans. B. Mueller (Woodbridge, Conn.: Ox Bow Press, 1989; originally 1952); this volume includes selections "On General Theory."

Some of the most helpful commentaries on Goethe's science include: F. Amrine, F. Zucker, and H. Wheeler, eds. *Goethe and the Sciences: A Reappraisal* (Dordrecht: D. Reidel, 1987); H. Bortoft, *Goethe's Scientific Consciousness* (Nottingham, United Kingdom: Russell Press, 1986); H. Bortoft, *The Wholeness of Nature: Goethe's Science of Conscious Participation in Nature* (Hudson, N.Y.: Lindisfarne Press, 1996); E. Heller, Goethe and the Idea of Scientific Truth, in *The Disinherited Mind* (New York: Meridian Books, 1959); R. Magnus, *Goethe as Scientist*, trans. H. Norden (New York: Henry Schuman, 1949); T. Roszak, *Where the Wasteland Ends* (New York: Harper and Row, 1973), pp. 302–17; and L. L. Whyte, Goethe's Single Vision of Nature and Man, *German Life and Letters* 2 (1949): 287–97.

Also important to Goethean science is the valuable contribution made by the Austrian philosopher and spiritual teacher Rudolf Steiner (1861–1925), who developed a method of spiritual development called "Anthroposophy." Goethe's ideas played a major role in Steiner's philosophy, and both he and others touched by his work have written extensively on Goethean science. Works by Steiner on Goethean science include: *Goethe the Scientist*, trans. O. D. Wannamaker (New York: Anthroposophic Press, 1950); *Goethe's World View*, trans. W. Lindeman (Spring Valley, N.Y.: Mercury Press, 1985); and *Goethean Science*, trans. W. Lindeman (Spring Valley, N.Y.: Mercury Press, 1988). For an introduction to Steiner's thinking and the nature of Anthroposophy, see R. A. McDermott, ed., *The Essential Steiner* (New York: Harper and Row, 1984).

Perceptive Goethean studies that draw on Steiner's interpretation of Goethe in various ways include: J. Bockemühl, ed., *Toward a Phenomenology of the Etheric World* (Spring Valley, N.Y.: Anthroposophic Press, 1985); J. Bockemühl, ed., *Awakening to Landscape*, (Dornach, Switzerland: Goetheanum Research Laboratory, 1992); J. Bockemühl and A. Suchantke, *The Metamorphosis of Plants*, trans. N. Skillen (Cape Town, South Africa: Novalis Press, 1995); E. Lehrs, *Man or Matter: Introduction to a Spiritual Understanding of Matter Based on Goethe's Method of Training, Observation and Thought* (London: Faber and Faber, 1958); W. Schad, *Man and Mammals: Toward a Biology of Form* (Garden City, N.Y.: Waldorf Press, 1977); T. Schwenk, *Sensitive Chaos: The Creation of Flowing Forms in Water and Air* (London: Rudolf Steiner Press, 1965).

Perhaps the single most accessible introduction to Goethean science is Henri Bortoft's *The Wholeness of Nature*. For a comprehensive picture of research on Goethean science, see Frederick Amrine's invaluable multivolume study, *Goethe in the History of Science* (New York: Peter Lang, vols. 1 and 2, 1996). Also see Amrine's helpful annotated bibliography in *Goethe and the Sciences*, pp. 389–437. For one recent discussion of contemporary Goethean science in practice, see H. I. Brook, *Goethean Science in Britain*, Ph.D. diss., School of Independent Studies, Lancaster University, Lancaster, United Kingdom, 1994.

2. H. Spiegelberg, *The Phenomenological Movement: An Historical Introduction*, 3rd ed. (The Hague: Martinus Nijhoff, 1982) pp. 78–80; p. 109.

3. The nature of phenomenology is complicated and not easy to master. As phenomenologist Herbert Spiegelberg argues, there are as many phenomenologies as phenomenologists; see H. Spiegelberg, *The Phenomenological Movement*, p. 2. Part five of Spiegelberg's book, "The Essentials of the Phenomenological Method," is a helpful introduction to doing phenomenology. Perhaps the single most accessible introduction, especially for non-philosophers, is D. Stewart and A. Mickunas, *Exploring Phenomenology: A Guide to the Field and Its Literature*, 2nd ed. (Athens: Ohio University Press, 1990).

4. Portions of the following discussion on Goethe's method are based on D. Seamon, "Goethe's Approach to the Natural World: Implications for Environmental Theory and Education," in *Humanistic Geography: Inventory and Prospect* edited by D. Ley and M. Samuels (Chicago: Maaroufa Press, 1978), pp. 238–50.

5. Goethe, *Goethe: Scientific Studies*, p. 307. "There is a delicate empiricism which makes itself utterly identical with the object, thereby becoming true theory."

6. "Cautions for the Observer," in R. Matthaei, ed., *Goethe's Color Theory* (New York: van Nostrand Reinhold, 1971), p. 57.

7. Lehrs, *Man or Matter*, p. 111, p. 106.

8. Goethe, *Goethe: Scientific Studies*, p. 311.

9. Lehrs, *Man or Matter*, p. 125.

10. See Roszak, *Where the Wasteland Ends*, p. 304.

11. Goethe, *Goethe: Scientific Studies*, p. 275.

12. Matthaei, *Goethe's Color Theory*, p. 60.

13. Lehrs, *Man or Matter*, p. 85.

14. Ibid., pp. 84–85.

15. Goethe, *Goethe's Botanical Writings*, p. 235.

16. Ibid., p. 106.

17. Ibid., p. 111.

18. Roszak, *Where the Wasteland Ends*, p. 306. The Romantic poet Johann von Schiller complained to Goethe that his "ur-phenomenon" was synonymous with the Platonic ideal, but Goethe refused to accept that characterization. See R. H. Brady's chapter 5 in this volume.

19. Lehrs, *Man or Matter*, p. 125.

20. P. Salm, *The Poem as Plant* (Cleveland, Ohio: Press of Case Western Reserve University, 1971), p. 27.

21. George A. Wells, "Goethe's Scientific Method in the Light of His Studies in Physical Optics," *Publications of the English Goethe Society*, edited by E. M. Wilkinson et al. (Leeds: W. S. Maney, 1968), p. 102.

22. Matthaei, *Goethe's Color Theory*, p. 16. In practice, Goethe's method of seeing and understanding is much more complex and multidimensioned that I suggest in my description here. For a clear, extended picture of the method see Nigel Hoffmann's chapter 7 in this volume.

23. Lehrs, *Man or Matter*, p. 125.

24. Matthaei, *Goethe's Color Theory*, p. 76.

25. *Zur Farbenlehre*, in *Goethes Werke, Hamburger Ausgabe*, E. Trunz, ed., vol. 13 (Hamburg: Christian Wegner, 1948–); English editions of this work are: *Theory of Colours*, trans. C. L. Eastlake (Cambridge, Mass.: MIT Press, 1970; originally published in English in 1840); R. Matthaei, ed. *Goethe's Color Theory* (see note 6; this edition uses Eastlake's translation and also includes selections from Goethe's writings on method); and *Theory of Color*, included in *Goethe: Scientific Studies* (see note 1) and translated anew by Douglas Miller.

26. Goethe, *Goethe: Scientific Studies*, p. 163.

27. Goethe, *Theory of Color*, pars. 5–14.

28. Ibid., pars. 8, 6.

29. Ibid., par. 8.

30. Ibid., par. 38.

31. See N. M. Ribe, "Goethe's Critique of Newton: A Reconsideration," in *Studies in History and Philosophy of Science* 16 (1985): 315–35; Dennis L. Sepper, *Goethe contra Newton: Polemics and the Project for a New Science of Color* (Cambridge: Cambridge University Press, 1988). A useful discussion of the history of light, including Goethe's contribution, is Arthur Zajonc, *Catching the Light: The Entwined History of Light and Mind* (New York: Bantam Books, 1993).

32. Of all Goethe's scientific studies, *Theory of Color* (see note 25) is the work that most directly introduces students to his way of looking and seeing.

Particularly valuable as phenomenological exercises are the many prism experiments that involve the appearance of color when one looks through a prism (see Goethe, *Theory of Color*, pars. 205 and following). One aim of the experiments is to observe carefully how color appears in the prism and, in time, to arrive at a set of statements that describe the appearance accurately. For a lucid discussion of these prism experiments, see Bortoft, *Goethe's Scientific Consciousness*, pp. 13–20 (see note 1).

33. E. Heller, *Goethe and the Idea of Scientific Truth*, p. 11 (see note 1).

34. Schwenk, *Sensitive Chaos* (see note 1).

35. Also see H. Bortoft, *The Wholeness of Nature* (note 1). Other useful discussions of understanding the whole, all similiar in spirit to Goethe, though different in their methods, include: C. Alexander, S. Ishikawa, and M. Silverstein, *A Pattern Language* (New York: Oxford University Press, 1977); J. G. Bennett, *Elementary Systematics: A Tool for Understanding Wholes* (Santa Fe, N.M.: Bennett Books, 1993); and I. L. Stefanovic, Evolving Sustainability: A Rethinking of Ontological Foundations, *Trumpeter* 8 (1991): 194–200.

36. In fact, few academic thinkers have expressed interest in Goethe's work as it may be representative of "proto-phenomenological" efforts. In his comprehensive historical study of phenomenology, Spiegelberg recognizes parallels between Goethe's method and phenomenology, particularly in regard to the approach of *Theory of Color*. Apparently unaware, however, that Goethe's discoveries in that work have major bearing on such philosophical concerns as perception, epistemology, and conceptualization, Spiegelberg erroneously concludes that "Nevertheless Goethe's primary concern was not philosophy, but merely a natural science of the color phenomena different from Newton's" (Spiegelberg, *The Phenomenological Movement*, p. 23). One of the few mainstream philosophers to recognize the many commonalities between Goethe's way of science and phenomenology was Fritz Heinemann, who concludes that: "Goethe's phenomenology . . . may have some real value for the present situation, for an age whose watchword is 'the return to the concrete,' for the transition from Husserl's abstract phenomenology to the concrete phenomenology which will be needed to prepare the ground for the reformation of philosophical problems" (see F. Heinemann, Goethe's Phenomenological Method, *Philosophy* 8 [1934]: 81).

37. On the perspective and methods of Husserlian phenomenology, see Spiegelberg, *The Phenomenological Movement*, chap. 3. *Intentionality* is one concept in Husserl's phenomenological thinking that can be used to clarify Goethe's approach to understanding, though Goethe never used the concept explicitly himself. See R. H. Brady's discussion of phenomenology and intentionality in chapter 5 of this volume.

38. See J. Schmidt, *Maurice Merleau-Ponty: Between Phenomenology and Structuralism* (New York: St. Martin's Press, 1985), chap. 2.

39. For one useful overview of existential phenomenology, see R. S. Valle and S. Halling, eds., *Existential-Phenomenological Perspectives in Psychology* (New York: Plenum, 1989). On the methods of existential phenomenology, see

M. van Manen, *Researching Lived Experience* (Albany: State University of New York Press, 1990). An important effort to conduct "empirical" research in existential phenomenology is the work of the Duquesne School of Phenomenological Psychology; for an introduction, see A. Giorgi, A. Barton, and C. Maes, eds., *Duquesne Studies in Phenomenological Psychology*, vol. 4. Pittsburgh, Pa.: Duquesne University Press, 1983).

For a review of research in environmental phenomenology (which largely draws on the approach of existential phenomenology), see R. Mugerauer, *Interpretations on Behalf of Place* (Albany: State University of New York Press, 1994); D. Seamon, "Phenomenology and Environment-Behavior Research," in *Advances in Environment, Behavior, and Design*, edited by G. T. Moore and E. H. Zube, vol. 1 (New York: Plenum, 1987), pp. 3–27; and D. Seamon, ed., *Dwelling, Seeing, and Designing: Toward a Phenomenological Ecology* (Albany: State University of New York Press, 1993). For helpful examples of how the Goethean approach can be used to understand natural landscapes and built environments, see G. J. Coates, *Erik Asmussen: Toward a Living Architecture* (Stockholm: Byggförlaget, 1997); M. Riegner, "Toward a Holistic Understanding of Place: Reading a Landscape Through Its Flora and Fauna," in D. Seamon, *Dwelling, Seeing, and Designing*, pp. 181–215; and G. Trevelyan, *The Active Eye in Architecture* (Ross-on-Wye, Herefordshire: The Wrenkin Trust, 1977).

40. L. L. Whyte, *Goethe's Single Vision of Nature and Man*, p. 290.

41. I have explored this possibility in David Seamon, *A Geography of the Lifeworld: Movement, Rest, and Encounter* (New York: St. Martin's Press, 1979), especially in part III.

42. Bortoft argues that, in his way of working, Goethe sets the foundation for a science of intuition: ". . . intuition is connected with a change of consciousness, and moreover in a way which can be made quite precise and not just left vague. It . . . follows that Goethe's procedures are practical exercises for educating the mind to function intuitively instead of intellectually, leading to a science which is intuitive instead of organized intellectually" (Bortoft, *Goethe's Scientific Consciousness*, p. 34).

1

Arthur Zajonc

Goethe and the Science of His Time

An Historical Introduction

When Goethe undertook his scientific studies, he did so in an intellectual environment shaped by the forces of the Enlightenment. Jean Le Rond d'Alembert declared the eighteenth century to be "the century of philosophy, *par excellence.*"[1] Yet, his own century rested squarely on the genius of the past, not the present. The "century of philosophy" sought only to bring the scientific spirit, as it was understood at the time, into all aspects of human endeavor, thereby bringing to each the certainty of celestial or terrestrial mechanics.

The Enlightenment, therefore, was not an age of great scientific originality but rather one of elaboration, popularization, and the dissemination of a world view felt to embody the discoveries of previous centuries. Instances abound wherein we can see these ideals active. Voltaire, among many others, rendered Newton's 'natural philosophy' intelligible to those who were not master of the arcane mathematical arts required.[2] In his *Plurality of Worlds*, Bernard de Fontenelle permits us to eavesdrop on his own conversations with a Countess concerning the heavens, distant worlds, and their inhabitants.[3] In doing so he demonstrates the grace, urbane wit, and broad superficiality characteristic of a *philosophe*. Denis Diderot and his widespread army of collaborators gathered together and systematically ordered the knowledge of humanity in his *Encyclopédie*, including in their opus all the arts—scientific,

15

artistic, and industrial. Throughout, the encyclopedists communicated the accomplishments of science so that all might be freed from ignorance, superstition, and oppression. Reason was to act as final arbiter over all matters, whether technical, political, or moral. Thus, enlightenment was to transform individuals and nations.

To locate its foundations, we must turn to the scientists and philosophers of the previous century—such thinkers as Sir Isaac Newton, René Descartes, Sir Francis Bacon, and John Locke. In that century, the two streams of rationalism and empiricism found their clearest scientific development. During the Enlightenment that followed, the two mingled. In the words of Ernst Cassirer, "a new alliance is now called for between the 'positive' and the 'rational' spirit"[4] by such Enlightenment figures as Jean Le Rond d'Alembert and Etienne Bonnot de Condillac. The methodology they and others developed was patterned on Newton's physics. Reason was no longer a participation in divine nature as it had been but was now seen as an intellectual force that determined and guided the discovery of truth. Within the tradition of the French Enlightenment, the love of system led these thinkers to conceive of a universal physics in which every phenomenon could be placed. The faith in such an absolutely coherent universe was axiomatic not only for Descartes but equally for Diderot.

The perceived coherence of the universe rested on an explicit set of convictions shared by the *philosophes*, namely, the adoption of mechanical philosophy as the reigning metaphysics. In the same breath that they damned the sciences of the past for the presence of "occult qualities," they deified their own set of metaphysical, if materialistic, assumptions. And so, unaware, they fell into the same pitfall they had only just rejoiced in escaping, the mingling of physics and metaphysics. No longer did the substantial forms and occult qualities of medieval science haunt the explanations of their philosophy. In their place stood the clockwork universe constructed according to Newtonian or Cartesian blueprints.

Two examples will suffice to illustrate the spirit of the age in which Goethe lived. In his *Plurality of Worlds*, we find Bernard de Fontenelle in conversation with his enchanting hostess, the Countess. He is concerned lest his mechanical vision of the universe horrify her. But her response was certain to warm his own heart when she replied, "I esteem the universe all the more since I have known that it is like a watch. It is surprising that nature, admirable as it is, is based on such simple things."[5]

The mechanism envisaged was universal, including in its compass not only the inanimate world, but also the traditionally distinct kingdoms of plants, animals, and human beings. Progress had been made even since Descartes, who had exempted the human spirit from the extended material world (*res extensa*), the world of automata. By the time of Fontenelle, the "error" had been corrected by Thomas Hobbes, John Locke, and others.[6] When Julien La Mettrie explained that the human body is a time piece, he included the human soul and spirit as well: "The human body is a clock, but an immense one and constructed with so much artifice and skill that if the wheel which turns the second hand should stop, the minute hand would still turn and continue on its way."[7]

A keynote of the Enlightenment was the rise of an essentially secular, materialistic philosophy. The universe was material, both in order and being. The hierarchy of beings that had for centuries connected human beings to their Creator was replaced by an engine, the Artificer of which, if he existed at all, dwelt on the periphery. The palpable loss of the spiritual dimension to nature and humankind is at root one of the principal laments of the Romantic Age.

Yet, Romanticism need not be coupled with a detached longing for some other world beyond the present. Another side of the romantic nature was an emphasis on sensuality. Nature, as experienced through all the senses, commanded the Romantics' attention. In contrast, Enlightenment philosophy supposed a dusty textbook universe, as laid out, for example, in Diderot's *Encyclopédie* or d'Holbach's *System of Nature*, which, in his autobiography, Goethe describes reading in his youth:

> I mention as an instance, to serve for all, the "Système de la Nature," which we took in hand out of curiosity. We did not understand how such a book could be so dangerous. It appeared to us so dark, so Cimmerian, so deathlike, that we found it a trouble to endure its presence, and shuddered at it as at a spectre. . . . A system of nature was announced; and therefore we hoped to learn really something of nature,—our Idol. . . . But how hollow and empty did we feel in this melancholy, atheistical half-night, in which earth vanished with all its images, heaven with all its stars.[8]

The dissatisfaction that Goethe voices here is a sentiment echoed and reechoed for over a century. The complaint was that the accounts provided by scientific treatises did nothing to reach beyond the surface nature of things. In place of the spectacle and wonderment of nature, these presentations offered the "half-night" of abstraction. In England, John Keats would decry Newton's *Opticks* as the "unweaving of the rainbow," and William Blake lamented the scientific myopia that sees the world with one eye only and is blind to its true colors.[9] In America, Henry David Thoreau sounded a similar note as he watched a sunset on Christmas of 1851:

I, standing twenty miles off, see a crimson cloud in the horizon. You tell me it is a mass of vapor which absorbs all other rays and reflects the red, but that is nothing to the purpose, for this red vision excites me, stirs my blood, makes my thoughts flow, and I have new and indescribable fancies, and you have not touched the secret of that influence. If there is not something mystical in your explanation, something inexplainable to the understanding, some elements of mystery, it is quite insufficient. If there is nothing in it which speaks to my imagination, what boots it? What sort of science is that which enriches the understanding, but robs the imagination? . . . if we knew all things thus mechanically merely, should we know anything really?[10]

GOETHE AND THE "NATURE-PHILOSOPHERS"

Yet, it would be a great error to imagine that the Romantics, particularly Goethe, opposed science. The problem was not with science as such but with the specific kind of science then practiced. The task, therefore, was one of transformation, not rejection. Science was to be widened in scope; it was to reach deeper and higher. Many thinkers participated in the project, especially in Germany, where it took various forms. Perhaps best known is the *Naturphilosophie*, or "nature philosophy," associated with the names of Friedrich von Schelling, Georg Hegel, Lorenz Oken, Carl Gustav Carus, Henrik Steffens, and Karl Ernst von Baer. It is essential to distinguish Goethe's scientific efforts sharply from those of these "nature philosophers," his contemporaries. While they and Goethe shared a disenchantment with orthodox science, the routes pursued in consequence were very different— one might even say, diametrically opposed.

Goethe's understanding of science was gained primarily through the activity of empirical research. In observation or experimentation, his extraordinary perceptual abilities and refined sensibilities could flourish. One could term his a visual science, with the eye as symbol for the organ that perceives a unity as well as a diversity in nature. In contrast, the nature-philosophers were associated with German idealistic philosophy, which approached nature from the pole of pure thought. When one speaks of the "nature philosophy" of Schelling or Hegel, one must realize the enormous difference between these thinkers' style and Goethe's efforts. "For philosophy in the proper sense I had no organ," he declared.[11] Least of all did Goethe have the inclination to practice the kind of transcendental philosophy common to "nature philosophy. "This disinterest is not to deny the admiration or, at least, respect that existed between Goethe and his contemporaries. On more than one occasion we even find them as strange bedfellows in an awkward alliance against

Newtonian science.[12] One can quickly gain a sense for the depth of the difference by contrasting their treatments of a common subject. We might look, for instance, at Hegel's treatment of light and matter in his *Philosophy of Nature*:

> As the abstract self of matter, light is absolute levity, and as matter, it is infinite self—externality. It is this as pure manifestation and material ideality, however, in the self-externality of which it is simple and indivisible.[13]

This definition of light can be contrasted with the opening remarks made by Goethe in the preface to the 1810 edition of his *Theory of Color*. Speaking specifically of light and the means one can use to understand its nature, he writes:

> Indeed, strictly speaking, it is useless to attempt to express the nature of a thing abstractly. Effects we can perceive, and a complete history of those effects would, in fact, sufficiently define the nature of the thing itself. We should try in vain to describe a man's character, but let his acts be collected and an idea of the character will be presented to us. . . .
>
> Colors are the deeds of light; its deeds and sufferings: thus considered we may expect from them some explanation respecting light itself.[14]

As this passage suggests, Goethe distrusted the abstract art of reasoning as practiced, for example, by Hegel. He saw it as constantly prone to the danger of unsupported conclusions and speculations untested by nature. We gain a glimpse of these two in conversation through J. P. Eckermann's recollections of a tea given by Goethe in honor of a visit by Georg Hegel in 1827:

> The conversation turned to the nature of dialectics. "Basically," said Hegel, "it is nothing more than the regulated and methodically cultivated spirit of opposition inherent in every human being as a talent which shows its greatness in the distinction of the true from the false."
>
> "If only," interrupted Goethe, "such intellectual arts and skills were not frequently misused and misemployed to make true what is false and false what is true!"
>
> "I suppose that sort of thing is done," answered Hegel, "but only by people who are intellectually sick."
>
> "That is why I prefer the study of nature," said Goethe, "which does not allow such sickness to arise. For there we have to do with infinite and eternal truth that immediately rejects anyone who does not

proceed neatly and honestly in observing and handling his subject. I am also certain that many a person who is dialectically sick could find a beneficial cure in the study of nature."[15]

I describe Goethe's method of science more fully later, but it is nothing if not steeped in observation—a "delicate empiricism" that holds a deep distrust of pure reason unchecked by the constant presence of nature, though we must not single out Hegel in this regard. Goethe also noted, for instance, a profound difference between his own means of discovery and those of his mentor Johann von Herder to whom he wrote from Italy: "What you, through the power of your spirit, bring together out of tradition, that must I piece together in my own way from every region of the heavens, from mountains, hills and rivers."[16]

Novalis, too, in his short life, sought new pathways into nature and a "poetized" science.[17] He admired Goethe's efforts greatly, calling him the first since Plotinus to enter the sanctuary of nature: "Goethe is to become the liturgist of this physical science—he understands the temple service perfectly."[18] Still, while he appreciated what Goethe brought to scientific investigation, Novalis' own thinking moved in a freer, more inspired region. He knew much transcendental philosophy and sought a tran- scendental science, a "logical physics" that would serve his goal of the "romanticization" of nature. Similarly, in England, one finds thinkers such as Samuel Coleridge, who also sought to fashion new concepts and a philosophy to meet the demands of science at the turn of the nineteenth century. Others have explored these threads, and I will not attempt a summary of their findings.[19] Rather, having placed Goethe within the context of both Enlightenment thought and the "nature philosophy" of his countrymen, I next consider the nature and content of Goethe's science.

GOETHE'S STUDY OF NATURE

Goethe recognized two periods in his relationship to nature: one during the decade prior to 1780, until his thirty-first year, and the second taking him through the next fifty years to his death.[20] Each stage, he said, had its own special character.

Goethe's early interests in science can be seen already during his student years, 1765–1768, in Leipzig. While studying law, he also enrolled in science courses, studying anatomy and the theory of electricity and magnetism. In his *Autobiography*, we witness Goethe's lively interest in the medical discussions of his fellow boarders around the dinner table. In September of 1768, however, Goethe fell seriously ill, an event that provided the opportunity for another important influence. During convalescence at his Frankfurt home, Goethe was befriended by his mother's friend, Fräulein Susannah Katharina von Klettenberg, a dedicated member of a Pietist religious circle affiliated with the Moravian Brethren. Through her counselling and the visits of the teacher-physician J. F. Metz, Goethe became deeply interested in alchemy and, among other works, read the writings of Paracelsus.

At the hands of Metz and Klettenberg, Goethe regained his health and returned to his studies but now in the Alsatian city of Strasbourg. While there, Goethe continued his alchemical-cabalistic studies even though he separated from the Moravian brotherhood. During the fall of 1770 he wrote a letter to Klettenberg, giving his explanation for withdrawal from the brotherhood, but also making the telling admission, "Yet alchemy is still my veiled love."[21] In his academic work, Goethe devoted more time to lectures on medicine and science than to law. Thus, we can detect the twin themes of orthodox and hermetic sciences as influences in Goethe's student years.

During the next few years, Goethe's literary efforts flourished and led to an invitation in 1775 from Duke Karl August to come to his Weimar court, where Goethe would reside until his death in 1832. While there his fascination with nature engaged him in many enterprises. Initially they bore the stamp of Goethe's first period in his relationship to nature, which he saw as dynamic and the source of an elusive life that exhilarated but refused to be captive. This dance of nature as Goethe experienced it is vividly depicted in his essay "Nature," the opening sentence of which suggests the Goethe of "Storm and Stress"—the early Goethe who rose meteorically to fame with his *Sorrows of Young Werther*:

> NATURE! We are encompassed and embraced by her—powerless to withdraw, yet powerless to enter more deeply into her being. Uninvited and unforewarned, we are drawn into the cycle of her dance and are swept along until, exhausted, we drop from her arms.[22]

As we cross into the eighties of the eighteenth century, however, Goethe's dynamic phase matured toward a more practical and intellectual, if no less intense, interest in nature that radiated into and so infected the rest of the Weimar court that Friedrich von Schiller, who visited Weimar when Goethe was in Italy, would lament:

> The spirit of Goethe has molded everyone who belonged to his circle. He and his whole local sect are marked by a proud contempt of philosophical speculation and inquiry, coupled with an attachment to

nature sometimes driven to the point of affectation, a resignation to the five senses—in short, a certain childlike simplicity of the mind. They would rather hunt herbs and dabble in mineralogy than get lost in idle syllogism. It is an idea that may be well and good, but it can be driven to excess.[23]

Schiller's comments illustrate that Goethe's interest in nature was contagious, and its character was anything but philosophical. Once again we discern the observational tenor of Goethe's scientific temperament. During the three years from 1781 to 1784, Goethe studied anatomy and persuaded Professor Loder at Jena to spend a week demonstrating the structure of bones and muscles on two cadavers. Through these and associated activities, Goethe developed keen sensibilities in the new area of comparative anatomy, an effort that culminated in his first scientific essay, "An Attempt, Based on Comparative Osteology, to Show that Man Shares the Intermaxillary Bone in the Upper Jaw with Other Animals." The essay represents not only a significant scientific discovery, but also reflects Goethe's deep-set conviction that it was senseless to distinguish the human being from the ape on the basis of a single bone, as had been done by Pieter Camper and Johann Briedrich Blumenbach.[24]

The human being was, in Goethe's estimation, certainly no animal, for incarnate in its uniquely balanced anatomy was the high principle of the *entelechy*. The animal nature must rise to this principle: "In man the animal nature has been intensified (*gesteigert*) for higher purposes and put in the shade as it were, for the eye as well as the mind."[25] Or, "The final product of a Nature which keeps outdoing herself is the beautiful human being."[26] In short, one must look for other less material bases for the human being's high stature in this world—not the absence of a bone in the upper jaw.

Goethe also became involved in botanical studies, which dated back to his first years at Weimar and received an enormous impetus through his travels in Italy during 1786 and 1787. The variety of flora growing there in conditions so different from those of his homeland stimulated him to search for the unifying principle or archetype of the plant kingdom. While in Italy, he clarified and developed his thought concerning plant metamorphosis so that in 1790 he could publish his essay "An Attempt to Explain the Metamorphosis of Plants." By a detailed study of the graded series of leaf forms, Goethe strove to demonstrate that the "leaf" itself becomes all the organs of the plant: sepal, corolla, pistil, and so forth. In doing so he brought a new element into botany—the study of plant morphology.

From this time on Goethe's scientific activities never ceased. In the same year, 1790, while contemplating the skull of a sheep on the Lido,

Goethe formulated what he had pondered before—his vertebral theory of the skull. In this same year, Goethe began the study of color that would occupy him continuously until the publication of his *Theory of Color* in 1810. Few among Goethe's contemporaries appreciated his scientific investigations. Yet through them fruitful relationships developed, for example, with Alexander von Humboldt and especially Friedrich Schiller.

The first conversation between Goethe and Schiller, two titans within the German cultural landscape, is recounted for us by Goethe years later.[27] Meeting Schiller coincidentally at the end of a scientific meeting in Jena, Goethe presented him his theory of plant metamorphosis. The lively conversation that ensued, each man firm in his respective position, entwined their destinies with science: ". . . and thus through the great duel between objective and subjective, we sealed a bond which lasted uninterruptedly and accomplished much good for ourselves and others."[28]

In the last years of the eighteenth century, Goethe studied insect metamorphosis, the phases of the moon by telescope, and followed the scientific discoveries in chemistry and physics with keen interest. Each Wednesday, to an audience of Weimar ladies, Goethe lectured from his growing knowledge in these many areas. In the years following 1803, Goethe spent much time and personal resources in reorganizing the scientific collections of the University of Jena. All the while he continued his botanical and color studies, expanding also into such areas as mineralogy, geology, and meteorology.

His studies of nature continued through to his last years. In 1815, when he was sixty-six, Luke Howard's newly developed system of cloud classification ignited Goethe's long-standing interest in the sky.[29] From 1817 to 1824, he published his volumes "On Natural Science" and "On Morphology," completing or rewriting many essays from years before, but also initiating new investigations. Goethe, now nearly eighty, could look back on his scientific accomplishments, the fruit of an activity essential to all aspects of his life, literary as well as scientific. For without those labors, he wrote, "I would never have come to know man as he is."[30]

During the end of 1831 and the early months of 1832, Eckermann informs us that "Goethe turned again wholly to his favorite studies, the natural sciences." Until his death on March 22, 1832, Goethe sought for the insights that could reveal the world around him as the image of the universal idea. He sought them not through a speculative philosophy but through the phenomena of this world. "The idea is eternal and unitary. . . . All that of which we become aware and of which we can speak are only manifestations of the idea."[31]

TOWARDS "INTUITIVE JUDGMENT": GOETHE'S METHOD

As explained above, Goethe held that the investigator should begin not with the pole of speculative thinking or first principles, but with observation, and should take care not to replace observations with abstractions. He expressed this approach in his *Theory of Color*:

> [The student] should form to himself a method in accordance with observation, but he should take heed not to reduce observation to mere notion, to substitute words for this notion, and to use and deal with these words as if they were things.[32]

The practice of such restraint is difficult, yet without it that which stands before us becomes empty, even dead: "Yet how difficult it is not to put the sign in the place of the thing; how difficult to keep the being (*Wesen*) always livingly before one and not to slay it with the word."[33] It is not that Goethe abhors theorizing. In fact, he recognizes it as present in our every act of observation, explaining that: "Every act of seeing leads to consideration, consideration to reflection, reflection to combination, and thus it may be said that in every attentive look on nature we already theorize."[34] Rather it is a question of fully recognizing the deeply structured, "theory-laden" form of our seeing. An essential aspect of the scientific enterprise becomes, therefore, the conscious schooling of that capacity for ever deeper insights. Where, then, is a theory of color to be found? Goethe's emphatic reply is in the proper seeing of archetypal instances of color. He sees the sunset and blue sky as, in this case, the rightful end point of investigation:

> The highest thing would be to comprehend that everything factual is already theory. The blue of the heavens reveals to us the fundamental law of chromatics. One should only not seek anything behind the phenomena: they themselves are the theory.[35]

Thus, Goethe valued the rational as well as the empirical dimension of science. He sought to bring the rational element consciously into science, but not as an autonomous activity operating upon observation. Rather, he endeavored to imbue seeing itself with the rational. The result was what he termed a "gentle empiricism" possessed of perceptive seeing rather than mathematical techniques:

> There is a gentle empiricism that makes itself in the most intimate way identical with its objects and thereby becomes actual theory. This

heightening of these spiritual powers belongs, however, to a highly cultivated age.[36]

In an exchange from 1787 with Schiller, we find one of the clearest expositions of the steps along the way to this cultivated means of investigation.[37] One begins with ordinary "empirical phenomena," the simple observations any attentive observer might make. From these one can rise to a higher awareness by varying the conditions under which the phenomenon appears. By doing so, the essential preconditions for its appearance become apparent. Such instances he termed "scientific phenomena." Goethe explained that some thinkers would have one rest content with this level of understanding, but he sought a higher level of recognition—what he called "pure phenomena" or, later, "archetypal phenomena" (*Urphänomen*).[38] We find an echo of this same progression in his later *Theory of Color*:

> . . . the circumstances which come under our notice in ordinary observation are, for the most part, insulated cases, which with some attention, admit of being classed under general leading theoretical rubrics which are more comprehensive and through which we become better acquainted with certain indispensable conditions of appearances in detail. From henceforth everything is gradually arranged under higher rules and laws, which, however, are not to be made intelligible by words and hypotheses to the understanding merely, but, at the same time, by real phenomena to the senses. We call these archetypal phenomena (Urphänomen), because nothing appreciable by the senses lies beyond them, on the contrary, they are perfectly fit to be considered as a fixed point to which we first ascend, step by step, and from which we may, in like manner, descend to the commonest case of everyday experience.[39]

THE ARCHETYPAL PHENOMENON

Goethe considered the archetypal phenomenon to be the highest level of experience attainable. He writes that the natural scientist:

> should forebear to seek for anything further behind it: here is the limit. But the sight of an archetypal phenomenon is generally not enough for people; they think they must go still further; and are thus like children who after peeping into a mirror turn it round directly to see what is on the other side.[40]

Although archetypal phenomena are the fixed points from which one can "descend to the commonest case of everyday experience," Goethe distinguishes them from first principles from which all else is derived. Rather, it is a question of *seeing*, within nature's multiplicity, the single, archetypal instance. Five years before his death, Goethe wrote in this vein to Christian Dietrich *v.* Buttel:

> Moreover, an archetypal phenomenon is not to be considered as a principle from which manifold consequences result; rather it is to be seen as a fundamental appearance within which the manifold is to be held.[41]

These descriptions indicate how heavily Goethe relies on the metaphor of seeing. Understanding, he believed, is not so much a discursive, explanatory process as a moment of seeing—what he called "*aperçu*," or "insight." Once this insight is attained, its formal elaboration in discursive or mathematical terms is of strictly secondary interest. In a letter of 1823 to Frederic Soret, he wrote, "In science, however, is the treatment null, and all efficacy lies in the *aperçu*."[42] Once we realize this, we can read the *Theory of Color* differently. We should not search for explanations of the phenomena in the usual sense but, more importantly, we should relive the experiments and experiences he describes so that we, too, may have the insight—the *aperçu* that weds together subsequent experiences. The result is that we see not only the isolated instance, but also more general, universal patterns and relationships. This clarity is guarded and not readily apparent in the ordinary phenomena that confront us, but we can school our perceptual capacities and eventually see that:

> The True Is god-like: it does not appear unmediated, we must guess it from its manifestations. . . . Only in the highest and most general do the Idea and the Appearance meet.[43]

Goethe is therefore uninterested in causes as such and goes so far as to state that to separate effect from cause is an error. Rather, the phenomenon should be taken as a whole. Instead of causes, one searches for the essential "circumstances under which the phenomenon occurs."[44] Goethe writes: ". . . man in thinking errs particularly when inquiring after cause and effect; the two together constitute the indissoluble phenomenon."[45] Or, "It is rightly said that the phenomenon is a consequence without a ground, an effect without a cause."[46]

Science, then, should attend closely to the appearances of nature, which becomes the gentle yet demanding teacher. Even the faculties of cognition required to perceive the archetypal phenomena must be formed under nature's care. These faculties are like the eye, which:

owes its existence to the light. Out of indifferent animal organs the light produces an organ corresponding to itself; and so the eye is formed by this light for the light so that the inner light may meet the outer. . . . If the eye were not sunlike how could we perceive the light?[47]

The "gentle empiricism" that Goethe advocates evokes these organs within us needed for the deeper understanding of nature. Again the metaphor of seeing is omnipresent: "Every new object, well contemplated, opens up a new organ within us."[48] The intimate intertwining of the human being into nature in this way does much to overcome the experience of alienation common to "objective" Enlightenment science. Scientific investigation becomes individualized—a process profoundly dependent on the person and his or her capacities to see pattern, form, and the archetype within the multiplicity of nature.

We find, therefore, the theme of human development, or *Bildung*, to be an essential feature of Goethe's mode of scientific investigation. In addition, we witness his attempt to reaffirm experience over abstraction and to remain with the phenomena even when they become a symbol or emblem of the ideal. Goethe believed that the dusty textbook universe of Baron Ruel-Henri-Dietrich d'Holbach would thereby be avoided.

The ambitions of the young Goethe succeed in that his science is one wherein the full, rich content of nature is retained but now penetrated and illumined by human faculties shaped by the hand of nature itself. Nature includes not only what impresses the eye as color or form, but also inner dimensions, for example, the moods of colors. Goethe called these dimensions the "moral" (*sittlich*) aspects of experience, and he believed deeply that they are also part of our experience of nature and, ultimately, must be included in scientific knowledge.

For Goethe, the world is no mere surface reality but a living cosmos that we can gradually learn to see if only we do not abandon a "gentle empiricism" for the attractions of mechanical philosophy.

NOTES

1. Jean Le Rond d'Alembert, "Pensées. Philosophie. Tableau de l'esprit humain au milieu du dix-huitième siècle," in *Oeuvre de d'Alembert*, edited by Condorcet (Farls: Eugene Didier, 1853), p. 217.

2. François de Voltaire, *The Elements of Sir Isaac Newton's Philosophy*, trans. John Hanna (London: Cass Library of Science Classics, 1967).

3. Bernard de Fontenelle, *A Plurality of Worlds*, trans. John Granvill (London: Nonesuch Press, 1929).

4. Ernst Cassirer, *The Philosophy of the Enlightenment*, trans. Fritz Koelln and James P. Pettegrove (Princeton, N.J.: Princeton University Press, 1951).

5. Fontenelle, *A Plurality of Worlds*, p. 79.

6. Edwin A. Burtt, *The Metaphysical Foundations of Modern Science* (London: Routledge, 1967).

7. Julien Offray de la Mettrie, *Man a Machine*, trans. G. C. Bussey and M. W. Calkins (Chicago: Open Court, 1927).

8. J. W. von Goethe, *Autobiography*, trans. John Oxenford (Chicago: University of Chicago Press, 1974), 2:108–11.

9. John Keats, "Lamia," in *The Poems of John Keats*, ed. Jack Stillinger (Cambridge, Mass.: Belknap Press of Harvard University, 1978).

10. Henry David Thoreau, *The Journals of Henry D. Thoreau*, eds. Francis H. Allen and Bradford Torrey (Boston: Houghton Mifflin, 1906), 3:155–56.

11. J .W. von Goethe, "Einwirkung der Neueren Philosophie," *Goethes Werke, Naturwissenschaftliche Schriften 1*, ed. Erich Trunz, *Hamburger Ausgabe*, 14 vols. (München: C. H. Beck, 1981), 13:25. Hereafter this edition will be referred to as *HA*. A translation appears in "Influence of the New Philosophy," *Goethe's Botanical Writings*, trans. Bertha Mueller (Honolulu: University of Hawaii Press, 1952), p. 228.

12. G. W. F. Hegel, *Philosophy of Nature*, ed. and trans. M. J. Petry, 3 vols. (London: Allen, 1970), 2:139ff.

13. Hegel, sec. 276, II:17.

14. Goethe, *HA*, XIII:315.

15. J. P. Eckermann, *Conversations with Goethe*, ed. H. Kohn, trans. G. C. O'Brlen (New York: Frederick Ungar, 1964), pp. 125–26; the conversation of October 18, 1827.

16. J. W. von Goethe, *Goethes Briefe*, HA, III (25 January 1787).

17. See for example the books by John Neubauer, *Bifocal Vision: Novalis' Philosophy of Nature and Disease* (Chapel Hill: University of North Carolina Press, 1971), and *Novalis* (Boston: Twayne, 1980).

18. Friedrich von Hardenberg, "Fragmente I," *Novalis Werke/Briefe*, ed. Ewald Wasmuth (Heidelberg: Lambert Schneider, 1957), 2:142, fragment no. 452.

19. Owen Barfield, *What Coleridge Thought* (Middletown, Conn.: Wesleyan University Press, 1971).

20. Goethe, "Commentary of 'Nature,'" in *Goethe's Botanical Writings*, pp. 244–45. Here Goethe terms the two his "comparative" and "superlative" periods.

21. Gustav Roethe, ed. *Die Briefe des Jungen Goethe* (Leipzig: Insel Verlag, n.d.), p. 113. Quoted in Alice Raphael, *Goethe and the Philosophers' Stone* (London: Routledge and Kegan Paul, 1965), p. 25. Alchemy remained a love veiled from most of his associates, including Herder. In his *Autobiography*, Goethe wrote: "But, most of all, I concealed from Herder my mystico-cabalistical

chemistry, and everything relating to it; although, at the same time, I was still very fond of secretly busying myself in working it out more consistently than it had been communicated to me" (2:22).

22. Goethe, *HA*, XIII:45; *Goethe's Botanical Writings*, pp. 242–44. This essay has been the focus of continual controversy, inasmuch as Goethe did not sign the original publication nor recalled writing it. However, he himself thought that it stemmed from his own hand, and recognized the sentiments as entirely characteristic of his early period, which is sufficient for my purposes. See his "Erlauterung zu dem aphoristichen Aufsatz, 'Die Natur'" *HA*, XIII:48.

23. From a letter of 1787 by Schiller to Koerner. Quoted in Rudolf Magnus, *Goethe as a Scientist*, trans. Heinz Norden (New York: Henry Schuman, 1949), p. 18.

24. See G. A. Wells, *Goethe and the Development of Science 1750–1900* (Alphen aan den Rijn, The Netherlands: Sijthoff and Noordhoff, 1978), pp. 12–18.

25. Goethe, quoted in Karl Victor, *Goethe the Thinker*, trans. Bayard Morgan (Cambridge, Mass.: Harvard University Press, 1950), p. 137.

26. Goethe, quoted in Victor, *Goethe the Thinker*, p. 162.

27. Goethe, "Propitious Encounter," *Goethe's Botanical Writings*, pp. 215–19.

28. Ibid., p. 218.

29. Arthur G. Zajonc, "The Wearer of Shapes. Goethe's Study of Clouds and Weather," *Orion Nature Quarterly* 3:1 (winter 1984):34–43.

30. J. W. von Goethe, quoted in A. Wachsmuth, *Geeinte Zwienatur* (Berlin: Aufbau-Verlag, 1966), p. 6.

31. Goethe, *HA*, XII:366, no. 12.

32. Goethe, *HA*, XIII:482; *Theory of Colours*, trans. Sir Charles Eastlake (Cambridge, Mass.: MIT Press, 1970), p. 283.

33. Goethe, *HA*, XIII:452.

34. Goethe, *HA*, XIII:317.

35. Goethe, *HA*, XII:432, no. 488, trans. F. Amrine.

36. Goethe, *HA*, XII: 435, no. 509, trans. F. Amrine.

37. Goethe, *HA*, XIII:23; *Goethe's Botanical Writings*, p. 228.

38. Goethe, *HA*, XIII:317; *Theory of Colours*, p. xl.

39. Goethe, *Theory of Colours*, pp. 71–72.

40. J. P. Eckermann, *Conversations with Goethe*, trans. Gisela C. O'Brien (New York: Frederick Ungar, l964), 18 February 1829, p. 147.

41. *Goethes Briefe*, *HA*, IV:231, letter to Christian Dietrich *v.* Buttel 3 May 1827.

42. Goethe, quoted in Rike Wankmueller, "*Farbenlehre*: Goethes Methode," *HA*, XIII:616, as in a letter to Soret, 30 December 1823.

43. Goethe, *HA*, XIII:366, nos. 11 and 14.

44. Goethe, *HA*, XIII:25; *Goethe's Botanical Writings*, p. 228.

45. Goethe, *HA*, XIII:446, no. 591.

46. Goethe, *HA*, XIII:446, no. 590.

47. Goethe, *HA*, XIII:323–24.

48. Goethe, *HA*, XIII:38.

I

Goethean Science
Philosophical Foundations

2

Frederick Amrine

The Metamorphosis of the Scientist

Startling as the claim might sound to those who would prefer to cast him as a Romantic reactionary or even a kind of scientific Luddite, Goethe can be shown to have anticipated many of the most important tenets of contemporary philosophy of science.[1] In an early attack on conventional scientific historiography, Paul Feyerabend even held Goethe up as a model, arguing that he had anticipated contemporary objections to the "dogmatic" treatment of Newton's theory, and praising Goethe's "critical sense" as a historian of science.[2] Goethe's warning that "[t]he most destructive prejudice is that which would put any branch of scientific research under the ban" sounds rather like Feyerabend (although there are other more fundamental differences).[3] Goethe also doubted the possibility of "rational reconstruction" in science, arguing in a strikingly contemporary idiom that "the history of science is science itself."[4] Most important, Goethe was well aware that there is not and cannot be any neutral language of observation:

> An extremely odd demand is often set forth but never met, even by those who make it: i.e., that empirical data should be presented without any theoretical context, leaving the reader, the student, to his own devices in judging it. This demand seems odd because it is useless simply to look at something. Every act of looking turns into observation, every act of

33

observation into reflection, every act of reflection into the making of associations; thus it is evident that we theorize every time we look carefully at the world.[5]

Indeed, Goethe was even present when the "opening shot" of the revolution in theory was fired, for at the head of his epoch-making chapter on the "theory-ladenness" of perception, N. R. Hanson placed as an epigraph Goethe's "If the eye were not sunlike, the sun's light it would never see."[6] If it was Hanson who fired the "opening shot" of this revolution, it was Thomas S. Kuhn who won the decisive battle. The paradigm shift in the philosophy of science inaugurated by his book has been so profound that one might want to divide the history of that discipline into B.K. and A.K.— "before Kuhn" and "after Kuhn"—with suitable typological allowances for earlier "prophets" such as Alexandre Koyré, N. R. Hanson, and Stephen Toulmin.[7] The main argument of his book is too well known to require extensive recapitulation. Suffice it to say that, while others had argued that reductionism was not borne out by the historical evidence in this or that individual case, Kuhn applied the argument to the history of science as a whole and, more important, was able to tell us why it does not work.

Yet, Kuhn's *The Structure of Scientific Revolutions*, to which has been attributed "a wider academic influence than any other single book of the last twenty years," nevertheless leaves a number of important and troubling questions unresolved.[8] If reductionism does not work—and the consensus is that it does not—can there be progress in science in any real sense?[9] If the history of science is so discontinuous that it cannot be rationally reconstructed and if paradigm shifts are by nature so radical that the resulting paradigms remain incommensurable, is science doomed to be governed by subjectivity and historical accident?

Moreover, the unresolved questions extend not only to the history of science. At the same time, serious doubt has been cast upon fundamental aspects of scientific method. Let us recall that, for Kuhn, nearly all scientific activity is "normal science," merely the extension and elaboration of an already existent paradigm, while the all-important moment of discovery remains entirely outside the purview of scientific method itself—"logically unscripted," as P. B. Medawar explains.[10] If that is so, the most important aspect of scientific method would seem to be extra-scientific as well, with all the dubious consequences that would imply: doubts about intersubjectivity, control, repeatability, testability, objectivity, and so forth. The central moment in scientific research would be at best a matter of psychology or sociology.

Assuming that one accepts Kuhn's account of "normal science," it follows that real scientific progress (as opposed to mere elaboration and substantiation of that which has already been gained) takes place not principally *within* paradigms but, rather, *between* them. And it is just these revolutionary, "extra-paradigmatic" moments about which Kuhn has nothing to say, indeed, cannot have anything to say, either on the "micro" level at which individual hypotheses are formed or on the "macro" level of the history of science as a whole. In a sense, Kuhn has written a book that confesses ignorance of its proper subject matter and might be better entitled "The Structure of Normal Science." A study of the structure of scientific revolution in Kuhn's sense has never been written, and by his own lights never could be, since the history of science reveals the succession of paradigms to be governed ultimately by non-scientific prejudices such as aesthetics. According to Kuhn, one cannot account for the structure of scientific revolutions because they are ultimately unstructured and extra-scientific. How then can the progress of science be explained? How controlled, augmented, fostered?

Nor is this the scientist's only dilemma. According to the prevailing methdology, not only are we unable to say anything about the generation of hypotheses. The impossibility of scientific induction dictates that we are also unable to validate them conclusively once they arrive.[11] According to the hypothetico-deductive method, one frames a hypothesis to account for a particular perception or phenomenon (the origin of the hypothesis is inconsequential, and thus again treated as extra-scientific), then invents an artificial context in which the factor that is held to be crucial is isolated, and, finally, predicts a result logically deducible from the hypothesis. Depending upon the result of the experiment, one's hypothesis is then either confirmed or disconfirmed. Supposedly, scientists are prepared to abandon cheerfully any hypothesis the moment it has been falsified. However, because one can never induce universal laws from particular instances—the method is in that sense a one-way street—no hypothesis can ever be conclusively affirmed. According to Karl Popper, the chief theorist of the hypothetico-deductive method, "science" is anything but the bastion of unassailable truths portrayed in the high school science texts, in the popular media, and—disingenuously—in the popular writings of certain scientists. It is rather the set of hypotheses we have not yet succeeded in falsifying. We can never know with certainty whether any of our hypotheses are valid.

That conclusion would seem dismal enough, but the scientist's dilemma is actually much more acute, for even the possibility of falsifying hypotheses that have been disconfirmed is now open to doubt. Kuhn, Feyerabend, and others have shown convincingly on the historical evidence that falsification through experimentation almost never happens in science.[12] More recently, Kuhn has made this point even more strongly, arguing that "in the final analysis it is the individual scientist rather than the current theory that is tested."[13]

Moreover, there seem to be good theoretical reasons for doubting whether such testing of hypotheses against phenomena is even possible. The scientist has been trained within a paradigm and is invariably already committed to a research tradition. Scientists are taught from the very beginning to see phenomena in a certain light, and phenomena not predicted by the paradigm are seldom noticed. These are deep dilemmas, to which there would seem to be no solution.

A New Way of Seeing

Nevertheless, I would like to argue that, just as Goethe anticipates many of the central tenets of the most recent philosophy of science, he also offers a solution to its central dilemmas in both theory and practice. For it would seem from Kuhn's account that if there is anything like progress in science, it is a matter of developing in a rigorous and controlled manner new ways of seeing. It is not the data that change in a "Gestalt switch." Rather, it is we who change.[14] If the historical progress of science is like a series of Gestalt switches (as Kuhn and others have argued), it follows that the growth of science resides neither in the accumulation of brute facts nor in the reduction of one way of seeing to another. Rather, it resides in the controlled development of new ways of seeing as such.

That Goethe understood this is clear not only from his more systematic pronouncements on science, as I shall argue below, but even from more casual comments. Full of excitement about the new species of plants and fish that he had seen in Sicily, he wrote to his friend Karl Ludwig von Knebel (18 August 1787) that if he were ten years younger, he would undertake a trip to India, "not in order to discover anything new, but rather to view that which has already been discovered in [my] own way." One is reminded of Goethe's companion in the poem "The Metamorphosis of Plants" (1798) who is asked (with intentional ambiguity) not merely to observe the flowers but to "consider them growing":

> All the shapes are akin and none is quite like the other;
> So to a secret law surely that chorus must point,
> To a sacred enigma. Dear friend, how I wish I were able
> All at once to pass on, happy, the word that unlocks!
> Growing consider the plant and see how by gradual phases,
> Slowly evolved, it forms, rises to blossom and fruit.[15]

As this passage intimates, Goethe's scientific ideal is to allow oneself to be transformed in following the transformations of the phenomena. Thus for Goethe, the ultimate aim of science is nothing other than *the metamorphosis of the scientist*. To that end, he developed fundamentally different notions of hypothesis-formation and experimentation. For Goethe, the hypothesis is not something abstracted from the phenomena, but rather the pattern of the phenomena themselves.[16] One's initial "theorizing" (Goethe always understands this term in its etymological sense, as our "way of seeing") is not tested against logical axioms deduced from an abstract hypothesis; rather, it is continually tested directly against the *phenomena themselves*. Unlike Kant, for example, Goethe has confidence in the phenomena—confidence that they are transparent to the underlying idea.[17] For Goethe, the active idea is found within the phenomena themselves. However, unlike David Hume or Sir Francis Bacon (and like Immanuel Kant), he believed that the idea is not given immediately in experience. It must be sought in the labor of experimentation and practice.

In Goethe's version of scientific method, one does not abandon the phenomena, imagine a mechanism or cause, and then proceed to test one's abstract hypotheses by constructing an artificial experience in which individual phenomena are torn out of context. Rather, one stays with the phenomena; thinks *within* them; accedes with one's intentionality to their patterns, which gradually opens one's thinking to an intuition of their structure.[18] Always moving forwards and backwards through the graded series, between the phenomenon and its environment, one watches the structure of the phenomena precipitate gradually out of the dynamic of the interaction between the observer and observed. In the preface to his *Theory of Color*, Goethe offers a fine analogy for this procedure: "We labor in vain to describe a person's character, but when we draw together his actions, his deeds, a picture of his character will emerge."[19] Otherwise lost in abstraction, the characteristic qualities one seeks can be captured within such a phenomenological dynamic.

The essence of Goethe's procedure is that one remain as open as possible and allow his or her way of seeing to be shaped by the phenomena, just as one's "theorizing" co-creates what he or she sees. It was for this reason that Goethe warned against interposing instruments between the perceiver and the phenomena, claiming that it is instead the *scientist* who is—or can become through practice—the most precise scientific instrument:

> Insofar as he makes use of his healthy senses, the human being is the greatest and most precise scientific instrument that can exist. And precisely this is the greatest disservice of modern science: that it has

divorced the experiment from the human being, and wants to know nature only through that which is shown by instruments—indeed, wants to limit and demonstrate nature's capacities in that way.[20]

In direct contrast to prevailing scientific methdology, Goethe's ideal scientist tries consciously *not* to reduce phenomena to a schema but, rather, to remain inwardly mobile. The ideal is to become, as P. H. Bideau has characterized Goethe's student Carl Gustav Carus, an "âme interieurement plastique" (inwardly mobile soul).[21] The aim is to cultivate as many "modes of representation" as possible, or better, to cultivate the mode of representation that the phenomena themselves demand. Thus, while mathematical formalism may be the most appropriate *Vorstellungsart* for mechanics, it may well be entirely inappropriate for chromatics. Goethe felt this, and it was the real basis of his polemic against Sir Isaac Newton.[22] Above all, the scientist must strive not to fall into habits of perception, for even the most rigorous and severe scientific discipline becomes mere habit the moment one ceases to be conscious of the limitations inherent in any *Vorstellungsart*—which is to say, the moment one ceases to be self-conscious.

In this way, the scientist gradually elevates ordinary empirical phenomena into "scientific phenomena" by arranging them in graded series. Goethe's fullest treatment of this aspect of his method is in his essay "Der Versuch als Vermittler zwischen Objekt und Subjekt" ("The Experiment as Mediator between Object and Subject"). There he argues that the scientist must allow the phenomena to order themselves out of themselves in a way he compares—rather surprisingly, perhaps, given his "fear of abstraction"—to mathematics:

> In the first two parts of my *Contributions to Optics* I sought to set up a series of contiguous experiments derived from one another in this way. Studied thoroughly and understood as a whole, these experiments could even be thought of as representing a single experiment, a single piece of experimental evidence explored in its most manifold variations.
>
> Such a piece of empirical evidence, composed of many others, is clearly of a higher sort. It shows the general formula, so to speak, that overarches an array of individual arithmetic sums. In my view, it is the task of the scientific researcher to work toward empirical evidence of this higher sort—and the example of the best men in the field supports this view. From the mathematician we must learn the meticulous care required to connect things in unbroken succession, or rather, to derive things step by step. Even where we do not venture to apply mathematics we must always work as though we had to satisfy the strictest of geometricians.[23]

Goethe's method is "mathematical" not in its formal abstraction but, rather, in its rigor. Hjalmar Hegge has rightly described Goethe's chromatics in just these terms: "What Goethe attempts here, therefore, is an axiomatization of the domain of colour qualities. And why should not an axiomatizing be as possible for color qualities in the science of color as it is for curves, planes, etc. in geometry? . . . . Goethe is aiming at a deductive system for the phenomena of light and colour, but without quantification of the phenomena."[24] Goethe himself argues: "What is exact in mathematics except exactness itself? And this again, is it not a consequence of the feeling for truth?"[25] In a geometric proof, for example, each step is self-evident because it is created anew each time upon the stage of our mind. We intend the relationship and participate fully in the process. As a result, nothing remains opaque. Goethe seeks to extend this mathematical transparency to the empirical sciences as well by developing a nonreductive, yet thoroughly rigorous approach to *qualities*. The lawfulness of the phenomena is revealed by recreating them in their ideal sequence. When the phenomena are arranged "axiomatically," the law shines through and moves between the phenomena, like the melody that moves between the notes in a piece of music.[26]

The resulting intuition constitutes a "pregnant point" from which it is possible to "deduce" (*ableiten*) all the phenomena in their ideal relationships.[27] Yet, the word *point* is misleading, for what is accessed in this moment is a pure activity that is nevertheless saturated with empirical content and thus not abstract. It is an immediate intuition of unity-*in*-diversity. Like the Hegelian absolute, it is the *concrete* universal that emerges at the end of one's cognitive labors, bearing its full empirical content within—the oak tree, not the acorn.[28] It is a living idea rather than a dead hypothesis because it is generative, plastic, multidimensional—a series of structured activities rather than a static structure.

And just as the "point" Goethe indicates as the proper goal of scientific hypothesis-formation is nothing static, the "deduction" that we then perform from this intuited ground is not any kind of logical entailment but, rather, a synchronic *seeing*. The "pregnant point"—let us now call it by the name Goethe usually employs, the "*Urphänomen*"—is ideal without being abstract. From this vantage point, all possible lawful phenomena can be immediately *intuited*. Hence, Goethe's claim in a letter to Johann von Herder that his "archetypal plant" would enable him to invent plants that exhibited an inner necessity even if they did not actually exist:

The archetypal plant shall be the most marvelous creature in the world, and nature herself shall envy me for it. With this model and the key to it one can then invent plants *ad infinitum* that must be consistent, i.e. that could exist even if they do not in fact, and are not just picturesque or fanciful shadows and shows, but have instead an inner truth and necessity.[29]

REFINING PERCEPTIONS

As the *Urphänomen* is not an abstract *terminus* (in either sense of the word) but a pure activity, it can be accessed and realized only through practice. Thus, Goethe conceives of the scientific experiment as the systematic exploration, practice, and elaboration of a mode of representation. In the hypothetico-deductive method, one begins by projecting a structure upon one's observations, then isolates what is held to be the crucial factor, thereby cutting oneself off entirely from the phenomenal context. As we have seen, what takes the place of an abstract hypothesis in Goethe's method is an intuition that arises within the graded series. It is the pattern of the phenomena as a whole. The source and guide of one's thinking is the *energeia* of the phenomena. As in Aristotle's theory of perception, there is a real sense in which one *becomes what one perceives*. Thus, for Goethe, the conventional method of isolating phenomena is tantamount to wearing blinders. In the conventional method, one is not led through a process; having already abstracted from the phenomena, one can no longer *develop with them*.

Moreover, the conventional mode of experimentation not only abrogates the developmental process whereby the phenomena shape one's perceptive faculties, but it also tends to freeze thinking. Ironically, P. B. Medawar, one of the most thoughtful scientists, has gone so far as to argue that the best experiment is one that circumvents the need for thinking entirely: "It is a truism to say that a 'good' experiment is precisely that which spares us the exertion of thinking: the better it is, the less we have to worry about its interpretation, about what it 'really' means."[30] For the conventional scientist, mathematics is the sole guarantor of certainty, while perception and thinking are the sources of all error. Consequently, the thrust of modern science has been to quantify everything that can be quantified (and much that properly cannot), while banishing the remainder to the realm of subjectivity. Goethe rightly saw this as an impoverishment of cognition.

Conventional science seeks its refuge in axiomatic islands insulated from the threats of perception and thinking. Goethe seeks to access through experimental practice the underlying activity in which the two are inseparably joined and thus mutually transformative.[31] Hence, his characterization of the scientific experiment as "mediator between object and subject." Out of this activity of ordering phenomena, something ideal gradually precipitates. The "phenomena of a higher kind," arranged in a graded sequence, gradually become transparent to their own underlying structure, which then can be immediately intuited.

The goal of experimentation in Goethe's sense can be viewed as a kind of empirical counterpart to the "intellectual intuition" of post-Kantian philosophy—an experience at the phenomenal pole that is otherwise remarkably like Johann Fichte's "activity into which an eye has been inserted."[32] Universal and particular, idea and experience enter into a relationship that transcends logical subsumption. They become reciprocally determinative and, in that sense, a unified and organic whole. The context of discovery becomes simultaneously the context of justification, and that same congruence and simultaneity becomes the basis of explanation. Universal and particular each appear within and through the other—or, rather, the universal shines through the particular, while inseparable from it as in a symbol.[33] Hence, Goethe's contention that inquiry should cease with the apprehension of the *Urphänomen*; abstracting further can only lead away from this fullness of understanding to reduction.

An excellent example of Goethe's method is his procedure in paragraphs 38–54 of his *Contributions to Optics* (*Beiträge zur Optik*), part one, which Hans Gebert recapitulates succinctly:

First, Goethe asks the observer to look at the surroundings through the prism and to note the variety of colored fringes. Next, we are to look at the unclouded blue sky and to notice that no color appears but that color comes into being immediately when the tiniest cloud comes into view. Now he asks us to use some of the specially prepared printed cards sold with the book. We start with irregularly curved black and white lines which give a confused lot of colored boundaries. Next comes a regular pattern of squares which give already a more regular set of fringes. Cards with narrow black and white stripes and with broken black and white lines show how the fringes change when the stripes are oriented differently with respect to the refracting edge. We now come to a white stripe on a black background and a black stripe on a white background to be viewed parallel to the refracting edge; we see the Newton and Goethe colors respectively if the prism is far enough from the cards. Finally, we use a card which is half black and half white with a straight boundary parallel to the refracting edge. Now we have the pure boundary colors which constitute the 'ur-phenomenon' for this set of observations. There follow a number of experiments with more complicated arrangements to show how in each the boundary colors are manifest.[34]

As Gebert then points out, it is extremely unlikely that this order of experiments duplicates the actual order in which Goethe made his discoveries. The reason why Goethe does not follow the more usual procedure of demonstrating immediately the simplest form of the boundary colors, then giving the procedure for deriving the more complicated phenomena, is that for him, the process of working through the series as a whole is more important than the end result. Experiments must become concentrated, ongoing experiences through which one learns new ways of seeing.

Given this displacement of product by process, one can understand Goethe's repeated insistence that his scientific work needed to be *done* to be understood. For example, he writes from Italy that his "plant system" is "hard to write in any case and impossible to comprehend from mere reading, even if everything were written ever so sharply and properly."[35] Goethe's subtle notion of multiple *Vorstellungsarten* reveals how profoundly he understood that all perception is "theory-laden." It was partly for this reason that Goethe was so adamantly opposed to Newton's *experimentum crucis*, arguing that a single experiment proves nothing.[36] Equally important was his fundamentally different notion of scientific experimentation. For Goethe, the experiment is not like a single, practical syllogism but rather like artistic practice directed towards the refinement of one's perception over time. Again we see that the primary aim of science, as Goethe understands it, must be self-development, *the metamorphosis of the scientist.*

MORPHOLOGY AND CHROMATICS

The centrality of metamorphosis to Goethe's concept of scientific method helps also to explain, perhaps, why he chose to work primarily in the disciplines of plant morphology and chromatics. That metamorphosis is fundamental to plant morphology is self-evident; yet Goethe also saw color phenomena as dynamic and in that sense "metamorphic." Like botanical phenomena, colors also are governed by the archetypal principles of "polarity" (*Polarität*) and "enhancement" (*Steigerung*). As Gernot Böhme has argued, this very different conception of color is one of the most important grounds for Goethe's polemic against Newton:

Since Newton establishes the basis for explaining color phenomena in the characteristics of light, he attempts in his experiments to exclude as far as possible the influence of "conditions." Goethe censures these experiments consistently for their very neglect of conditions (such as size of image, distance, incidence of light, conditions of brightness, etc.), for it is precisely these conditions which in his theory are the bases of explanation. In connection with this, Goethe frequently reproaches Newton for regarding the prismatic image as something complete, or finished, instead of something in the process of becoming. . . . For Goethe, there are no colors until the last condition is determined. He thus rejects the synthesis of white from the spectrum because no finished image exists in advance of the second prism.[37]

Both the central, "didactic" part of Goethe's *Theory of Color* and the "polemical" part he calls "Exposure of Newton's Theory" (*Enthüllunq der Theorie Newtons*) repeatedly insist upon the "metamorphic" nature of color. Thus, in section 217 of his *Theory of Color*, Goethe declares that "[i]n all that we have observed we should always remember that the phenomenon must not be thought of as fixed or complete, but rather as evolving, growing, and open in many ways to modification."[38] And in section 710 he underscores the "changeability [or mobility] of color" that manifests itself above all in the phenomena of "intensification" and the internal metamorphoses of the color circle: "We have already had to consider the changeability of color in intensification and traversal of the circle, but colors also move back and forth across the circle, quickly and of necessity."[39]

In his polemic against Newton, he warns that even the colors arising through prismatic refraction must be viewed as "ever mobile and becoming"; that one cannot "operate" upon these without modifying them in the process, and that even then one can do so only "for a moment, under the greatest limiting conditions."[40] And in section 544 of the "Exposure of Newton's Theory," Goethe adduces Newton's own eleventh experiment as evidence against him, arguing that "his finished, eternally immutable colors are here reduced, sublated (*aufgehoben*), inverted, and place right before our senses the true nature of the prismatic colors as becoming, continually *in statu nascendi*, and ever mobile."[41] Goethe sees color as an active entity that moves—indeed arises only in the tension *between* light and dark. In the Preface to the *Theory of Color*, he even terms colors "the deeds of light, what it does and what it endures."[42]

Nor are these the only scientific disciplines in which the phenomena are seen to structure themselves "metamorphically." Rather surprisingly, perhaps, Goethe sought to extend this dynamic conception into geological studies as well. Neil M. Ribe has characterized this aspect of the geological works succinctly, citing as an example Goethe's attempts to construct all the transition forms between granitic and porphyritic rock textures as a continuous series, taking as his criterion the relative grain sizes of the different minerals:

Granite is characterized, according to Goethe, by a perfect balance among its three component minerals, quartz, feldspar and mica, such that that which contains is indistinguishable from that which is contained. The metamorphosis of granite occurs when one of its components becomes dominant, giving rise to a whole series of transition forms leading to the porphyritic texture in which *continens* and *contentum* are clearly distinguishable . . . the balanced diversity of the granite mineralogy may be seen as an elementary threefold polarity, a kind of geological *Urphänomen* upon which the multiplicity of rock forms is elaborated through metamorphosis.[43]

Moreover, Goethe sought to treat osteology and even meteorology in a similarly "metamorphic" manner. Since metamorphosis is most immediately evident and most readily rehearsed in plant morphology and chromatics, however, these areas of study remained the focus of Goethe's scientific activity.

REUNITING
SUBJECT AND OBJECT

Yet, there is perhaps another, deeper reason why plant morphology and chromatics remained central to Goethe's scientific work. Both topics represent boundary situations—threshold experiences in which it can become immediately evident that *all* perception is grounded in a realm beyond the split between subject and object.[44] When following botanical development, we do not *see* movement but rather *intend* it, in the way that we unify intuitively the very different projective views of an object as we walk past.[45] Nor do we actually see light but rather only the ways in which it is darkened by objects. Hence, color is also in a very real sense an intentional construct.[46]

Thus for Goethe, botany and chromatics were valuable not only for the intrinsic interest and dignity of their subject matter, but above all because of their propaedeutic value—because there the contribution of the perceiving subject to the construction of the phenomenon is most immediately apparent. Plant morphology and chromatics are the disciplines in which it is easiest to comprehend, control, and even rehearse an intentional activity that we must infer to be at work in all other modes of scientific perception, although it remains much less conscious. Here scientific research most readily becomes a field for practice and self-development.

But where the line between subject and object becomes blurred, must we not fear subjectivity?[47] How do we know that the patterns we are seeing are *objectively* present? Does one not surrender in this way all the ground that science has won, in all its battles against dogma, prejudice, and superstition? Must not every scientist worthy of the name subscribe to Karl Pearson's dictum that "the scientific man has above all things to strive at self-elimination in his judgements"?[48]

This is indeed a deep problem, but it is not Goethe's alone. For here all the difficulties outlined above come home to roost. As we have seen, the hypothetico-deductive method remains incapable of validating any hypothesis conclusively, while the inescapable "theory-ladenness" of all perception simultaneously undermines our ability to falsify them. Contrary to popular belief, the "objectivity" of conventional science is not borrowed from phenomenal objects. They, too, are seen as a source of potential error. Their status is thus nearly as "extra-scientific" as the formation of hypotheses. Neither the kind of thinking that frames hypotheses nor the evidence of the phenomena is to be trusted fully. Thus, the scientist retreats into the unassailable fortress of mathematical axioms. Not only does this distort or exclude from science altogether phenomena that resist mathematical explanation, but also such mathematical axioms can seldom even be compared with empirical phenomena.[49] Experiments are conducted not to test the scientist's hypotheses, but rather to manufacture phenomena that confirm the axioms deduced therefrom. That is what "normal science" is about. Reduction is the price we pay for protection against subjectivity. The only alternative would seem to be arbitrariness.

I submit that Goethe's is a far more attractive solution to this dilemma. His counsel is twofold: first, trust in the appearances; and second, accept the role of the thinking self in perception, but reflect its powers back upon the self in striving for a higher kind of objectivity.[50] As Goethe himself puts it in one of many analogous formulations: "We are adequately equipped for all our genuine earthly needs if we will trust our senses, and develop them in such a way that they continue to prove worthy of our confidence."[51]

Moreover, these seemingly antithetical activities are actually related, even mutually dependent. For, while phenomena appear only in the light of a certain "paradigm" or way of seeing, it is only in the mirror of phenomena that one comes to see oneself. If allowed, the phenomena will always show us the limitations of our *Vorstellungsart*—of any single *Vorstellungsart*—in the face of the richness and complexity of nature. In confronting the phenomena selflessly, we come to know ourselves. But to know oneself is to change oneself. Self-knowledge is already the beginning of self-transformation. The transformed self, cocreative, constructs enhanced phenomena in turn. Neither of these two poles is primary. Rather, what is primary is the activity that precedes the distinction between subject and object, and calls both into being.[52] Out of this pure activity, the particular subject and particular object are precipitated as moments of a larger dynamic.[53] Thus, it is the ground of a higher objectivity. And it is upon *this* ground that Goethe would found the proper activity of science.

Hence, the ideal of the "Goethean" scientist is to remain inwardly mobile through participating in the metamorphosis of the phenomena themselves: "The form is immediately transformed again, and, if we wish to achieve a contemplation of nature that is somewhat alive, we must see that we remain as mobile and plastic as the example nature provides us."[54] Having elaborated disparate phenomena into graded series, ordered them through sympathetic participation in the self-structuring of the phenomena themselves, the scientist's thinking can then operate upon the series "freely." As Goethe writes: "Above all, true researchers must observe themselves and see to it that their organs remain plastic, and also remain plastic in their way of seeing, so that one does not always insist rudely on one mode of explanation, but rather knows in each case how to select the most appropriate, that which is most analogous to the point of view and the contemplation."[55]

Yet, the prerequisite for this freedom is that the scientist remain scrupulously phenomenological in moving from empirical to "scientific" phenomena, and remain severely self-critical at every stage. Goethe describes his own efforts to accomplish this in a letter to his friend Friedrich Jacobi of 27 December 1794:

> The material [his "optical studies"] is, as you know, extremely interesting and the elaboration a mental exercise (*Übung des Geistes*) of a sort that I perhaps would not have gained in any other way. To grasp the phenomena, to fixate them into experiments, to order one's experiences, and to come to know all the ways in which one might view them; to be as attentive as possible in the first case, as exact as possible in the second, to be as complete as possible in the third, and to remain many-sided enough in the fourth, requires that one work through one's poor ego in a way I had else hardly thought possible.[56]

Or, as Goethe argues in an all-important passage in the preface of his *Theory of Color*, the scientist's progression from "looking" (*Ansehen*) to "observing" (*Betrachten*) to "reflecting" (*Sinnen*) to "associating" (*Verknüpfen*) must be accompanied by consciousness, self-knowledge, freedom, and finally—Goethe calls it a "daring word"—by irony.[57] Only then are we freed from recourse to reduction (Goethe calls it "the abstraction that we fear"); only then does science become "beneficial" and "alive."

AN ACTIVE INDETERMINATION

In this free activity that oscillates between self-reflection and selfless immersion in the phenomena, we have discovered the heart of Goethe's science. But we have found something else besides. Here is the ground from which all our *Vorstellungsarten*—all scientific "paradigms"—arise. We have found the *desideratum* of Kuhn's book, what moves *between* the paradigms, the source of the revolutions themselves.

Of course, Goethe himself does not speak of "paradigms" or "revolutions." Yet, it should be clear by now that he means very much the same thing. Seen in this light, some of Goethe's more startling (and often intentionally provocative) assertions become readily comprehensible, as for example the conversation in "The Collector and His Circle" (*Der Sammler und die Seinigen*):

I: Every experience needs the appropriate organ.
Guest: Some special organ I suppose?
I: No, not a special one, but it must have a specific quality.
Guest: And what might that be?
I: It must be able to produce.
Guest: Produce what?
I: Experience! There is no experience which is not produced, brought forth, created.[58]

Kuhn would say that phenomena appear only in the light of a particular paradigm, and those that the paradigm does not illuminate are often not seen at all.[59] Goethe's claim that "every new object, well contemplated, opens up a new organ of perception within us" reveals itself to be an extremely condensed version of the entire scientific procedure described above.[60] Again, one is reminded of Fichte's striking notion of "an activity into which an eye is inserted"—in other words, the goal of science is not to end with an abstract theorem but rather with new capacities that are themselves incitement to ever greater activity and ever enhanced perception. In contrast, abstract theorems (which Goethe terms "hypotheses") "are lullabies with which the teacher soothes his pupils to sleep."[61] The danger of hypotheses is that they "hinder the *anagnorismos*, the reconsideration of the phenomena in question, their examination from all sides."[62] They restrict the mobility of one's thinking and imagination, upon which "the metamorphosis of the scientist" and, with it, the growth of science depend.

The freedom of the scientist, like the freedom of the artist, is active indetermination and, thus, perpetual revolution.

NOTES

1. A slightly different version of this essay originally appeared in *Goethe Yearbook: Publications of the Goethe Society of North America* 5 (1990): 187–212. The essay is used with permission of the editor of *Goethe Yearbook*.

2. Paul Feyerabend, "Classical Empiricism," in *The Methodological Heritage of Newton*, edited by Robert E. Butts and John W. Davis. (Toronto: University of Toronto Press, 1970), pp. 150–70. Cf. p. 158, fn. 6: "Up till now the historical literature concerning Newton has been full of the kind of dogmatism he himself tried to put over on his contemporaries and successors. (There were a few exceptions, such as Goethe, but they were mostly regarded as cranks. However, German scientists were put in a difficult position by their joint veneration of their chief poetic father and of what they thought was proper scientific method.) For example, it has been taken for granted, almost universally, that Newton established the nature of white light. This situation is now at last changed by the appearance of Dr. Sabra's *Theories of Light from Descartes to Newton* (London: Oldbourne, 1967). This, as far as I can see, is the first consistently critical analysis of Newton's optics and the first account that explicitly considers his methodology and its role in the theory of colours." That Feyerabend means "first consistently critical analysis" within the accepted academic literature—that is, that he does not exclude Goethe from consideration for this honor on other grounds is clear from a later passage in the same essay (fn. 9, p. 162): "We know today the reason why pyramids are *seen* even if the *physical light* should happen to terminate in a semicircle. . . . We may suspect that Newton, who also dealt with the physiology of sight, had an explanation of this kind in mind. However, he did not give the explanation but simply redescribed what he saw in order to turn it into a physically useful phenomenon. And in this redescription he introduced the machinery of the very same theory he wanted to prove. Goethe's question, 'for how should it be possible to hope for progress if what is inferred, guessed, or merely believed to be the case, can be put over on us as a fact?' addresses itself to this feature of the theory . . . Dr. Sabra . . . apart, I do not know of a single historian of science whose critical sense matches Goethe's in this connection." Feyerabend's continuing interest in Goethe is evidenced by the section on "Goethe versus Newton" that he included in *Kunst und Wissenschaft*, edited by Paul Feyerabend and Christian Thomas (Züruch: Verlag der Fachvereine an den Schweizerischen Hochschulen und Techniken, 1984), pp. 95–158.

Moreover, it has recently emerged that Goethe was a seminal influence on two of the main protagonists in yet another revolutionary contemporary scientific development, namely "chaos theory." In his remarkable study, *Chaos: Making a New Science* (New York: Viking, 1987), James Gleick argues that both Mitchell Feigenbaum and Albert Libchaber were inspired in important ways by Goethe's work in chromatics and plant morphology, respectively.

3. Goethe, *Maximen und Reflexionen*, No. 481. See Johann Wolfgang von Goethe, *Goethes Werke. Hamburger Ausgabe*, 5th ed. (Hamburg: Christian Wegner, 1966), XII:431. Henceforth, references to the *Hamburger*

Ausgabe are abbreviated *HA*. Except where otherwise noted, translations are the author's.

4. This in the preface to his *Theory of Color (Farbenlehre)* (*HA*, XIII:319). The English translation is from Johann Wolfgang von Goethe, *Scientific Studies*, ed. and trans. Douglas Miller, Goethe Edition. vol. 12 (New York: Suhrkamp, 1988), p. 161.

5. Goethe, *Scientific Studies*, Preface, p. 159 (*HA*, XIII:317).

6. In calling the profound shift that has occurred in the philosophy of science since the 1950s and, especially, since the publication of Thomas S. Kuhn's *The Structure of Scientific Revolutions*, itself a kind of "scientific revolution," I follow Harold I. Brown's excellent study *Perception, Theory and Commitment: The New Philosophy of Science* (Chicago: University of Chicago Press, 1977).

The original German is: "Wär nicht das Auge sonnenhaft, Die Sonne könnt es nie erblicken." See N. R. Hanson, *Patterns of Discovery. An Inquiry into the Conceptual Foundations of Science* (Cambridge: Cambridge University Press, 1958), chap. 1: "Observation," p. 4. Hanson's translation ("Were the eye not attuned to the Sun, the Sun could never be seen by it") misses the radical monism of *sonnenhaft*: not "attuned to the sun," but rather something like "of the nature of the sun itself." One might add here that Goethe also anticipated the eventual rejection of induction in the twentieth century (without giving himself over to the kind of metaphysical deduction one sees in *Naturphilosophie*). Viewed in the light of contemporary philosophy of science, it is not Goethe, but rather the classic "refutations," such as Hermann von Helmholtz's, that have come to seem outmoded.

7. Kuhn credits Koyré's *Études Galiléennes* (Paris: Hermann, 1939) as having been a seminal influence upon his own work (*The Structure of Scientific Revolutions*) [Chicago and London: University of Chicago Press, 1970], p. vi.

In regard to Toulmin, see, for example, his discussion of changing "Ideals of Natural Order" in *Foresight and Understanding: An Enquiry into the Aims of Science* (Bloomington: Indiana University Press, 1961; Westport, Conn.: Greenwood Press, 1981).

8. Gary Gutting, *Paradigms and Revolutions: Appraisals and Applications of Thomas Kuhn's Philosophy of Science* (South Bend, Ind.: University of Notre Dame Press, 1980), p. v.

9. See H. I. Brown, *Perception, Theory and Commitment*, part II, for an excellent overview.

10. P. B. Medawar, *Induction and Intuition in Scientific Thought* (Philadelphia: American Philosophical Society, 1969) p. 30.

11. For an excellent overview of this problem, see P. B. Medawar, *Induction and Intuition*.

12. See Thomas S. Kuhn, *Scientific Revolutions*, p. 26: "No process yet disclosed by the historical study of scientific development at all resembles the methdological stereotype of falsification by direct comparison with nature."

13. Thomas S. Kuhn, *Criticism and the Growth of Knowledge: Proceedings of the International Colloquium in the Philosophy of Science*, London, 1965,

vol. 4, eds., I. Lakatos and A. Musgrave, (Cambridge: Cambridge University Press, 1970), p. 5.

14. H. I. Brown is excellent on this point (see, e.g., p. 81 ff.).

15. Johann Wolfgang von Goethe, "The Metamorphosis of Plants," Lines 5–10, in Christopher Middleton's translation *Selected Poems*, edited by Christopher Middleton (Boston: Suhrkamp, 1983), p. 154. [*HA*, I:199–201].

16. See R. H. Brady's essay, "Goethe's Natural Science: Some Non-Cartesian Meditations," in *Toward a Man-Centered Medical Science*, edited by K. Schaefer, H. Hensel, and R. Brady (Mt. Kisco, N.Y.: Futura, 1977), pp. 137–65. Also see R. H. Brady's "Form and Cause in Goethe's Morphology," in *Goethe and the Sciences: A Reappraisal*, edited by Frederick Amrine, Francis J. Zucker, and Harvey Wheeler (Dordrecht: D. Reidel, 1987), pp. 257–300; and R. H. Brady's chapter 5 in this volume. On Goethe's science, generally, see my extensive annotated bibliography in *Goethe and the Sciences*.

17. To be more precise, unlike the Kant of the First Critique, although perhaps very much like the Kant of the Third—but elaboration of this difficult and interesting point would greatly exceed the bounds of this essay.

18. On the relevance of the phenomenological term *intentionality* to Goethe's scientific procedure, see R. H. Brady, "Goethe's Natural Science," and his chapter 5 in this volume.

19. Goethe, *Scientific Studies*, p. 158 (*HA*, XII:315).

20. Goethe, "From Makaria's Archive," *Wilhelm Meister's Journeymanship* ("Aus Makariens Archiv," *Wilhelm Meister's Wanderjahre, HA*, VIII:473). See the strikingly similar remarks by one of the great experimenters of our time, Edwin Land: "I am convinced," he said, "that this kind of naive and direct relationship to nature by the experimenter is a vital part of this sort of scientific development. Only by looking with your own eyes can you know the feeling that red is not red, and green not green, and blue is not blue, unless some other color is in the field of view. As you cover the lenses of two of the projectors, leaving any one of the three uncovered, the so-called saturated color [meaning, roughly, pure and intense color] ceases to be saturated. But it becomes vivid instantly when one of the other colors is allowed to pass to the screen. I submit that it is the visual experiences at a time like this that lead to convictions which lead to hypotheses which lead to science. . . ." In concluding his lecture, Land speculated that the eye was made for looking at natural objects, and that therefore the subtlety of its operation was entirely lost when it was subjected to rigorously analytic experiments, based on spectroscopes and the matching of spots of color in which "no images are involved." (From Land's acceptance speech "The Case of the Sleeping Beauty," given upon receiving the Progress Medal from the Society of Photographic Engineers, May 1955, as reported by Francis Bello, "An Astonishing New Theory of Color," in *Fortune 59* [1959]: 200.)

21. P. H. Bideau, "Carl Gustav Carus Lecteur et interprète de Goethe. Goethe 'au point de vue purement physiologique'," *Études Germaniques*, 27 (1972): 341–63; 580–600.

22. On this polemic, see especially two recent studies: Neil M. Ribe, "Goethe's Critique of Newton: A Reconsideration," in *Studies in History and Philosophy of Science* 16 (1985): 315–35, and Dennis L. Sepper, *Goethe contra Newton: Polemics and the Project for a New Science of Color* (Cambridge: Cambridge University Press, 1988).

23. Goethe, *Scientific Studies*, p. 16 (*HA*, XIII:18).

24. Hjalmar Hegge, "Theory of Science in the Light of Goethe's Science of Nature," *Inquiry* 15 (1972): 371 (reprint with minor additions in *Goethe and the Sciences: A Reappraisal*, 195–218). Originally published in Norwegian as "Noen vitenskapsteoretiske sporsmal belyst ved Goethes naturvitenskap," in *Norsk filosofisk tidsskrift* 2 (1967).

25. Goethe, *HA*, XII:455.

26. See Brady, "Goethe's Natural Science," p. 157f.

27. Goethe, "Significant Help Given by an Ingenious Turn of Phrase" in *Scientific Studies*, p. 41; "Bedeutende Fördernis durch ein einziges geistreiches Wort" (*HA*, XXIII:40).

28. See Fritz Heinemann, "Goethe's Phenomenological Method," in *Philosophy* 9 (1934): 67–81. The metaphor of the acorn and the oak is borrowed of course from the "Preface" to Hegel's *Phenomenology*.

29. Goethe, *Italian Journey*, Naples, 17 May, 1787 (*HA*, XI:323).

30. P. B. Medawar, *Induction and Intuition*, pp. 14–15.

31. Thus, Goethe's interest in, for example, physiological optics, and his insistence that it belongs at the beginning of any study in chromatics (where it stands in his own *Theory of Color*), for here we can easily watch the subject being transformed in conformity with the phenomena themselves. Cf. Arthur G. Zajonc, "Goethe's Theory of Color and Scientific Intuition," *American Journal of Physics*, 44 (1976): 327–33. In this regard see also Arthur G. Zajonc, "Facts as Theory: Aspects of Goethe's Philosophy of Science," in *Goethe and the Sciences: A Reappraisal*, 219–45; and Fredrick Amrine, "Goethean Method in the Work of Jochen Bockemühl," ibid., 301–18.

32. See Dieter Henrich, "Fichte's Original Insight," in *Contemporary German Philosophy*, vol. 1 (University Park: Pennsylvania State University Press, 1982), pp. 15–53. Originally published as "Fichtes ursprüngliche Einsicht," in *Subjektivität und Metaphysik, Festschrift für Wolfgang Cramer*, edited by Dieter Henrich and Hans Wagner (Frankfurt/Main: Vittorio Klostermann, 1966), pp. 188–232.

33. See Ernst Cassirer, "The Idea of Metamorphosis and Idealistic Morphology: Goethe," in Ernst Cassirer's *The Problem of Knowledge: Philosophy, Science, and History since Hegel* (New Haven: Yale University Press, 1950), chap. vii, esp. pp. 145–46, where Cassirer quotes yet another Goethean analogy of the relationship between particular and universal that is reminiscent of Fichte.

34. Hans Gebert, "Goethe's Work on Color," *The Michigan Academician* 8 (1976): 263–64. Gebert relies in turn upon C. Gögelein, "Zu Goethes Begriff von Wissenschaft auf dem Wege der Methodik seiner Farbstudien," *Einzelarbeiten*

aus dem Max-Planck-Institut zur Erforschung der Lebensbedingungen der wissenschaftlichtechnischen Welt 1 (München: Hanser, 1972).

35. Goethe, *HA*, XI:400.

36. Goethe argues this at several different points in his polemic against Newton. For the contemporary position, see Harold I. Brown, *Perception, Theory and Commitment*, part II; and John Losee, *A Historical Introduction to the Philosophy of Science*, 2nd ed. (Oxford: Oxford University Press, 1980) pp. 189–218.

37. Gernot Böhme, "Is Goethe's Theory of Colors Science" in *Contemporary German Philosophy*, translated by Joseph Gray vol. 4 (University Park: Pennsylvania State University Press, 1984), pp. 262–86. Originally published in German in *Studia Leibnitiana* 9 (1977): 27–54; reprinted in Böhme's *Alternativen der Wissenschaft* (Frankfurt/ Main: Suhrkamp, 1980) pp. 123–53.

38. Goethe, *HA*, XIII:377.

39. Goethe, Scientific Studies, p. 269 (*HA*, XIII:480).

40. *Enthüllung der Theorie Newtons*, §136.

41. *Enthullung*, §544.

42. Goethe, *HA*, XIII:315; Goethe, *Scientific Studies*, p. 158.

43. Neil M. Ribe, "Science and Symbol in Goethe's Geology," (paper presented at the annual meeting of the History of Science Society, Ann Arbor, Mich., June, 1982.) Ribe is careful to distinguish this distinctly Goethean sense of metamorphosis from the modern petrographic concept.

44. The breakdown of any absolute subject/object is evident in contemporary philosophy of science but by no means restricted to that discipline. Indeed, an important model—perhaps even the main impetus—for that "revolution" was a series of developments in the psychology of perception that began already with the Gestalt theorists. Cf. R. L. Gregory's argument (in summarizing the results of recent research) that "perception involves a kind of inference from sensory data to object-reality . . . a kind of problem solving—a kind of intelligence" (*The Intelligent Eye* [New York: McGraw-Hill, 1970], p. 30). See also Patrick A. Heelan, *Space-Perception and the Philosophy of Science* (Berkeley: University of California Press, 1983), an important study that proceeds via phenomenology and the psychology of perception to a notion of scientific method remarkably like Goethe's, namely, science as a means of transforming one's own modes of perception.

45. See Brady, "Goethe's Natural Science."

46. The best exposition and interpretation of this subtle Goethean notion is to be found in the work of Michael Wilson; see, especially, his "Goethe's Colour Experiments," in *Year Book of the Physical Society* (1958), pp. 3–12, and "Goethe's Concept of Darkness," *Journal for Anthroposophy* 24 (1976): 43–57.

47. Objections of this kind to Thomas S. Kuhn's book were immediately raised from a number of different quarters; see, especially, I. Lakotos and A. Musgrave, *Criticism and the Growth of Knowledge*, and Israel Scheffler, *Science and Subjectivity* (Indianapolis, Ind.: Bobbs-Merrill, 1967).

48. Karl Pearson, *The Grammar of Science* (London: Dent, 1911), p. 11. Quoted in Joseph Weizenbaum, *Computer Power and Human Reason: From Calculation to Judgement* (San Francisco: W. H. Freeman, 1976), p. 25.

49. E.g., Kuhn, *Scientific Revolutions*, p. 26.

50. See Brady, "Goethe's Natural Science."

51. *Maximen und Reflexionen* (*HA*, XII:1061). A strong argument along similar lines is advanced by Thomas R. Blackburn (with explicit reference to Goethe and Newton as competing models) in his article "Sensuous-Intellectual Complementarity in Science," *Science* 172 (1971): 1003–7: "What is urgently needed is a science that can comprehend complex systems without, or with a minimum of, abstractions. To 'see' a complex system as an organic whole requires an act of trained intuition, just as seeing order in a welter of numerical data does. The conditions for achieving such perceptions have been discussed at length among scientists (with little discernible impact on the way we train scientists). The consensus, if any, is that they follow only after long periods of total immersion in the problem. The implication for the present discussion is that the intuitive knowledge essential to a full understanding of complex systems can be encouraged and prepared for by: (1) training scientists to be aware of sensuous clues about their surroundings; (2) insisting on sensuous knowledge as part of the intellectual structure of science, not as an afterthought; and (3) approaching complex systems openly, respecting their organic complexity before choosing an abstract quantification space into which to project them. . . . If we do learn to know complexities through the complementary modes of sensuous intuition and logical abstraction, and if we can transmit and discuss the former as reliably as the latter, then there is hope for a renaissance in science as a whole comparable to that which occurred in physics between 1900 and 1930" (p. 1007).

52. The analogy to Johann Fichte is clear; again, see D. Henrich, "Fichte's Original Insight." That Goethe's scientific work must be understood in conjunction with Fichte's philosophy was argued already in 1886 by Rudolf Steiner in his *A Theory of Knowledge Based on Goethe's World Conception: Fundamental Outlines With Special Reference to Schiller*, translated by O. D. Wannamaker (Spring Valley, N.Y.: Anthroposophic Press, 1940); originally published in German as *Grundlinien einer Erkenntnistheorie der goetheschen Weltanschauung mit besonderer Rücksicht auf Schiller* (1886; reprint, 7th ed, Dornach/Schweiz: Rudolf Steiner Verlag, 1979).

53. Johann Fichte terms these the "divisible self" and the "divisible not-self."

54. Goethe, "The Purpose Set Forth," *Scientific Studies*, pp. 63–66 (the translation of this passage, however, is the author's); "Die Absicht eingeleitet," *Zur Morphologie* (*HA*, XIII:56).

55. Goethe, "Preliminary Studies for a Physiology of Plants" (Vorarbeiten zu einer Physiologie der Pflanzen), *Goethes Werke, Weimarer Ausgabe* (Weimar: Hermann Böhlau), II.6:349.

56. Goethe, *Goethe Briefe, HA*, II:192.

57. Goethe, *Scientific Studies*, p. 159; *HA*, XIII:317.

58. Goethe, "The Collector and his Circle," in Johann Wolfgang von Goethe, *Essays on Art and Literature*, edited by John Gearey (New York: Suhrkamp, 1986) p. 146; "Der Sammler und die Seinigen" (*HA*, XII:85).

59. Kuhn, *Scientific Revolutions*, p. 24.

60. Goethe, "Significant Help," *Scientific Studies*, p. 39. "Jeder Gegenstand, wohl beschaut, schliesst ein neues Organ in uns auf" (*HA*, XIII:38). I have modified Miller's version somewhat, translating "*wohl beschaut*" as "well contemplated" rather than "clearly seen."

61. Goethe, *HA*, XII:441.

62. Goethe, *HA*, XII:441.

3

Walter Heitler

Goethean Science

In the last several years, much has been written about Goethean science.[1] The spectrum of opinions extends from a brusque rejection, which grants these writings at best some artistic, but no scientific worth whatsoever, to an unconditional veneration that interprets Goethe's work as the only admissible and infallible scientific method. During his lifetime and long thereafter, Goethe's efforts were largely ignored by scientists. For his critics who were physicists, this rejection was particularly easy, since Goethe's *Theory of Color* includes mistakes and false conclusions that appeared to place Goethe's polemic against Newton on a false factual basis from the start. The result, unfortunately, was that the didactic part of Goethe's *Theory of Color* was discredited as well.[2]

Today, one encounters a great deal of disquietude regarding the question of Goethe's science; this uncertainty can be viewed as a sign of reconsideration. For example, botanists have worked fruitfully according to Goethe's indications, but these studies have been few. The attitude toward Goethean science one encounters most often today is a benevolence that recognizes high artistry and perhaps even deep insight, that occasionally appreciates certain scientific contributions, but that for the most part remains uncommitted.

What is the goal of Goethean science? How is it different from conventional scientific work? Does it seek something different from that which is sought by what has commonly been termed "natural science"? All scientific undertakings, to the extent that they exist today and deserve the name "science," can be placed over a single common denominator: Scientific cognition always consists in tracing a single natural phenomenon back to something universal. With this idea Goethe is in agreement. What, however, is this universal? Here Goethe and conventional science part company and travel separate paths.

MECHANICAL MODELS

Let us consider two examples from mechanics: an object falls to the ground; the moon circles the earth. Both phenomena can be traced back to the universal law of gravity. Here we have something to which these otherwise entirely different phenomena are both subject—a law or cause.[3] Both phenomena can be derived logically and mathematically in all their particulars by reason of this law and the law of motion.

To understand better Goethe's way of science, it is helpful to review briefly the history of physics, in which the first area of investigation was mechanics. From the beginning, Galileo, its creator, sought to explain other areas of physics in terms of mechanics as well. Light, for example, was supposed to be "in reality" something mechanical, which becomes our subjective experience of light only through sense perception. The thesis could hardly be more bold. Today we encounter and grow accustomed to such mechanical representations from childhood on and hold them to be far more self-evident than they actually are.

Newton sought the first experimental proof of Galileo's thesis. His conception of light was a mechanical model consisting of tiny balls, one type for each color. Later physicists replaced his model with another—the little balls became electromagnetic waves—but the essentially mechanical nature of the representation did not change. Let there be no misunderstanding: the truth of this conception of light is beyond doubt, in the sense that these waves exist and comprise a certain part of the reality of light.

Yet, these waves are not the whole reality, since no system of any sort that is built upon a mechanical model (and we include electromagnetism within mechanics) contains the concept of color. Consequently, a valid science of color can never be derived in this way. The mechanical conception of light is useful in many ways—an understanding of refraction and above all of diffraction phenomena are some of its most important fruits. It can make no claims, however, about those things that do not occur within its system of concepts and can never occur there. If physicists now and at that time have been able to make assertions concerning color based on their theories, then it is for this reason: they assume a heuristic relationship between wavelength and color—we have all learned this in school—which can be proven in many cases by mere observation, but in many cases is quite simply false.

Thus physics, in the usual sense, teaches very little about color *as color*. Yet can a science of color exist? It is from this critical standpoint that we must judge Goethe's attempt to formulate his color theory.

A SCIENCE OF QUALITIES

Goethe radically rejects every mechanical model of light. His reasons and motives are many, and they are in part profound. They form the basis of Goethe's extremely emotional polemic against Newton—a polemic that often had no basis in fact. It would be of no use to take up the part of Goethe's polemic that seeks to prove Newton's experiments and conclusions factually false. Of course, Newton's pioneering work has weaknesses which may be attacked, but his genius shows itself in that he was able to draw from imperfect experiments virtually correct conclusions that opened the way to a new science of light. Here Newton is beyond reproach. And yet a science of colors did *not* arise out of Newtonian physics.

But Goethe's motives lie deeper. Can one represent light—the life-giver, which appears and inspires us anew in a thousand different phenomena, without which life in all forms is unthinkable—as a dead, mechanical substance or even maintain that it *might* be mechanical? Goethe calls this interpretation the "skeleton of light." To maintain that an evening sky glowing red was nothing more than little balls or waves that strike our eyes was something that Goethe simply could not accept. In prose and in verse he expressed his abhorrence of this "mechanization" of nature or derided it. I believe that now, a century and a half later, we have reason to contemplate this side of Goethe's genius with profound earnestness.

Goethe rejects on principle any application whatsoever of mathematics to physics: "Physics must clearly differentiate itself from mathematics. The former must exist in resolute independence and seek with love, veneration, and piety to enter into nature's holy life. . . . Mathematics must, on the other hand, declare itself independent of everything external, must proceed according to its own spirit and laws."[4] Clearly, what is here understood as "physics" is for the most part qualitative natural phenomena we perceive (colors, for example), which cannot and should not be understood in terms of measurement and calculation. Mathematics, which Goethe admired as such and termed an art "in its execution," has no place in nature. Here he parts company with the greater part of contemporary science.

The coalescence of natural phenomena and mathematics, while it has led to profound insights, has also had widespread and profound effects everywhere. Having transformed the method into an absolute, this approach to science led to an untenably narrow *Weltanschauung* that has carried over into every other realm of thought. The world is viewed as a set of cogwheels turning mathematically, and as a result the whole world has become "technological." Goethe did not recognize the mathematical conception of natural phenomena as a path to cognition. In prescience of its consequences, he rejected it in practice. The evolution of physics did not follow Goethe's indications. What we term physics today pursues a measuring, mathematical approach to natural phenomena to the greatest extent possible. With color, however, which is almost entirely "quality," this quantification is not possible.[5] Physics knows but few qualities, such as mass, length, and so forth. The plenitude of qualities that the senses perceive, however—among them the colors—are not denizens of its realm.

The quantitative-mechanical, then, could not become the basis of a valid theory of colors. Goethe observed instead nature itself, including the phenomena of color. Many of his observations follow simply from the physics of that time or today and the above-named relationship between wavelength and color. These observations can thus be understood in terms of contemporary theories. Yet, Goethe made other discoveries that clearly contradict this assumed relationship, and with it Newton's theses. One such observation is the phenomenon of "colored shadows." Take, for example, a snowy sunset landscape illuminated yellow or red. The shadow of a tree should be white, for snow is white if it is not illuminated by colored light. The shadow appears, however, deep blue or green, the colors complementary to yellow and red. Such phenomena suggest that a science of color must be something quite different from Newtonian physics.

The two scientific methods do not coincide; one cannot be formulated in terms of the other. Thus, the inevitable questions: Can a science of color exist? How can we proceed? We can recall the words of one of Goethe's great contemporaries, Immanuel Kant: "Yet I maintain that any particular natural theory contains only so much true science as it contains mathematics." If we accept Kant's declaration as true, then right from the start we must renounce any attempt to formulate a theory of color. Yet, it is precisely this thesis of Kant's that Goethe refutes, and Goethe's incomparable achievement lies in his demonstration that this thesis is false—that rigorous, clear science is possible within the realm of the purely qualitative as well. Goethean science does not deal with a mechanistic, measurable substrate of light (although this dimension exists) but the simple color itself as we see it.

Color, as it is *seen*, is the object of this science. Here Goethe quite consciously severs himself from René Descartes, who separated the world into two parts: first, an external object independent of us that can then be imagined as a mechanism, and, second, our own inner life. Our everyday sensory perception, however, has no place within this scheme. Color, for example, belongs to both the external world and to our inner experience—the two are an indivisible unity as Goethe expresses in one of his poems:

> In the contemplation of nature you must
> Regard the One as All;
> Nothing is within, nothing is without.
> Grasp thus without delay
> A holy open secret.[6]

THE ARCHETYPAL PHENOMENON

Here is revealed a problem that equally concerns science and philosophy. Sense perception can be understood neither by natural science as it is practiced today, which studies only "external objects," nor by psychology, which studies only "inner experiences." The Cartesian split completely blocks the path to understanding. Only a mode of thought that overcomes this split and perceives the unity of "outside" and "inside" in all our everyday perceptions can gain insight into this problem.

What form must such a science of colors take? "Science" implies tracing individual instances back to a universal. Here we are dealing with phenomena of color. What would be the universal? Intimate observation of nature shows that there are many individual phenomena of one type, phenomena that have something in common. Let us gather them together and attempt to grasp that which is common to them, the universal. We stand, and shall remain within the realm of phenomena. The universal is, however, no longer an individual phenomenon; it is, as Goethe calls it, the *idea* of a whole group of phenomena, or, in the parlance of modern science, the point of convergence of a certain class of phenomena. Just as the point of convergence of a mathematical series is not identical with any one of its members, so this phenomenon at the outward boundary of physics is something that has no concrete existence. It is, as was said, the idea of a phenomenon, which Goethe terms the *archetypal phenomenon* (*Urphänomen*) and describes thus:

ideal, as that ultimately perceivable;

real, as perceived;

symbolic, because it comprehends all instances; identical with all
   instances.[7]

Each line has a profound meaning. "Ideal" can best be understood in
a platonic sense—that is, that which is "ultimately perceivable." Here,
however, we can agree with Goethe only if we do not step outside the
circle of his phenomenology. The inclusion of other occurences (in the
realm of physics, for example) would not allow the archetypal phenomenon to appear as "that ultimately perceivable." We perceive this
"idea" as something entirely "real," not as our own fantasy, for it permeates natural phenomena as a principle that calls forth the phenomenon. It comprehends all individual instances and is thus representative
or "symbolic," at work in every individual instance that it calls forth.
Thus, it is identical not only with the individual instance but also with
the totality of instances.

Let us consider two examples. One of Goethe's archetypal phenomena is that light, in passing through a turbid (*trübes*) medium,
appears yellow-red, while a dark background viewed through such a
medium appears blue. Another example is the general thesis from that
part of Goethe's *Theory of Color* entitled "Physiological Colors": the eye
has the tendency to call forth inwardly the color opposite to the color
viewed. This "opposite color" is, in modern terminology, the "complementary color." The phenomenon of colored shadows is one instance;
another is the after-image that we see when we stare at a colored dot for
a certain time and then close our eyes. The dot appears in the complementary color. This general principle can be called an "archetypal phenomenon," which is within the realm of phenomena what a law is within
the realm of the quantitative-mechanisms of physics.

We would wish to reach a point where we could trace all appearances of color back to one or at least to very few archetypal phenomena.
This is also what Goethe wished and believed he had more or less
accomplished. His archetypal phenomenon (the passing of light through
a turbid medium) supposedly allowed the colors to come forth out of
light and was therefore to be the basis of all appearances of color. Yet, he
did not succeed in showing this. The colors that arise through diffraction
or refraction in a prism, for example, can hardly be understood so. His
Theory of Color remained incomplete.

It is difficult to say whether the *Theory of Color* belongs to the realm
of physics, physiology, or psychology. It belongs to none of these and, at
the same time, to all. The division of science into the specialized fields
that we recognize today stems from the Cartesian "split" and is entirely

inappropriate. This mode of thought wishes to sever the human being from the world and thereby to claim objectivity. In actuality, however, one human capacity—measurement and abstract thought—is singled out and alone is allowed access to the external world. Thereby we perceive all sorts of mechanisms that appear in nature—everything that can be grasped quantitatively, but nothing about color. The other side of this "split" is the realm of pure psychology.

Goethe's standpoint was precisely the opposite; he makes no divisions. All scientific efforts proceed from the human being. Consequently, a sound science should allow every human capacity, to the extent that it has access to nature, to come forth and play its part. In this sense, Goethe's scientific approach is different and new. The human capacity upon which he principally relies is a *viewing*, intuitive observation (*Anschauung*), not analytical thought. We shall return to this point more fully later.

Moreover, Goethe does not limit himself to a single aspect of nature as Galilean science does. His view of nature is more comprehensive; it is not science alone but, rather, extends into art, aesthetics—even into the sphere of religion. Who would deny that an evening sky contains eminently artistic elements? An entire chapter of the *Theory of Color* is dedicated to aesthetics, or what Goethe calls the "Sensory-Moral Effects (*sinnlich-sittliche Wirkungen*) of Colors." His spirit strives to attain a totality and must seek to unite every aspect of color into a unified whole, in the center of which stands the human being.

THE REALM OF PURE FORM

Let us now turn to another area within Goethean science, that of plant morphology. *The Metamorphosis of Plants* is a pioneering work in which entirely new approaches were methodically developed and at the same time a new field of scientific investigation opened. Here Goethe undertakes nothing less than to show that a rigorous science of form (*Gestaltbildung*) is possible. In Goethe's time, Carl Linnaeus's system for the categorization of plants was strongly influential. An immense amount of material had been classified according to one constant criterion—the number of stamens. Goethe saw that, on one hand, much that was similar had been separated, while, on the other hand, much that was dissimilar had been grouped together according to a rigid, arbitrary criterion. He wrote of Linnaeus that he had learned an immeasurable amount from him, but no botany.

Goethe observed the forms of plants in their individual organs and watched how they metamorphosed during the growth of a single plant and then from plant to plant within related species. The sensually perceptible forms of a leaf, for example, can transform themselves continually until they appear outwardly quite different, yet they remain true to the "formative idea" (*gestaltmässige Idee*). Within a single plant, the leaf continually transforms itself into the calyx, the petals, and even into the pistil.

Goethe saw a genetic connection between these forms. Moreover, the same organ is continually transforming itself from plant to plant. As with the cactus, the leaf can atrophy to a barely recognizable remnant and still remain a "leaf," while the axial buds become the characteristic needles. The perception of these affinities, or "homologies," as they have come to be called, leads to the recognition of a general "building plan," a "blueprint" common to all seed plants. The outward forms may change in countless ways, yet the idea of this formative principle remains the same. Goethe called this formative principle the "archetypal plant" (*Urpflanze*). The archetypal plant is no specific plant existing anywhere in nature, nor is it to be understood temporally. Like the archetypal phenomenon, it is the principle underlying the morphological structure of all seed plants.

A conversation with Johann von Schiller sheds some additional light on the nature of the archetypal plant, of which Goethe makes a sketch about which Schiller then says: "That is not an experience, but an idea." Goethe responds: "Then I can be very glad that I have ideas without knowing it, and even see them with my eyes."[8] This last remark points to Goethe's enormous imaginative power. The "eyes" of which Goethe speaks are naturally not the bodily eyes, and he surely means "idea" in the Platonic sense.

Related, if not *mutatis mutandis* identical with the concept of the archetypal plant, is the concept of the *type*, which Goethe employs above all in zoology. The skeletal systems of all mammals are given shape throughout by the same formative principle: they all belong to the same type. The individual bones may take the most various forms—they are all present in the proper place and in the same relationship to one another. This universal idea of the type led Goethe to his well-known discovery of the intermaxillary bone, which is atrophied in human beings. No single animal represents the type itself: "no individual can be the pattern of the whole."[9] The type is not an experience but an idea.

We have said that science consists of tracing an individual instance back to something universal. If we succeed in tracing a certain plant's morphological structure back to the archetypal plant and fully identifying each organ with the organs of the archetypal plant, then we can speak of true scientific cognition. It is a kind of cognition entirely different from that to which we have accustomed ourselves in the exact sciences. There cognition implies knowing, for example, that an individual mechanical process is a special instance of a general law and can be derived completely from that law. The analogy within the realm of the organic would be a law according to which, for example, the growth of the plant could be derived from the seed. Thereby a great deal is demanded, and we are still very far from such an understanding.

Yet, within this law, the general morphological principle—the archetypal image—must be included. The tracing back of a specific plant to this morphological principle is then only a partial cognition but no less important for that reason. It is a partial cognition that relates directly to form, something that hardly exists in the realm of physics and lifeless matter. How the plant manages to transform the formative principle into a morphological deed, so to speak, is the secret of life—still entirely unknown to us.

Today we are so dazzled by the successes of Galilean science that we are often unwilling to recognize anything else as "scientific." Only the quantitative, material, and mechanical are considered valid science. The fundamental importance of Goethean science for us lies in its demonstration that rigorous science is possible both within the realm of pure form and the qualitative, and that this science is as valid as the Galilean.

In contrast to the *Theory of Color*, Goethe's morphology has found its adherents. The emergence of Darwin interrupted its development, yet it was taken up again in the twenties by Wilhelm Troll and others, and it has been developed further since.[10] To be sure, the static idea of the archetypal plant is no longer sufficient today; morphology must also be seen within the framework of the historical evolution of life, but this issue is beyond our current theme.

On the other hand, it might be good to compare the archetypal plant to analogous ways of thinking within modern molecular biology. According to contemporary thought, the hereditary factors of an organism are located within the genes of the chromosomes, the chemical substrate of which is the so-called *DNA* molecule. According to biologists, the gene corresponding to a certain inherited trait is simply a specific, localized section of the long, ribbon-like molecule. Since the form of the plant is inherited as well, they believe that the morphology of the organism is anchored in the chemical structure of *DNA*, even if other types of molecules come into play. One speaks of the "blueprint" or the "morphological information" contained in these molecules.

That a connection exists between the chemical structure of these molecules and morphology may well be true. But nothing would be farther from the truth than an attempt to identify the archetypal plant with *DNA* itself. "Blueprint" and "information" are not chemical or

physical concepts. They originate in the human mind to explain something that clearly exists in the plant but which cannot be grasped
chemically. The molecules can only be a material substrate for just this
idealike formative principle or archetypal plant.

If we may draw an analogy, the structure of the *DNA* molecule is to
the archetypal plant as the ink-smeared type in the printer's press is to the
poem that it will print. In no way at all do we understand what the
relationship between the chemical structure and the formative principle
actually is (just as we have no idea of the real relationship between
physics and color), or how the plant goes about changing the formative
principle into form.

Intuitive Perception

The next question to ask is how one arrives at knowledge in the Goethean
sense. The contemporary researcher, following in the steps of Galileo, has
but one access to nature: questioning nature by experiment, hypothesizing, and using measurement wherever possible, followed by abstract
logical thinking. The Goethean approach is entirely different. Experimentation and measurement in themselves were repugnant to Goethe when
used outside mechanics. He felt it to be an unpardonable encroachment:
"Nature becomes mute under torture. Its true answer to an honest question is: 'Yea, yea; Nay, nay: Whatsoever is more than these cometh of
evil.'"[11] Is to experiment, then, to torture nature? Newton's procedure
and that of all his successors is appropriate to understand light only in
terms of one single aspect of nature: the quantitative-mechanical. Yet
everywhere, in light as well as in biology, Goethe saw the divine in nature
(*Gottnatur*) and not just nature's "skeleton." Might it not very well be to
torture to demand only the latter from nature?[12]

One cannot say that Goethe was consistent in his rejection of the
experiment. He experimented often himself (and conscientiously at that).
For the most part he was moderate, however, and his method was quite
different. What remains when we reject the experiment? Clearly, bare
observation—a contemplative, intuitive perception of nature, which
Goethe developed to a degree unattained since. "Judgment through Intuitive Perception," the title of a very short essay by Goethe, characterizes
the method well in a few words.[13]

To perceive connections between botanical forms, one needs
analytical, logical thought far less than a view of the form in its totality.
The word *exact* reminds us that here imagination and speculation are not
given free rein. As is always the case in science, the results of one's
observations must pass the test of critical judgment. The danger of erring

into fantasy and arbitrariness is great. Let above all those who wish to expand and further Goethe's method take heed of this potential difficulty. Only critical and self-critical judgment can lead to clarity and true science.

In the aforementioned essay, Goethe takes issue with Kant's thesis that would restrict human cognition to "discursive judgement" (logical, serial thought), but which also admits that one could imagine an understanding that "is intuitive, proceeding from . . . the viewing of a whole to the parts (*intellectus archetypus*)."[14] Goethe believed that Kant meant by this a divine understanding, while human understanding is expressly characterized as discursive. Yet, this is precisely what Goethe rejects. The following sentence may be especially helpful in developing an understanding of Goethe's science: "Yet, if we may raise ourselves within the moral sphere through faith in God . . . into a higher region and approach Primal Being, such may also be the case within the sphere of the intellectual—that through the observation of eternally creative nature we make ourselves worthy of spiritual participation in its productions."[15] Then Goethe writes that his spirit had always striven to find the archetypal, for example, the archetypal plant.

Much of importance comes to expression here. Goethe claims that intuitive perception of a whole is a valid scientific method. Through perception of archetypal images (*Urbilder*), we participate in the creative process within nature's innermost spiritual core—an entirely Platonic position. The parallel Goethe draws between contemplative observation of nature and the raising of oneself through religion into a higher region shows just how highly Goethe valued this method. He had no such praise for the analytic-mathematical method that dominates science today. Another utterance goes yet further: "He who would deny that nature is a divine organ, would at the same time deny all revelation."[16] Here, natural cognition—the perception of nature's archetypal images—is addressed directly as divine revelation.

LIVING NATURE OR TECHNOLOGY?

The last question that we wish to raise is the most central: What stand must we take today with regard to Goethean science? How must we regard the more prevalent type of science that proceeds by means of mathematical analysis? We shall hardly go so far as to equate natural science of any sort with the divine revelation that has been transmitted to us through the great religions. Nevertheless, we can and must agree with Goethe's view: there can be no doubt that the method of exact intuitive perception leads to valid scientific knowledge, and this within a realm hardly accessible to the analytical mode of thought—the realm of qualities and relationships between forms. Above all we must agree with Goethe that the "archetypal images"—the formative principles behind phenomena—are *spiritual realities* accessible to our cognition, and we must view them as a part of the spiritual content of nature. If we wish, we may view these understandings as a reflection of the Spirit that created them. This phrasing brings us somewhat closer to Goethe's conception of the "divine organ."

Whether we may or even should grant to the natural law of exact science an equal rank is another question altogether. The mathematically formulated natural law is also something spiritual, an archetypal structure according to which lifeless (and to a considerable extent living) matter orders itself. We perceive this archetypal law (not to be confused with the ultimate components of matter, the elementary particles) with our minds as well. The discoveries made during the past century in the area of the exact sciences can be incomparably profound and beautiful. Here lies knowledge that may claim the highest spiritual rank. We must view these discoveries as archetypal images of universal laws and not, as positivism does, degrade them to a comfortable summary and "description" of data. Johannes Kepler held this, again, more or less Platonic view, and it is no accident that Goethe admired Kepler rather than Newton, seeing in Kepler a kindred spirit.

Such laws were alien to Goethe, however, and we cannot expect a suitable appreciation from him. There exists, of course, an essential difference between the laws of lifeless matter and the archetypal images of living nature that Goethe sought. The former cannot penetrate into nature's vital, creative center because physical law is rigid, lifeless, and inexorable. Or, to emphasize the negative side that Goethe saw, one is dealing with the "skeleton" of nature. Yet let us not forget that a crystal is something "frozen," and a crystal has a beauty of its own. With this in mind we can view the laws of exact science—of physics, chemistry, and so forth—as Spirit proceeding from the Creative Spirit, as archetypal images within the realm of lifeless matter, just as Goethe saw them in living nature—for example, in his archetypal plant.

On the other hand, we cannot help feeling great concern about positivist science. The Galilean-Newtonian approach led to an ever-increasing abstraction, to a detachment of science from humanity in the name of a misconceived objectivity. Only that which had nothing to do with human beings was to be considered objective—only that which could be measured and analyzed.

Goethe warned against these abstractions. A world conceived without the human being is no longer a whole and healthy world in which people can live. Let us also remember that all of our sensory perceptions (colors, sounds, and so forth) do not allow such an objectification of the external world. The realm in which abstract laws—above all those of the new physics—are conceived has also become somewhat alien to our experience. We find them principally in a laboratory experiment conducted under strict conditions or in a machine. It is more a human-made than a natural world. Newtonian science has led directly to contemporary technology and, to a great extent, is practiced only for the sake of technology. Goethe was in no way averse to the practical application of science—for example, one section in *Theory of Color* is devoted to dyeing. The promoter of technology in the modern sense, however, is not the Creator of nature, but Mephisto.

Our world and our thought today are permeated by a symbiosis of Newtonian science and technology. The countenance of both the earth and human beings has been and will be further altered by technology. This mode of science, which is only the half of science, manipulates nature to further its own ends, and has taken possession of our thinking. It lays claim to everything and even makes preparations for controlling people biotechnically, transforming the human being into an object of technology. Here we need not go so far as to mention the modern means of mass annihilation that are also its progeny. Can one doubt that Goethe's dark and gloomy premonitions have proved justified, and that Mephisto is indeed at work here? And since technology is so closely bound to the Newtonian mode of science, must we not then already see in it Mephisto's bald pate and all-too-clever profile?

This last question overtaxes our ability to answer. Perhaps the answer depends on us and the way in which we view and practice science. Let us suffer no delusions: the human being stands in the middle between God and the devil, and the last thing we wish is to declare war against "diabolic science." Yet, a great task lies before us, the size of which is still incomprehensible: we must see that we do not sign away our souls to a monomaniacal belief in progress through science and technology. We are already on the way, and such a belief could well cost more than just a drop of blood. If we wish to survive and remain human, we must resist the temptation of this one-sided "progress."

There may be many paths to that goal, and they may split and lead in many different directions. But one precondition is indispensable—a more penetrating look at Newtonian science and an understanding of its one-sidedness despite its enormous success in this one direction. As yet the achievements of Goethean science cannot match those of Newtonian science. Little has been done, but what has been done is extremely important. This work lies in the broad field beyond the narrow Newtonian road, in a field of qualities and forms that is also occupied by human beings. The Newtonian path is a rough road leading outward from this field, always farther and farther away. Goethean science always proceeds from the center of this field and always plows in the near vicinity. In this sense, Goethean science can help us to realize the proper limitations of the Newtonian world view and the technology that has changed our environment, sometimes in destructive ways. Should we succeed in further developing a Goethean science—far beyond that which has been indicated here—we would have a counterbalance to resist Mephisto's temptation to see Newtonian science and technology as our only salvation.

NOTES

1. This essay was originally entitled, "Die Naturwissenschaft Goethes: Eine Gegenüberstellung Goethescher und modern-exakter Naturwissenschaft," and read before the *Berliner Germanistentag* in 1968. It was first published in *Der Berliner Germanistentag, 1968: Vorträge und Berichte*, edited by K. H. Borck and R. Henss (Heidelberg: Carl Winter Universitätsverlag, 1970), pp. 13–23; and reprinted in Walter Heitler, *Naturphilosophische Streifzüge* (Braunschweig: Vieweg, 1970), pp. 66–76. The essay was translated by Frederick Amrine.

2. E.g., E. Buchwald, *Naturschau mit Goethe* (Stuttgart: Kohlhammer Verlag, 1960), and H. Fischer, *Goethes Naturwissenschaft* (Zürich: Artemis-Verlag, 1950). Although I disagree with several of his points, I also recommend Werner Heisenberg, "Die Goethesche und die Newtonsche Farbenlehre im Lichte der modernen Physik," *Geist der Zeit* 19 (1941): 261–75; reprinted in Werner Heisenberg, *Wandlungen in den Grundlagen der Naturwissenschaft: Sieben Vorträge*, 10th ed. (Stuttgart: S. Hirzel, 1973), pp. 85–106.

3. Here, Heitler makes a point that cannot be rendered in English concerning the etymology of the German word for "cause," *Ursache*. The word is a compound, consisting of the root *Sache* (matter, affair) and the prefix *Ur-*, which can be rendered as "primal" or "archetypal." Thus, a "cause" is, in German, quite literally that which existed at the very beginning, that which originally underlay the phenomenon. Trans.

4. Goethe, "Maxims and Reflections," No. 644, in *Werke: Hamburger Ausgabe*, edited by Erich Trunz (Hamburg: Christian Wegner, 1948–1960), XII:454. Henceforth, references to the *Hamburger Ausgabe* are abbreviated *HA*.

5. Colorimetry makes possible a limited application of quantitative methods within the realm of color.

6. Goethe, "*Epirrhema*," *HA* I:358.

7. Goethe, "Maxims and Reflections," *HA*, XII:366.

8. Goethe, "Propitious Encounter," *Goethe's Botanical Writings*, trans. Bertha Mueller (Honolulu: University of Hawaii Press, 1952), p. 218.

9. Goethe, *Naturwissenschaftenliche Schriften*, I:244.

10. Cf. Lothar Wolf and Wilhelm Troll, "Goethes morphologischer Auftrag," *Botanisches Archiv*, 41 (1940): 1–71; later published as *Goethes morphologischer Auftrag: Versuch einer naturwissenschaftlichen Morphologie*, 3rd ed. (Tübingen: Neomarius, 1950). The application of the concept of form contained in this monograph to the inorganic and molecular world appears to be an unwarranted projection that threatens to obliterate once again the fundamental difference between inorganic matter and life. The form of the flower blossom with its various attributes and the "form" of a molecule are of fundamentally different natures and origins.

11. Goethe, "Maxims and Reflections," *HA*, XII:498.

12. It is good to keep in mind—at least in the realm of atomic physics—that each experiment is an encroachment that changes the object of that experiment. It is not unthinkable that an experiment on light such as Newton conducted altered precisely that which Goethe saw in light: the natural phenomenon as it touches us directly appearing as artistic-aesthetic effect, even as a revelation of God. Let it also be clear in our minds that experimentation in biology such as is common today in our exclusive continuation of the methods of physical measurement has led to no small amount of animal torture. Our guilt in this matter grows daily.

13. Heitler requested that I not translate the essay title, "Anschauende Urteilskraft," literally. Trans.

14. Goethe, *HA*, XIII:30.

15. Goethe, *HA*, XIII:30–31.

16. Goethe, "Maxims and Reflections," *HA*, XII:2.

4

Herbert Hensel

Goethe, Science,
and Sensory Experience

Human cognition rests upon experiences of various kinds, among which sensory experience occupies the rank of an indispensable and irreplaceable foundation.[1] This fact is true not only for our everyday and naive view of the world, but also for all the positive sciences whose activity is directed towards exploration of the world of the senses. Even the empirical disciplines that are most abstract and remote from sensory experience, such as physics, cannot avoid calling upon sensory experience as their final witness—no matter how far they go in transcending naive perception with their conceptual systems.

Let it be emphasized here that our everyday sensory experience cannot stand as purely phenomenal, for it is already shot through with conceptual determinations and categorical structures. In general, our everyday experience is governed by a naive objectivism. Anyone who thinks this through clearly will see that one has need of a special method to achieve the pure, uninterpreted phenomenon. One can term this method, with Edmund Husserl, "phenomenological reduction," or, in its more rigorous form, introduced into the theory of sensation principally by Y. Reenpää, "analytical reduction."[2] Its leitmotif is a methodical withholding of judgment or "epoché." By bracketing all conceptual interpretations, positing, valuations, and judgments, we proceed from the categorically preformed world of things to pure phenomenality.

71

There has been no lack of attempts on the part of philosophers and scientists to discuss away the fundamental function of sensory perception, to deny and reinterpret sensory phenomena, to classify them as deception, deceit, and illusion. This mistrust in the senses goes back to the Presocratics, and found its most pregnant expression in Parmenides' dictum: "To think what exists and to be: these both are one and the same."[3] Parmenides explains that sensory phenomena are deceit and deception, and that human beings can gain knowledge of the truth only through the pure thinking that takes no notice of experience.

PRIMARY AND SECONDARY QUALITIES

A radical reversal took place at the beginning of the modern age with the rise of scientific empiricism and positivism. It is at the same time an evolutionary step that allowed the modern consciousness to think the concepts object and subject in full clarity. Positivism sees the only legitimate access to reality in sensory experience, while granting to thinking only a pragmatic role in summarizing experiences to a particular end. Positivism also falsifies our relationship to the senses by granting objectivity only to the part of the sensory world that can be numbered, measured, and weighed, the so-called primary qualities, while it locates the secondary qualities in the subject. Galileo, especially, represents this development:

> I hold that there exists nothing in external bodies for exciting in us tastes, odours and sounds other than sizes, shapes, numbers, and slow or swift motions; and I conclude that if the ears, tongue and nose were removed, shape, number and motion would remain but there would be no odours, tastes or sounds, which apart from living beings I believe to be nothing but names.[4]

In more recent sensory theory, it was Johannes von Müller who sought to give this conception a physiological interpretation:

> Sensation, therefore, consists in the communication to the sensorium, not of the quality or state of the external body, but of the condition of the nerves themselves, excited by the external cause. We do not feel the knife which gives us pain but the painful state of our nerves produced by it. The probably mechanical oscillation of light is itself not luminous; even if it could itself act on the sensorium, it would be perceived merely as an oscillation; it is only by affecting the optic nerve that it gives rise to the sensation of light. Sound has no existence but in the excitement

of a quality of the auditory nerve; the nerve of touch perceives the vibration of the apparently sonorous body as a sensation of tremour. We communicate, therefore, with the external world merely by virtue of the states which external influences excite in our nerves.[5]

Müller's pupil Emil Du Bois-Reymond expresses himself even more radically; for him, the objective world is dark, mute, and without qualities.[6] These thinkers' theses are both epistemologically untenable, for all comprehension of the objective world already presupposes sensory perception. If there are "in reality" no qualities, then one also cannot speak in a naive way of sensory nerves. Rather, one would then have to say that the representation of an external world acts upon the representation of a nerve—a blatant incongruity.[7]

Today, we have become more reticent. Not every scientist will, for example, declare wavelengths to be the sole objective reality and colors to be a purely subjective illusion. And yet the opinion is widespread that an unambiguous relation exists between color and wavelength. But the definition of the fundamental physical quantities rests predominantly upon free conventions that hardly take into consideration immediate sensory experience. Thus, from the outset, one cannot expect that an isomorphic reproduction of phenomenal experiences by means of physical concepts will be possible. This fundamental state of affairs has not yet been given sufficient attention.

An example of this confusion: the experience of the color yellow is phenomenally unambiguous and simple—that is, unable to be reduced further. Yet, one cannot at all reproduce it unambiguously in the language of physics by means of a simple quantity. A specific shade of yellow can correspond to a single wavelength (for example 589 nm), or, in accordance with the laws of so-called additive color mixing, a combination of wavelengths (for example 671 and 537 nm). The phenomenal appearance of yellow does not reveal which physical situation is present in the individual case. And even these conditions are not yet sufficient, for the phenomenal appearance of yellow can arise also as a successive contrast after the presentation of violet or as simultaneous contrast, as in the case of colored shadows.[8]

Thus, one would have to augment one's explanation by introducing concepts from physiology, whereby the conditions of reproduction become entirely indefinable. When Hermann Ludwig von Helmholtz, another of Müller's pupils, says that sensory phenomena, while not the physical reality, are yet signs of it that unambiguously reproduce the reality, we know from our example that his thesis is untenable.[9] In fact, the relationships between sensory phenomena and physical objects remain to this day totally opaque and impossible to reduce to a single denominator. Thus, sensory qualities are independent realms of being that can be neither logically reduced nor isomorphically reproduced from each other. Between the various realms of qualities there gapes a *hiatus irrationalis*.

GOETHE'S SCIENTIFIC METHOD

If we consider Goethe's scientific method, we can characterize its point of departure as phenomenological, even if Goethe, characteristically, did not work out in detail its epistemological basis. He was deeply convinced of the primacy and immediacy of sensory phenomena. Sensory qualities are for him substantial irreducibles that are explicable only in terms of themselves. He sees no fundamental cognitive gain in any attempt to derive one qualitative realm from another, for example, the realm of color qualities from the colorless mechanical realm.

The insight that sensory phenomena are not secondary manifestations of an objective "reality" supposedly underlying them (yet a reality also imagined in a quasi-sensory manner) gives rise to a new trust in the senses: "Man is sufficiently equipped for all his genuine earthly needs if he trusts his senses and cultivates them in such a way that they remain worthy of that trust."[10] And elsewhere: "The senses do not deceive; it is judgement that deceives."[11]

The wealth of sensory qualities reveals itself only to immediate human perception. As Goethe explained, "The human being in himself, when he makes use of his healthy senses, is the greatest and most precise physical instrument that can exist, and just this is the greatest evil of modern physics: that one has as it were divorced the experiments from man, and wants to know nature only in that which artificial instruments show, to limit and prove thereby what nature can accomplish."[12]

Beginning with a phenomenology of the phenomenon, Goethe proceeds to erect a rigorous scientific method. His procedure becomes especially clear in his *Theory of Color*, which shall serve as an example in what follows.[13] The decisive thing is not whether Goethe is guilty of particular mistakes but, rather, the systematic rigor and internal consistency of his undertaking. A stance that adheres to a merely naive description of sensory phenomena as presented by nature could be termed "phenomenalism." Goethe is anything but a phenomenalist, for he progresses from this more passive stance to an active cognition that corresponds to the modern evolution of consciousness. The human being no longer desires merely to receive impressions that approach him or her as it were from without; rather, he or she wants to enter into the process of cognition as an ego—a self-motivated agent. The expression of this modern cognitive stance is the scientific experiment that shapes the conditions under which nature manifests.

In his "The Experiment as Mediator between Object and Subject," Goethe set forth his notion of the scientific experiment, which in many regards deviates from—and is in essential points even antithetical to—the current conception of experimentation.[14] Having warned insistently against the numerous pitfalls in drawing overhasty conclusions from isolated experiments, he comes to the nucleus of his experimental method. It is not the single experiment that is decisive but, rather, the systematic multiplication of experiments—the establishment of an uninterrupted series of variations from which the underlying lawfulness is revealed of itself as "higher-order experience within experience." This higher-order experience Goethe terms *Urphänomen*. Instead of verifying or falsifying a hypothesis conceived ideally, outside of experience, the important thing is to order the experiments in such a way that, in progressing through the series of experiences, the underlying idea becomes immediately intuitive. Through completing inwardly the movement that manifests itself in the experimental series, the experimenter reaches an intuitive grasp of the *Urphänomen*.

Goethe's methodological approach restricts itself severely to that which can be experienced and avoids the dualism of idea and experience, of theory and fact. "The highest thing would be to comprehend that everything factual is already theory . . . seek nothing behind the phenomena: they are themselves the theory."[15] As for experimental relationships, here Goethe speaks in an exemplary manner of "conditions" in the sense of that which can be exhibited phenomenally.

To be scientific means, for Goethe, to hold fast to the inner identity of a realm of quality and to penetrate within this realm to the higher lawfulness of the *Urphänomen*. Thus, in the experiments in his *Theory of Color* he remains within the realm of the colored itself and does not attempt to import as explanatory principle a colorless realm postulated behind the color phenomena. This in no way excludes the possibility of connections between the colored and the non-colored and that these connections in the broader sense belong entirely to the essence of the colored. It is only that in order to be consistent, one cannot place them at the beginning of a theory of color.

The uncovering of the *Urphänomen* can be characterized as a phenomenal axiomatic. Just as the mathematician progresses in rigorous, logical sequence from the diversity of mathematical relations to the axioms that underlie them, so also does Goethe progress from the multiplicity of phenomena to the *Urphänomen*. Contrary to the popularly held view that he had no understanding of mathematics, Goethe himself saw his experimental method as thoroughly mathematical in spirit:

The circumspection of proceeding by only one step at a time, or rather, of deducing one step from its immediate predecessor, is something that we must learn from the mathematicians; and even when we attempt no calculation we must work as though we were liable to justify ourselves to the most rigorous geometer. For actually it is the mathematical method that, because of its circumspection and purity, reveals immediately every leap in the assertion, and its proofs are actually but detailed expositions to the effect that what has been brought forth in conjunction was there already in its simple parts and its entire sequence; that it has been surveyed in its entire scope and found to be correct and irrefutable under all conditions.[16]

What Goethe seeks is a procedure that is quintessentially mathematical. What he dismisses is the misuse of mathematics through its restriction to the quantifiable. One fundamentally misunderstands if he or she accords to Goethe the capacity for an empathetic description of phenomena, but finds him otherwise incapable of being truly scientific. To be sure, whoever equates science with causal analysis, which seeks to reduce the wealth of phenomena to the mathematical-mechanical realm, can hardly arrive at any other conclusion. In fact, Goethe develops an exemplary, self-consistent notion of science, which, according to J. Hoffmeister, involves "the striving to investigate and order a circumscribed realm of inquiry according to methods appropriate to that realm, to subsume the wealth of the data gained in this way under comprehensive principles, and to explain the data thereby."[17] What is decisive is that the principles of a science are developed out of its own field of inquiry, not borrowed from other realms.

Goethe's scientific method exhibits a balance between selflessness in contemplating phenomena and the activity of the self in structuring experimental conditions. Theory enunciates itself in the intuitive grasping of the *Urphänomen* and is not foisted upon the phenomena from without. This is a cognitional stance that points to the future; here, the human being ceases to exercise power over nature in the process of cognition.

If the activity of the self predominates in a one-sided way, then the cognitional stance of "operationalism" arises as the antithesis to phenomenalism. In this regard, C. F. von Weizsäcker writes: "The experiment is the exercise of power in the service of cognition. It makes possible, conversely, the application of knowledge in the service of power. Its gifts and dangers are the gifts and dangers of power."[18] Immanuel Kant had already expressed a similar conclusion:

Reason, holding in one hand its principles, according to which alone concordant appearances can be admitted as equivalent to laws, and in the other hand the experiment which it has devised in conformity with these principles, must approach nature in order to be taught by it. It must not, however, do so in the character of a pupil who listens to everything that the teacher chooses to say, but of an appointed judge who compels the witnesses to answer questions which he has himself formulated.[19]

This standpoint is represented in extreme form by the modern theory of science, which strives to separate theory and fact. What remains unclear is the extent to which the so-called facts already harbor theories. This severing of theory from fact results in its losing the ground of reality beneath its feet: any assertion can be a theory, so long as it is interpreted in retrospect by means of experimental data. W. Stegmüller speaks in this regard of "interpretive anchors"; through these "anchors," points of the theoretical network are bound to the level of observation. At these points of contact "the blood of empirical reality flows through the connecting lines out into the nodes of the network furthest removed from the level of observation."[20] The decisive thing here is not experience but, rather, the mathematical model according to which the experiments are fashioned:

> The model that science constructs appears to us more serious, more important and more real than experienced reality. Contradictions are not merely eliminated; they become mistakes that are regarded as a breakdown. Thus today we must expand Galileo's description of modern scientific method by saying: to measure everything measurable; to make everything which is not measurable measurable; and to deny everything which cannot be made measurable.[21]

GOETHE'S APPROACH TO SENSORY PHENOMENA

The universal leitmotif of conventional science is objectivism—the idea of an external world independent of the observing subject. This idea is considered valid even where it is only incompletely realizable. The result is that science judges that which is sense-perceptible only with regard to its objective validity and excludes everything that does not fit into the model.

Phenomenology, on the other hand, is generally uninterested in the objectivity of its objects. It does not ask, "Is a phenomenal color 'real'? Does it belong to the external world, or to the perceiving subject?" Rather, the emphasis is an investigation of the sensory phenomena as such. One would be entirely unjustified in terming them "subjective" at this stage of investigation because, on the phenomenal level, there is nothing to be said in this regard. That I have a certain sense-impression is immediately certain. It is an entirely different question whether what I perceive exists in an objective, external world. Thus, Goethe also places unabashedly, at the beginning of his *Theory of Color*, the physiological colors—a realm of phenomena eliminated by objectivistic science as "subjective."

The precondition for any phenomenological investigation of the sensory as experienced is our ability to order qualities according to the criteria of equality or inequality, similarity or difference, independence or dependence. The variety of sensory phenomena can be described on the basis of their qualitative content and interrelationships without transgressing the phenomenal realm. A good example is the phenomenological ordering of the colors represented by Goethe's color circle. The structure of this ordering of the colors is totally invariant with regard to their subjectivity or objectivity. It is valid regardless of whether one is dealing with surface colors, the colors of light, after-images, or hallucinations. The color circle does not correspond to the physically defined structure of the scale of wavelengths; neither its self-contained structure nor the complementary colors have adequate correspondences within that scale.

In experimental science fashioned after mathematical "modelism," sensory experience is reduced to a minimum, for example, reading correlations from measuring instruments. The sensory quality is in the end fortuitous and interchangeable, since it stands only for a bit of abstract information within the mathematical model. For Goethe, in contrast, the human being making use of his or her healthy senses is the greatest and most precise physical apparatus. Here it is a matter of the complete and unrestricted human capacity for perception. This capacity for perception is, however, nothing fixed and finished. Rather, it is something that can be practiced, further developed, and refined. Thus, the practice of science for Goethe does not merely provide abstract knowledge; it entails at the same time a transformation and development of the human being.

For human perception, the sensory quality is in no way a matter of indifference; it is no mere x; rather, it presents itself as a specific experience that cannot be interchanged at will with other qualitative experiences. Every sensory quality is significant to the human being. Thus, for example, red has a very specific meaning completely different from that of, say, green. Sensory qualities present themselves to everyday perception and its discursive elaboration as simple entities not susceptible to further logical analysis. One cannot define conceptually what red is—only experience it. We can only accept the fact of various qualities;

because of the *hiatus irrationalis* standing between them, they cannot be logically deduced. The elementary sensory experiences are, in their essential content, purely phenomenal; confronted with them, the analytic understanding must come to a halt without being able to dissolve them into parts.

THE COMPLEXITY OF SENSORY EXPERIENCE

To be sure, more is required for the perception of the essential features of the qualitative realm than just the physical sense organs. A more subtle perceptual capacity includes the emotional, aesthetic, and spiritual aspects of sensory qualities. In *Theory of Color*, Goethe speaks of the "sensory-moral effect" of colors, which speaks not only to the eye but also to the soul.

Viewed in this way, the so-called unilocal sensory experiences reveal themselves to be no longer simple but complex. On the suprarational level, the qualitative sensory realms separated by a *hiatus irrationalis* enter into inner relationships. Thus red, unlike blue, is experienced very distinctly as a "warm" color and reveals thereby a relationship to experiences of temperature. Moreover, red is experienced as advancing spatially and enters thereby into relationship with the sense of movement and spatial experiences. When we speak of red as a "loud" or "shouting" color, we give expression to its connection with the sense of hearing. In this way, we advance from an absolute separation of the sensual qualities to a higher unity.

The "sensory-moral" effect of colors has been described at all times and by the most various researchers in an astoundingly similar way. Thus, in a publication of the Modern American Color Association edited by F. Birren, red (signal red, medium red), is characterized as "passionate, exciting, fervid, active."[22] When we penetrate to the hidden functions and energies of red as they are expressed in the imagination of the painter, in color psychology, in language, and in color symbolism, a new and richly articulated qualitative world opens up to us in the unity of sensory red. The endpoint of the discursive-conceptual analysis can become the starting-point for the discovery of the suprarational realm of qualities by means of an imaginative experience.

In two addenda to *Theory of Color*, Goethe offers a characterization of the psychological and spiritual meaning of colors: "In red is seeking and desiring; in yellow, finding and knowing; in white, possessing and enjoying. In green, on the other hand, is hoping and expecting; in blue is noting and thinking; in black, forgetting and renouncing."[23] Elsewhere, he lists some of the other polarities associated with the polarity of yellow and blue:

Yellow	Blue
Plus	Minus
Activation	Deprivation
Light	Shadow
Bright	Dark
Strength	Weakness
Warmth	Cold
Proximity	Distance
Repulsion	Attraction
Affinity to acids	Affinity to bases.[24]

In the face of their intersubjective validity, it would be a mistake to term the suprarational qualities of substance and expression purely subjective. That would constitute a regression into the mistake of subjectivism such as that made with regard to secondary qualities. Epistemologically, one may term subjective only that which belongs to the subject in the intentional act of perception. Yet, this does not hold true when considering the aesthetic qualities of colors—one can term both these and other color qualities objective with equal justification.

Conventional science tends by nature toward separation and isolation of the various levels of being. Behind this division stands the primal separation of subject and object. Goethe moves in the opposite direction. In place of the principle of division and objectivization, he substitutes a coherent and interrelated ordering of appearances:

> All the effects, of whatever kind, that we note in experience cohere in the most persistent way, pass over from one into another; they undulate from first to last. That one separates and opposes them; that one conflates them is unavoidable. Yet this had to give rise to boundless opposition within the sciences. Sclerotic, divisive pendantry and mystical transports both bring evil in train. But those activities, from the basest to the highest; from the tile that crashes down from the roof to the luminous spiritual insight which rises up in you and which you communicate—all these join themselves into a continuous series. We shall attempt to express it: accidental, mechanical, physical, chemical, organic, psychic, ethical, religious, genial.[25]

The concept of the *Urphänomen*, unlike the concept of the object, signifies immediately that the perceiving and cognizing self forms an indissoluble unity with the objects of cognition. Thereby, the inner identity of the *Urphänomen* manifests the inner identity of the ego. We stand here before the highest goal of Goethean science: the progression from the single phenomenon to the thoroughgoing interrelationship between appearances and the unification of the human being as knower with the entirety of existence.

NOTES

1. Translated from the German by Frederick Amrine.

2. Edmund Husserl, *Husserliana*, 9 vols. (den Haag: Martinus Nijhoff, 1950–1962); Y. Reenpää, *Allgemeine Sinnesphysiologie* (Frankfurt a.M.: Vittorio Klostermann, 1962).

3. H. Glockner, *Die europäische Philosophie, von den Anfängen bis zur Gegenwart* (Stuttgart: Reclam, 1958), p. 17. [I have translated Glockner's German translation directly into English; two different alternatives are given in G. S. Kirkland and J. E. Raven, *The Presocratic Philosophers: A Critical History with a Selection of Texts* (Cambridge: Cambridge University Press, 1971), p. 269 [= 344,1.8; Fr.3]: ". . . for the same thing can be thought as can be (construction above, literally the same thing exists for thinking and for being).

4. A. C. Crombie, *Augustine to Galileo*, 2nd ed. (Cambridge, Mass.: Harvard University Press, 1961), II:302.

5. J. Müller, *Elements of Physiology*, trans. W. Baly (Philadelphia: Lea and Blanchard, 1843), p. 588.

6. Emil Du Bois-Reymond, *Reden*, 2nd ed., 2 vols. (Leipzig: Veit, 1912).

7. This fundamental epistemological objection was brought forth already during Emil Du Bois-Reymond's lifetime by Rudolf Steiner; see Rudolf Steiner, *The Philosophy of Freedom*, trans. M. Wilson (London: Rudolf Steiner Press, 1964), pp. 50–59.

8. H. Hensel, "Die Sinneswahrnehmung des Menschen," *Musiktherapeutische Umschau*, 1 (1980): 203–18.

9. H. von Helmholtz, "The Facts of Perception," in *Selected Writings of Hermann von Helmholtz*, edited by R. Kahl (Middletown, Conn.: Wesleyan University Press, 1971), pp. 366–408.

10. J. W. von Goethe, "*Maximen und Reflexionen*," No. 1061, in *Werke: Hamburger Ausgabe*, edited by E. Trunz, 14 vols. (Hamburg: Christian Wegner, 1948–1960), XII:514 (abbreviated hereafter *HA*).

11. Goethe, "Maximen," No. 295, *HA*, XII:406.

12. Goethe, "Aus Makariens Archiv," No. 90, Wilhelm Meisters Wanderjahre, *HA*, VIII:473.

13. Goethe, *Zur Farbenlehre: Didaktischer Teil*, *HA*, XIII: 314–523. The best English translation is Douglas Miller's *Goethe, Scientific Studies* (New York: Suhrkamp, 1988).

14. Goethe, "Der Versuch als Vermittler von Objekt und Subjekt," *HA*, XIII: 10–20.

15. Goethe, "Betrachtungen im Sinne der Wanderer," No. 136, *Wanderjahre*, *HA*, VIII:304.

16. Goethe, "Der Versuch," *HA*, XIII:18–19.

17. J. Hoffmeister, *Wörterbuch der philosophischen Begriffe*, 2nd ed. (Hamburg: Felix Meiner, 1955), p. 761.

18. C. F. Weizsäcker, "Das Experiment," *Studium generale*, 1 (1947):8.

19. I. Kant, *Critique of Pure Reason*, trans. N. K. Smith 2nd ed. (London: Macmillan, 1929), p. 20.

20. W. Stegmüller, "Wissenschaftstheorie," *Philosophie*, Das Fischer Lexikon, eds., A. Diemer and I. Frenzel (Frankfurt A.M.: Fischer Bücherei, 1958), p. 341.

21. H. Pietschmann, *Das Ende des naturwissenschaftlichen Zeitalters* (Wien/ Hamburg: Paul Zsolnay, 1980), p. 29.

22. F. Birren, *Color Psychology and Color Therapy: A Factual Study of the Influence of Color on Human Life* (New Hyde Park: University Books, 1961), p. 250.

23. Goethe, "Nachträge zur Farbenlehre," in *Sämtliche Werke*, 30 vols. (Stuttgart: Cotta, 1851), 3: 54.

24. Goethe, *Farbenlehre*, Sec. 696, *HA*, XIII: 478.

25. Goethe, "Nachträge," p. 56.

5

Ronald H. Brady

The Idea in Nature

Rereading Goethe's Organics

As historians of science who touch upon the matter are fond of remarking, Goethe's approach to natural science is not that of the present scientific community. He makes a rigid separation among the sciences—his organics will not reduce to chemistry or physics. He speaks of a "Nature" that can have "ideas," one of which was the *Urpflanze*, the primal or archetypal plant. It is hardly surprising that when the Swedish historian Erik Nordenskiold produced his sizable history of biology in 1928, he wrote that Goethe's Botany "is Romantic nature philosophy from beginning to end; it bears no resemblance whatever to modern natural research."[1] The "nature philosophy" that he had in mind is German *Naturphilosophie*, which later scientists rejected as impossibly philosophic. It is a commonplace of the history of science that Goethe's work is an expression of that movement, and suffers from the same weaknesses—that is, that it is more philosophic and speculative than empirical.

Nordenskiold provides a minor epiphany, however, when he implies that Goethe is to be rejected because he does not *resemble* modern science. For those who have actually bothered to read him, Goethe does not appear to be merely philosophizing; his texts are largely accounts of observation. But the sort of observations that he makes and his reasoning about them does not fit with science as we know it. By suggesting that his work should be seen as "Romantic nature philosophy," Nordenskiold makes its difference into a difference *from*, rather than within, science. He was hardly alone in that solution.

After having absorbed the usual accounts, readers who turn to Goethe's own texts may be somewhat surprised that he made his own interpretation of the difference between his project and the science of his day. This part of the story is usually truncated or omitted entirely.[2] As his commentaries make clear, he had problems with the methods of normal science, faulting them *for speculating beyond the phenomena*. Surely there is something significant in the fact that Goethe and the representatives of modern natural research accuse each other of the same mistake.

The writers of scientific histories are unable to perceive what they cannot conceive. When Goethe's complaint is freed from the misreadings fostered by the language of the period, it is fundamental and, if sustained, could lead to a new form of science. His argument has been neglected so often, however, that unless one wants to indulge in conspiracy theory he or she must suppose that it was neglected because it was invisible. This was to be expected when Goethe wrote, for he was ahead of his age.

Today, however, that argument seems peculiarly modern, raising issues similar to those found in N. R. Hansen and Thomas S. Kuhn, although addressing them in another fashion.[3] It is time that Goethe's erroneous placement within the confines of a speculative *Naturphilosophie* were corrected by a proper identification. Since Goethe's address to the problems he formulates has recognizable connections to a *phenomenological* outlook, it is profitably examined on this ground. A familiarity with this form of thought is hardly automatic, however, and a review is in order.

PHENOMENOLOGY

In the first years of this century, Edmund Husserl founded the philosophic movement that he termed "phenomenology." With his work, a major stream of European thought took a new turn.[4] The insight was so broad that it quickly transformed the face of European thought. Phenomenology is now a form of philosophizing rather than Husserl's philosophy, and the philosophers on whom it exercised profound influence include most of the major names in recent continental philosophy, for example, Martin Heidegger, Maurice Merleau-Ponty, Jean Paul Sartre, Paul Ricoeur, and Emmanuel Levinas.

Through his work, Husserl had come to the conclusion that the Western sciences were in a crisis of their own making. The Western mind had come into conflict with its own cultural impulse, which was the drive toward a fully realized science of "being" in all its appearances. Unfortunately, by means of a formulation of objectivity erected on the Cartesian split between mind and extended substance, a limitation was fostered upon scientific knowing that had betrayed Western culture and even science itself.

To see how this critique arises, let us review the web of difficulties into which the search for objectivity seems to lead. We shall find that problems arise through antagonisms between two principles: one, the principle of experience, which demands that an empirical science limit itself to what is given by experience; two, objectivity, which postulates that the external world has no share in mind or in any other content that is derived from the constitution of the observing subject.

Galileo's separation of primary and secondary qualities was an attempt to meet these demands by distinguishing the content of experience that was derivable from subjective constitution (color, smell, taste, in fact, all sensations, since these depend upon the activity of our sense organs) from those relations which were not separable from the extended body in space (for example, number, position, figure, and motion). Ever since, this distinction has been fundamental to physical science.

Since Immanuel Kant, however, the relations found within experience, including the primary qualities, have come under scrutiny. If sensation is not innocent, why should the relations between sensations be above suspicion? The more one studies the act of perception, the more it appears to be mental as well as physical. For instance, what about the corrections to visual perception that we introduce without making any changes in the aim and focus of the eye? In twilight it is easy for a shrub to seem a cat or a cow to seem a bush, but we do not blame this confusion on a defect of the eye. When we obtain a new image it is not the eye *but the mind* that refocuses.

If this integral relationship between the physical and mental is a correct description of experience, then those relations that Galileo thought so secure are actually impossible to find within the sensible report without the formulaic activity of the mind. In a sense then, the resultant facts are, at the same time, theories, for nothing in experience can be abstracted from the human subject; we cannot separate a purely objective element.

The contradiction can be given a more general form. It is only common sense that the world of appearances, the things about us, are out there over against the observing subject. This "outness" of phenomena, as Samuel Coleridge called it, is an experienced quality and no mere hypothesis. We can hardly deny what we can see so plainly. But just because this is so certain we can conclude that what we are seeing is *not* a basis for Cartesian externality, which is external to mind. The qualities of immediate experience cannot be divorced from the formulaic activity of the mind, but the "outness" of experience is itself such a quality. Of course, at this point the game is up. If the Cartesian split between mind and outer world is itself a formulation of mind, it does not disclose an objective realm beyond mind.

It appears that we cannot be certain that "external" reality is objective, that is, that it is divorced from mind. That is the contradiction within the Cartesian outlook, but there is another possibility. If this formulation of "objectivity" forces a compromise of the principle of experience, we might just as well suspend the objectivity postulate to allow a total restriction to experience. After all, my experiences are manifestly there, which is a good deal more than I can say for the unperceived world that may be the ultimate cause of these experiences.

All that I am sure of in experience is the mere experience as given—the way the thing *seems*. As I mentioned above, a second glance may make the experience seem quite different. But with all its troubles, this recognition is at least a definite beginning. I may never be sure how a thing really is, but I am not deceived about how it seems to me. Consciousness, as René Descartes himself demonstrated, cannot doubt its own existence without falling into self-contradiction. But consciousness is always consciousness of something, always has an object, and it can no more doubt *of what* it is conscious than it can doubt *that* it is conscious. In this we have Husserl's starting point. We can know whatever is directly given to our consciousness. Our interpretation of appearances may be merely hypothetical, but the appearances themselves, qua appearances, cannot be doubted.

The reason, given above, for our inability to separate appearances from consciousness now becomes the basis for the intimacy of my knowledge. The mind is not a passive spectator before its experiences. Awareness is essentially active—an act of attending. But to attend to anything is to take it for something. The mind must have a seeming of some sort to focus upon, and therefore needs discriminations. This directional quality of attention, the fact that one must mean or intend some particular thing, Husserl termed "intentionality." The result of this analysis links his point about appearances directly to Descartes' proof of the indubitability of the activity of thinking.

We do not notice, in ordinary mental life, the intentional act, but this usual lack of awareness only indicates that we must enter into a special state to observe our own activity. When I look at a table, I am aware of the object, but not of my attending to it. I may think, "there is the table," but I do not usually add, "I am thinking the table." When I attend to some image, since I am not at the same time attending to my act of attention, I do not notice the formulaic activity of intentionality.

In special circumstances, however, I may discover it. For example, consider figure 5.1, in which the deliberate ambiguity of construction

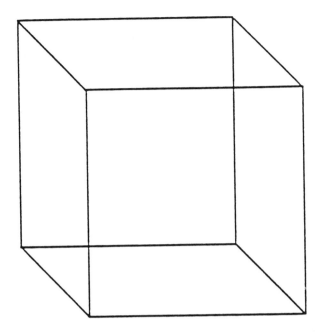

Fig. 5.1. What does one see in this figure?

allows me to bring my contribution to appearances to consciousness. If the average audience is asked what they see in the figure, some will reply that they see a cube slanting down and to the right, others a cube slanting up and to the left, yet others will say they see both and perhaps add further formulations. With practice, everyone will see both cubes, and with greater effort, a flat pattern.

These differing configurations are not added by thought after the object is perceived but are intended by the perceiver in the act of perceiving. The observer who attempts to make the choice of cubes voluntary will find that to exchange one cube for another no further change is required than thinking (intending) the other cube. Simply look at the cube presently seen and think or imagine the alternate cube until it appears. The shift should take place in a few seconds. Only an intentional change is required to produce the difference, for the alternate cube represents an alternate set of relations rather than a new sensible report.

The viewer makes these shifts by assigning the spatial relations to the elements in the diagram—particularly those of depth. After all, we must take the elements of the perceptual field to be at specific depths to reach this or that figure. Even the flat pattern presents no exception, for we can come to it only by seeing all elements on the same plane. Since, to see a figure, one must grasp the spatial relations of the same, seeing is also cognizing. Cognition in this sense is not a proposition about what is perceived but an activity that actualizes the perception. *Each act of seeing is necessarily an act of understanding.* The grasp of geometric relations that we use to understand the cube, once seen, is the same one that we use to see it in the first place. We do not perceive and then bring forward a concept to understand. We focus our understanding to bring forth a perception.

Once I reach the point where the appearance can be changed at will, intentionality is no longer tacit but self-conscious, and I am aware of my responsibility for the formulation of what I see. I can, in this state of awareness, examine the act of intentionality in detail, for it is my act. Once I make it conscious, it lies completely open to me.

I can discover, in this state, that although intentional formulation can be altered by conscious choice, perception cannot be voluntaristic. My act of intending does not create a perception *ex nihilo* but simply views the sensible report through a particular form of understanding. If the sensible can express nothing about itself through my focus, no perception will result, and I will have to try some other concept. Ambiguous figures, of course, must be constructed in such a manner as to allow me to see more than one image. Given figure 5.1, for example, I can see two cubes, a flat pattern, and so forth, but there are obvious limitations—the intention of rounded forms, for example. Here I encounter the same necessity that prevents me from making a stone look like a plant, or a plant an animal, or turning a pebble into an ice-cream cone and eating it. I must intend relations to become aware of them, but only those that are possible in the sensible report will ever result in a perception.

Because I can enter into the state of consciousness described, I can examine the structure of given appearances in depth. I can trace their very constitution, for this constitution, although *codetermined* by the sensible report, is yet *my* formulation, that is, it is the conceptual structure I have intended to make the sensible report visible. This phenomenological standpoint could be, then, the basis of an entirely rigorous science—rigorous in the sense that it could restrict itself entirely to the structures of appearance as given in experience. A descriptive morphology of the given appearances would result, and the possibility of such a morphology has immediate implications for the sciences.

PHENOMENOLOGY AND SCIENCE

The founding intuitions of mechanics were phenomenological in nature, but to show the full meaning of this claim requires a review of the ground. Let us remember that any change in perceptible bodies—change of position, of shape, of temperature—is correlated by the perceiver with a source or cause. The source can be located either within or without the body in question. We come to the sphere of mechanics when the source is located without, and the changes of a body are correlated with other changes external to its limits. To apply the concepts of mechanics, therefore, we need a realm of appearances in which bodies appear inert, which is to say, they seem to be moved only from the outside.

By now we can recognize the familiar situation of the body which is, for all present purposes, fixed and dead, because nothing happens to it if an outside force is not added. Such objects surround us at every moment. They *look* dead, or inert, before we reason about them through the application of mechanical laws, and this appearance is so compelling that it is always a bit disagreeable when one of these objects changes its appearance and joins the alert objects, for example, when a dead twig suddenly curves, revealing itself as an insect.

Reflection will show that the "inert" appearance is constituted by an intentional formulation on the part of the perceiver, by which the source of change is placed beyond the limits of the body. The formulation of appearances, therefore, has already included what becomes, when abstracted from appearances and expressed in words, the "law of inertia"— that is, a body will remain in its state of rest or motion unless altered through an impressed force. To abstract that principle is only to reflect, in a statement, how the appearances are constituted. But not every science is so founded.

The close connection between the laws of mechanics and the intentional structure of the appearances to which they were applied was not grasped by the scientific community. Thus, we see that the clarity and success of mechanics led researchers to suppose the problems set by other types of phenomena (organisms) could be solved by reduction to the concepts of mechanics, which were in themselves absolutely clear. If one assumes that all causality is external causality, the investigator need not take appearances to be fundamental. Faced with situations in which there can be no *direct* application of mechanical laws to phenomena, the scientist felt free to advance hypotheses as to the mechanical interaction *behind* the appearances that gave occasion to them. In this manner, the sciences abandoned any strict application of the principle of experience and evolved into a more speculative, less perceptually oriented viewpoint, even though the start made by mechanics was not actually of this nature.

The present willingness to apply interpretive principles to phenomena that do not contain those principles is maintained on the basis of a duality between external, objective nature and internal, subjective mind. Investigators must first discredit the given before they can reinterpret it through a reductionist logic. This is done in just the way I have proceeded in this discussion, by pointing to the impossibility of separating the content of experience from the activity of consciousness. To carry out such a program, however, the investigator must conveniently forget that the intuitions substituted were themselves originally given in experience.

A strict application of the principle of experience would demand that all laws be abstracted directly from the phenomena to which they are applied. Once no one form of experience is privileged over any other the tendency of the sciences to approach each other will be diminished. Chemistry and physics would obviously be more separate without the speculative models that unite them, but this separation could seem like a mere stream compared to the ocean that might open between organics, on one hand, and chemistry and physics, on the other.

That ocean was in place in Goethe's time, and he took it for granted that his audience understood the great difference between organics and the other sciences. Since two centuries of reductionism have eroded our ability to see this difference as clearly as it once appeared, a review is in order.

THE ORGANISM IN KANT'S ARGUMENT

In the eighteenth century, biology was still separated from physics and chemistry by a barrier. We still intuit the difference in the objects of these disciplines. As Aristotle once pointed out, unlike inert things, living ones may be termed self-movers or self-changers. They carry the principle of their change within themselves. The methods by which the inorganic world could be understood did not seem capable of crossing into the realm of life. Some thinkers assumed that one must invoke a creator to account for the difference, others assumed that it would be necessary to assume the existence of a vital force in addition to the forces already known. The next century would see the barrier crossed by a reductionist strategy, but on the eve of that change Immanuel Kant published his *Critique of Judgment* (1790), a work that foresaw both this solution and its cost.[5]

Kant pushed the Cartesian principles to their logical end rather than passing beyond them. He made phenomenal appearances so dependent on the human constitution that there was no possibility of knowing "the thing in itself"—the reality that was before we looked upon it. Since independent reality could not be known, Kant made science into a study of appearances aimed at bringing them under rational law, that is, if we could understand and predict appearances, our inability to understand their ultimate source would not be a serious debility.

Unfortunately there were some appearances that resisted this project. Kant was acutely aware that our notion of life was formed by the sense of inward unity, an agency that produced and governed the organism from within. This inner agency could not be brought to the understanding by a conceptual summary of its parts, as is the case with inorganic compositions. In its earliest stages, in fact, the organism had yet to develop the organs by which its later existence would be supported, making the inward unity *antecedent* to the developing parts, a whole which makes its own parts necessary rather than a result of the combination of the parts. To the degree that the combination of parts may be said to be causal, each part aided in the production and maintenance of all the others, and all the others did the same for each. As a result, the physical organs had to be recognized as both cause and effect of themselves. The linear chain of causes by which mechanical events were understood here curled up into a circle, depriving the chain of explanatory power.

If one reflects more deeply, it seems obvious that the mechanical laws do not show the requisite logical structure to explain life. Inert objects were moved from without by impressed forces. Laws governing their movement, therefore, are also "external" to the things moving, that is, the laws of mechanics sum up the interactions of objects while being perfectly indifferent to the individual natures of those objects.[6] The organism, however, could not be known in this abstract manner, and predictions concerning its changes were dependent on a knowledge of the species. Even the sort of materials out of which it was constructed are an expression of species identity, and thus the governing laws had to be identified with the object they governed, that is, such laws not only governed, but also produced, their objects. Or at least, Kant argued, these results express the way things *appear* to immediate perception.

By our experience, therefore, we are forced to conceive among natural objects a "thing-form" that will not submit to our rationality. Science proceeds by analysis, and analytic thought, which understands the whole through summing the effects of the parts, could not comprehend a whole that preceded the parts or accomplish a path of thought that moved from the general to the particular. Such a movement, Kant argues, would be that of an *intuitive* intellect, which humanity does not possess.[7] He concludes that "we cannot adequately cognize, much less explain" organisms by "mere mechanical principles," adding that:

> We can say boldly it is . . . absurd for men . . . to hope that another Newton will arise in the future who shall make comprehensible by us the production of a blade of grass according to natural laws that no design has ordered.[8]

A "rational organic"—a science that fully explained the constitution of phenomena—was out of the question, but this restriction did not mean that no science of biology was possible.

Arguing that there was a constant "dialectic" between teleology and mechanism, Kant suggested that biology could advance a study of the *parts* of the organism by mechanical principles, that is, making a close analysis of the physical and chemical constituents of life. It was only when the parts were assigned to their places in the organized *whole* that the recognition of life and internality must be invoked, along with the extra-mechanical element that this requires. Thus, although direct investigation of the unity of the organism was impossible, the analysis of the "parts"—literally anything graspable by analytic thought—would be the task of biology.[9]

Kant's subtleties were of no interest to scientists, who advanced through physical and chemical studies out of necessity, without serious attention to his work or to the apprehension of life. A mechanical analysis was treated as exhaustive, the residue of "antecedent unity" dismissed as subjective. The organism became, in a sense, a natural mechanism that *seems* "alive," rather than mechanical, due merely to the nature of our perceptual system.

Thus, although Kant was a central figure for the development of German thought and was very much revered in later years, this respect did not prevent Ernst Haeckel from invoking Kant's passage to announce, near the end of the next century, that in Darwin the world had found its "Newton of the organic world."[10] To make this claim, Haeckel ignored Kant's argument about the constitution of phenomena. Haeckel has remained in good company, since modern biology seems largely oblivious to the problem also.

REREADING GOETHE'S BOTANY

Goethe's *Attempt to Comprehend the Metamorphosis of Plants* is an early work, written at a time when he was breaking with the method of Linnaeus but had little understanding of the nature of the science he was creating.[11] He had been put off by a botany consisting of mere categorization of parts, shapes, species, and families without any insight into an underlying unity among them. He writes, in an essay, "The Author Relates the History of his Botanical Studies,"

> If I am to be consciously articulate about these circumstances, let the reader think of me as a born poet, who, in order to do justice to his subjects, always seeks to derive his terminology directly from the subjects themselves, each time anew. Imagine that such a man is now expected to commit to memory a ready-made terminology, a certain number of words and by-words, with which to classify any given form,

and by a happy choice to give it a characteristic name. A procedure of this sort always seemed to me to result in a kind of mosaic, in which one completed block is placed next to another, creating finally a single picture from thousands of pieces; this was somewhat distasteful to me.[12]

Goethe's distaste turned into rebellion as he attempted to classify plants according to the "mosaic" technique. He came to understand that the conventional vocabulary had as goals the ability to discuss plant phenomena

according to common agreement, and the elimination of all phenomena that are uncertain and difficult to represent. Nevertheless, when I attempted an accurate application of terminology, I found the variability of organs the chief difficulty. I lost the courage to drive in a stake, or to draw a boundary line, when on the selfsame plant I discovered first round, then notched, and finally almost pinnate stems, which later contracted, were simplified, turned into scales, and at last disappeared entirely. . . . The reader can imagine my embarrassing situation, a self-taught tyro torturing himself and fighting his way through.[13]

Following his own sense that the investigator should deal directly with experience, Goethe abandoned the terminological mediation that supported conventional botany. He made a close study of the transformation of plant appendages mentioned above, fastening on the very experience that led him beyond the accepted language. Since this is the departure that leads Goethe to a new methodology, we must consider it in some detail.

Goethe observed that the plant grows by lengthening and thickening the stem and extending appendages upon it. These appendages appear successively: cotyledons (seed leaves), stem leaves, sepals, petals, stamens, pistils, and so forth. Each stage of growth is an appearance of the plant. Each is a different, but not unrelated form.

Goethe found, for example, that though the stem leaves of many plants vary as they move up the stem, each shape was obviously a transformation of the preceding one. If the leaves of some plant species were laid out in the order of appearance on the stem, the alteration between stages was so gradual that they seemed to form a continuous movement. For example, if the reader studies the leaves illustrated in figure 5.2, picked from the stem of a common buttercup, the ability of the mind to grasp the graded series as a continuous transformation will become obvious. Given such a series, the observer sees clear reasons to recognize that all these forms are somehow the same thing.

In some plants, like the peony, one could follow a continuous trans-formation from cotyledons to stem leaves, stem leaves to sepals, sepals to

Fig. 5.2. Leaves taken from the common buttercup (*Ranunculus acris*). Ordered from bottom of stem (*lowest left*) to top (*bottom right*).

petals, petals to stamens, and so on throughout the entire range of plant organs in such small steps that it is impossible to say where one organ begins and another leaves off. Everything was a transformation of the leaf, Goethe declared, but what is the leaf, now that the stem-leaf constitutes but one metamorphosis of the leaf?

For Darwin the question must refer to the primordial appendage that the ancestral plant put forth. All later leaves, by such reasoning, must be transformations, by very gradual steps, of this original. Thus, Darwin looked at the stem leaf series as an indication of actual change—the first leaf had eventually evolved though all the stages—and the stem preserved something like a history of the transformation.[14]

Darwinian concepts have forced a consistent misreading on Goethe's texts, and in a certain sense his early language lent itself to a Darwinian interpretation. In an entry from the *Italian Journey* dated April 17, 1787, Goethe wrote of the Palermo Botanical Gardens:

"Here, where instead of being grown in pots under glass as they are with us, plants are allowed to grow freely in the open fresh air and fulfill their natural destiny, they become more intelligible. Seeing such a variety of new and renewed forms, my old fancy suddenly came back to mind: Among this multitude might I not discover the Primal Plant? There certainly must be one. Otherwise how could I recognize that this or that form was a plant if all were not built on the same model?"[15]

The language here is notable in its inability to resist reading according to the evolutionary habits of modern biology. A model for all plants sounds like a blueprint, and the suggestion that this model *might actually exist* as a physical plant is obviously destined to collapse into Darwin's common ancestor. If Goethe developed his notion in this manner he might properly be added to the list of Darwin's forerunners. The discovery of the Primal Plant, however, was from the first a very different project than the Darwinian might conceive. On May 17, 1787, a month after the above letter Goethe wrote to Johann von Herder:

"I must also tell you confidentially that I am very close to the secret of the reproduction and organization of plants, and that it is the simplest thing imaginable. The climate offers the best possible conditions for making observations. . . . The Primal Plant is going to be the strangest creature in the world, which Nature herself will envy me."[16]

Shortly after the publication of the *The Metamorphosis of Plants*, Goethe was forced to reread himself, a project he then continued for the rest of his life. The exercise forced him to clarify the difference between a purely sensible form and a higher experience of form, the "thing-form," which demanded an intuitive rationality. Here Kant had a useful influence, for Goethe himself admits that his notion of the archetype gained clarity when Friederich von Schiller attacked it from the Kantian perspective. The occasion for the conversation was a scientific meeting that both had attended in the end of July 1794. The two had met before but were not yet friends. Goethe remembers:

> We happened to leave the meeting at the same time and a conversation ensued. He seemed interested in the presentation, but commented intelligently and perceptively that such a fragmented way of dealing with nature could hardly appeal to any layman who wished to pursue the topic. I welcomed his remarks.
>
> I replied that this method would probably disconcert even the initiated, and that a different approach might well be discovered, not by concentrating on separate and isolated elements of nature but by portraying it as alive and active, with its efforts directed from the whole to the parts. He asked me to explain this point further, but was unable to conceal his doubts. He could not agree that what I described might be derived directly from empirical observation.
>
> We reached his house, and our conversation drew me in. There I gave an enthusiastic description of the metamorphosis of plants, and with a few characteristic strokes of the pen I caused a symbolic plant to spring up before his eyes. He heard and saw all this with great interest, with unmistakable power of comprehension. But when I stopped he shook his head and said, "That is not an observation from experience. That is an idea."[17]

Schiller's distinction was a modern one. He suggested that Goethe was hypothesizing something that *he could not actually find in experience.* Goethe was taken back, annoyed, and reminded of some earlier writings by Schiller that he had disliked:

> my old resentment began to rise in me. I collected my wits , however, and replied, "Then I may rejoice that I have ideas without knowing it, and can see them with my own eyes."[18]

THE INTERPENETRATION OF OBSERVING AND THINKING

Beginning with this exchange the two men, then Germany's most celebrated poets, became firm friends, and continued their conversation on scientific method until Schiller's death in 1805. The slightly angry rejoinder turned out to be a happy one, for it contained, if somewhat ironically, the key to the difficulty.

The reader will remember that, in the examination of figure 5.1, it was necessary to intend the configuration of a specific cube before that cube became visible. Since most readers saw a cube upon first glance, however, it would be easy to suppose, at that moment, that the visible figure had provided a concept of the same. As things turn out, the actual sequence is just the reverse. We must focus the mind as well as the eye and conceptualize to perceive. The perceiver is also a thinker in a manner that usually escapes notice, and what is thought in this manner is also seen—that is, the resultant image is an instance of our conceptual category.

The activity of intentionality, like other potential perceptions, escapes detection in ordinary consciousness because it is not brought to focus. While the observer reacts, for instance, to painted camouflage on roughly cubic buildings surrounded by foliage, the structures remain suppressed and invisible. Were the observer to look for vertical and horizontal lines, however, the buildings appear. Our activity of looking is a light that renders the world visible.

If we make this interpretation, with its metaphors of lighting and suppressing, the framework for Goethe's conversation, it generates a very consistent, if radical, reading. Goethe came to grips with the fact that his symbolic plant was an idea, but an idea that somehow became phenomenal in the world for the observer who could intend it. In his later discussions with Schiller and in papers written after Schiller's death, Goethe developed this reading not as a systematic philosophy of science but in a series of reflections on his work. Thus, he reads a commentary on his own work by a Dr. Heinroth, and finds the description of his method illuminating:

> Indeed, he calls my method of procedure unusual, saying that my capacity for thinking is *objectively* active. By this he means that my thinking is never divorced from objects, that the elements of the objects and my observation of them interpenetrate, become fused in the process of thought; that my observation is itself a thinking, and my thinking is a way of observation.[19]

Heinroth did not examine the respective roles of subject and object in his description and simply noted that thinking and observing interpenetrate. Goethe saw, however, that observation was not an independent content, to be penetrated by thinking, but already a result of thinking. In his *History of Color Theory*, he remarked that Galileo

> showed already in his early youth that for the genius a single instance stands for a thousand, in that he developed for himself from swinging churchlamps the theory of the pendulum and of falling bodies. In the sciences everything depends upon what one calls an *aperçu*—an

apperception of what actually lies at the foundation of the appearances. And such an apperception is fruitful ad infinitum.[20]

The *aperçu* is an illuminating intention, in Goethe's terminology also an idea, but one that is inseparable from the phenomena—that is, when we advance a new intention we generally become aware of what we have done by a new perception of the object (intentional activity in itself being tacit during the act of observation). Thus our consciousness of the idea, but not the idea itself, may derive from phenomenal experience:

> An idea cannot be demonstrated empirically, nor can it actually be proved. An individual not in possession of it will never catch sight of it with the physical eye.[21]

So here we have the effect of Schiller's influence, and while Goethe sustains Schiller's objection that the symbolic plant represented an idea, he alters the meaning of that term to explain how he can see his ideas before his eyes. His original empiricism has been made more self-conscious, but the goal of perceptual truth remains unchanged. Thus, he writes in *Maxims and Reflections* that the constant interplay between the search for intentions and the experience these produce leads to:

> . . . a delicate empiricism which makes itself utterly identical with the object, thereby becoming true theory. But this enhancement of our mental powers belongs to a highly evolved age.[22]

> The ultimate goal would be to grasp that everything in the realm of fact is already theory. The blue of the sky shows us the basic law of chromatics. Let us not seek for something beyond the phenomena—they themselves are the theory.[23]

INTENTION AND CONTEXT

Although current dialogue recognizes that observation is "theory-laden," this is understood in most quarters of science to refer to the *interpretation* of perception made by the observer after the event. Goethe understood, however, that the intentional idea structured the event itself and realized the implication for science.

His original naivete that led him to collide with Schiller's views became the perfect spur to develop Goethe's own perspective further. His later sophistication allowed him to recognize his earlier blindness with regard to his audience and write a series of essays aimed at explaining his approach.[24] These comments were too little and too late for his contemporaries, and later readers showed little interest in a departure from the path they knew.[25]

Yet, this departure carries Goethe's work into phenomenological science. If we are to portray—that is, intend—the organism, as Goethe said to Schiller, "alive and active, with its efforts directed from the whole to the parts," we will maintain the very aspect before which Kant thought science had to halt.

The approach is quite different from that normally taken by the scientific observer, who concentrates on that aspect which can lead over into mechanical analysis—the "fixed and dead." Thus, when Goethe wrote, in 1817, an essay "The Purpose Set Forth" introducing his morphological work, he argued that while the division of objects of nature, including living ones, into their constituent parts, had produced many advances, it also produced adverse effects when carried too far.

> . . . scientific minds of every epoch have . . . exhibited an urge to understand living formations as such, to grasp their outward visible, tangible parts in context, to see these parts as an indication of what lies within and thereby gain some understanding of the whole through an exercise of intuitive perception.[26]

A paragraph later, Goethe attempts to specify how this demand will be expressed in morphology:

The Germans have a word for the complex of existence presented by a physical organism: *Gestalt*. With this expression they exclude what is changeable and assume that an interrelated whole is identified, defined, and fixed in its character.

But if we look at all these *Gestalten*, especially the organic ones, we will discover that nothing in them is permanent, nothing is at rest or defined—everything is in a flux of continual motion. This is why German frequently and fittingly makes use of the word *Bildung* (formation, development) to describe the end product and what is in the process of production as well.

Thus in setting forth a morphology we should not speak of *Gestalt*, or if we use the term, we should at least do so only in reference to an idea, a concept, or to an empirical element that is held fast for a mere moment of time.

When something has acquired a form it metamorphoses immediately to a new one. If we wish to arrive at some living perception of nature we ourselves must remain as quick and flexible as nature and follow the example she gives.[27]

The older meaning of the term *Bildung*—a natural shape—had been overshadowed in the latter half of the eighteenth century with the notion of a development towards an ideal. The word now carried notions of "culture" and "cultivation"; the *Bildungs—Roman* was a novel of education and development, and Herder's work on the growth of human cultures used *Bildung* in the sense of "reaching up to *Humanität* (humanity and humane culture)."[28] Goethe's text, in its emphasis on the contrast with *Gestalt*, reflects the same concerns. To portray form as *Bildung* rather than *Gestalt* suggests an informing power placed within a context of becoming. The *Gestalt*, by contrast, is fixed because it is finished—it no longer possesses a connection to the antecedent unity and is no longer becoming.

The Aristotelian distinction of objects "changed by another" and objects "self-changed" is intuitive for most observers, but we do not usually reflect on how *complete* this distinction is. It is easy to suppose that the criterion refers only to the fact of alteration in an otherwise unremarkable form. For example, if billiard balls began to move by themselves, they would meet the test. But this is because we are attempting to derive the organic from the inorganic by a simple addition of one property.

The result, however, is disappointing because the billiard ball has no visible parts through which we can see purposive coordination. By contrast, living forms have parts that share a relation to each other and to the whole. This relationship cannot be gained by addition. There would be nothing in a self-moved billiard ball that prompted us to "see" a living thing. At best, we might propose that there was something alive within the ball.

The actual *appearance* of a self-changed entity requires a good deal more than one, or even several added properties. Consider the following passage which opens a recent text on the problems of scientific rationality:

> When friends meet, they smile. They greet each other warmly, and are glad to have met again. These sentences describe a common event in a simple and comprehensible way. But they are not "scientific." The warmth of the greeting cannot be measured by a thermometer, nor is the accompanying "gladness" observable. How then might friendship be described scientifically?
>
> Such a description might begin with the observation that a smile is a widening of the oral aperture, caused by contractions of the cheek musculature.[29]

Our normal perception of a human face comprehends a type of form that *is not fixed* and cannot be, since it is a visible manifestation of the self-changed. The configuration of shapes form a representative whole that is *continually* brought forth, that is, is continually *becoming*, since it is an immediate expression of the informing power. The expression is singular, although produced through manifold parts, because it becomes transparent to an inward and antecedent unity of consciousness. If facial physiognomy were a *Gestalt*, it would necessarily cease to be expressive since it would now be finished work severed from its formative cause— expression being expression only through immediate connection.

On the other hand, the scientific description of a smile is not a smile at all, but a portrayal of the physiognomy without the immediate connection or coordination of expression. To portray it in this manner we must divorce it from any inward whole; that divorce approximates the language of mechanics—that is, an elastic orifice is widened by the contraction of the elastic bands attached to it.

Of course, facial expression is a paradigmatic case for the appearance of life, but any living thing will demand an intentional context distinct from that utilized to make mechanical events visible. In the passage above, I have pointed to our tacit understanding that we cannot see a face *at all* without intending it in the context of expression. But if that insight is grasped, it should also become clear that animal life in general requires an expressive dimension to become visible. The animal *cannot appear as animal* unless it appears *behaving*, a term which, in its ordinary application, indicates a specific kind of causality.

Behavior is purposive movement that coordinates multiple parts. To be seen as purposive, we must view it as an expression of an inner unity, working outward through its "organs"—literally the means of carrying out its purpose. The fact that it does so appear means that we casually portray it, in Goethe's phrase, "from the whole to the parts."

GROWTH

I am aware, of course, that the animal not only behaves but also *grows*. But behavior is the manner in which an animal exhibits its animality; when we view that aspect, the immediacy of growth is suppressed because it is unfocused. If we want to examine an organism that exhibits its life— its internal potency for change—through growth, we must turn to the plant. Here again we will experience a difference between the living and the inert, but this time through growth alone.

Let us take an example that is easily constructed in the imagination. If, when leaving a restaurant which has surrounded diners with plastic plants, we discover to our surprise that the plant by the door is real, we have a sudden experience of just this difference. The overall impression is that of *movement*, not actual change but an inherent potential that the plastic, viewed as "fixed and dead," did not possess. Of course the actual changes brought about by growth are too slow to be seen as movement, but that is not the point.

Since plastic forms are fixed, we see them as finished work. Not so the actual plant. When the day is dry and reaches high temperatures, for example, many living plants temporarily wilt. In the drooping of the leaves and sometimes stem, we feel a loss of vitality. The next morning we are the more acutely sensitive to the vitality that has returned to full strength overnight. Both the weakening and the strengthening are seen in every part, not as something peculiar to that part, but as the expression of a unity. When a single shoot droops, we see that it has been somehow damaged and cut off from the whole. The plastic plant, as plastic, is unconnected to any whole that could express its activity in the gestures of the plant.

In this example, the connection between a sense of productive power and the *form* of the plant becomes more apparent, for the drooping reveals an important aspect of that form. The structure of the green shoot is somewhat delicate. The cut shoot wilts to an almost unrecognizable pile of limp tissue in a few hours. Leaves must be pressed if we are to artificially retain something of their shape.

Since the plant's forms are viewed in continuous connection to an antecedent unity, they become expressions of that power, and the plant can no more be cut off from it and appear "alive" than the face can lose its connection to an inner unity and remain a face. Because life must come to appearance through growth, plant form is never viewed as *Gestalt*, fixed and cut off from the process of production. This possibility would make it look like the plastic imitation. The actual plant must show a potential for change that it can only possess if its form is understand dynamically, as *Bildung*.

In other words, the distinction between "appearing alive" and "appearing inert" is not merely one of external evidence. No evidence is merely external, but all is the product of viewing some aspect of the world through a contextualizing intention. The phenomena of life arise when the living is viewed *as* living—through the intentions that organize appearances as if they were changed from within the changing body. Similarly, the phenomena of mechanics arise when mechanical events are viewed through intentions that take the elements of the field of vision to be changed from without.[30]

If one reverses these situations, viewing life through the contexting intentions of mechanics or the mechanical through the contexting intentions of life, the living will indeed appear somewhat mechanical and the nonliving somewhat alive, but these appearances are not stable. The plastic plant is an example of the latter, and produces an illusion of life only because it has been designed to imitate the living forms and then only at a distance.

Of course, the willful maintenance of an intentional context that does not entirely fit is possible, and thus, we can bring back the sense of life to the plastic plant by our own intentional effort, deliberately ignoring all details that do not fit the whole we are intending. Such willful maintenance of an intentional stance, however, does not produce true phenomena, which are enjoyed effortlessly once reached. Instead, the result is a form of distortion that demands constant effort.

Because the scientific mode of observing arose historically within physics, it was based on the intentional context of that science. If life is to be phenomenal, however, another context of intention is necessary as Kant himself noted. He despaired of raising a science on that foundation, and his judgment has been tacitly repeated by almost all biologists since. There is no logical impediment to such a foundation, however, once science itself is put on a phenomenological basis, by which I mean a science that draws its theoretical concepts from the structure of phenomena themselves rather than from an imperceptible reality assumed to lie behind them.

These theoretical concepts constitute a realm of phenomena because the sensible report becomes phenomenal only by the grace of intended conceptual contexts. As a result, all phenomena have a rational, conceptual structure. A full understanding of phenomena would bring their rational structure to self-consciousness, which must be the goal of phenomenological science. For such a science, the phenomena of life would be those in which life actually *appears*, rather than those derived from viewing the living within the contexts that serve to make inert substance visible. For example, the "second smile" is not an appearance of life, nor are any phenomena acquired by viewing the world through physical and chemical concepts.

THE IDEA

The emphasis above on experience may disturb some readers, who see a turn from "reality" to "appearance." It should take but a moment's reflection, however, to recognize that phenomenal appearance is a necessary basis of any true empiricism, and that unless we are looking *from* some contexting intention, we could find no object to look *at*. This relation is not open to subjective variation. The intention is a way of looking that raises potential phenomena to actuality, but these elements are objectively related—there is an exact correspondence between phenomenon and intention. If our mental context is lost, the object disclosed must also disappear. A science aware of this necessity would need an account of both phenomenon and contexting intention, or "idea" as Goethe called it in the realm of biology.

Goethe's "primal plant" was a first step toward a phenomenological biology. His search for what was common to all plants turned on the basis of *recognition*, which he understood to depend as much upon the "idea" in the observer as it did on the presence of the object recognized. If we look at Goethe's research in more detail, we see how this recognition is brought to a theoretical understanding.

As I've explained above, the organic, for Goethe, requires a form of cognition quite different from that of the inorganic. Kant saw this as well but stopped because he did not believe that another form of cognition could be developed. In keeping with Kant's terminology, Goethe calls the organ of organic cognition "*Vernunft*" (reason), while that by which the inorganic is thought is "*Verstand*" (understanding). In *Maxims and Reflections*, he wrote, "Reason concerns what is becoming; understanding what has become."[31] In this sense, becoming is the activity of life.

For Aristotle, becoming comes to actual appearance as the show of a potential-to-be-otherwise. The insight is particularly useful with regard to Goethe's thinking. When we observe a moving body—for example, a baseball perceived in the middle of its flight—the perception of its motion is at the same time the perception of its capacity to be in another position. The baseball will soon come to rest, but living bodies carry within them their own potency to change, which they need not derive from outside elements. A nonliving moving body has this potential only while in the condition of movement. In contrast, the organism has it while it is an organism—the corpse something quite different—and thus the potential-to-be-otherwise is an aspect of its being rather than its condition. We can easily sense this with any organism, since a loss of potency would amount to a loss of the organism. In the plant, however, the potency must be made apparent by the forms of growth alone.

The rational structure of this appearance is what underlies Goethe's investigation of *metamorphosis*. The concept did not refer to a historical relation but to the very nature of plant appearances. "I will go so far as to assert," he wrote, "that when an organism manifests itself we cannot grasp the unity and freedom of its formative impulse without the concept of metamorphosis."[32] Here we see Goethe's conviction that in metamorphosis the organism revealed the constant within change, which is a description of law even in the inorganic sciences. In mechanics, however, the law governs the relation of interacting bodies while remaining external to them. In organics, it constitutes the bodies as the unity indwelling in all and appearing in each.

Let us turn to the earlier example provided by figure 5.2, which presented a series of foliage leaves of the field buttercup—*Ranunculus acris*—arranged in a loop for better viewing. The forms of this graded series have the peculiar property of appearing to be arrested stages—we might call them "snapshots"—of continuous movement. If we begin with the first leaf on the stalk (*lower left*) and follow the transformation to the last (*lower right*), we have the sense that we are watching one form turning into another. In actuality, however, these leaves are adult stem forms, and none are stages of any other. The apparent transformation is a transformation of the formative process as it produces successive leaves on the stem.

The lawfulness of that process is immediately apparent. Consider, for a moment, how one could decide whether an additional form, not yet included in the series, could belong to it. By what criterion could the judgment be made? The solution is intuitive. Because we see the series in the context of intended movement, this very mode of seeing provides an adequate criterion for accepting or rejecting a new member.

The "movement" of the forms becomes more apparent to the degree that the "missing pictures"—the forms transitional between the shapes—are supplied. The movement we are *thinking* would, if entirely phenomenal, be entirely continuous, leaving no gaps. As gaps narrow, therefore, the impression of movement is strengthened. The technique by which a new form can be judged consists in placing that form within one of the gaps or at either end of the series and observing the result. When the movement is strengthened or made smoother, the new form may be left in place. If, however, the impression of movement is weakened or interrupted, the new form must be rejected. Contextualizing each form with an intended movement provides a principle of inclusion, because all potential forms in the series are now specified.[33]

There is an opposition between this context and each form viewed separately. To emphasize the continuity of the forms, Goethe suppressed their independence. If we intend movement, we cannot recognize the stasis of the empirical particulars in such a manner as to contradict that movement. In our intentional act, we suppress the sensible conditions by taking each individual form as an arrested stage of the transformation—a mode of perception that is, as I suggested above, akin to a series of photographs that break a continuous movement into a set of images transparent to the gesture they portray. We remain aware of the arrested stage, the *Gestalt*, but now only as an abstraction held in arrest by our sensible experience. Our attempt to detect the *relation* between forms makes them transparent to continuity.

This continuity among forms became the standard of inclusion by specifying, that is, generating, potential forms. Given the series, it is easy to imagine a form between any two neighbors within it. We should remember, however, that the *direction* of movement has no part in this result. We could, as Goethe suggests, let the movement run forward or backwards. The metamorphic relation does not depend upon direction.

By their inclusion within a context of metamorphosis, the single forms are no longer independent and complete in themselves. Whatever the direction of movement, each individual now appears to be coming from something as well as passing to something else, and by so doing *represents*, to our mind, *more than itself*, since each form can no longer be separated from its before and after. Indeed, its only distinction from these moments lies in the conditions of arrest—that is, we see it caught in the act of becoming something else. Each visible form now emerges as *partial* and becomes a disclosure of another sort of form.

Once we have worked up the context of movement (Goethe argues that we should do so in both directions) we intend each form not by itself but as representing the continuity of the whole as the passing note does in music. *Each must represent all others*, potential or actual. This capacity of the part to represent the whole is what Goethe terms the symbolic function of phenomena. Through it a supersensible form emerges from the sensible, as it did through the face.

In figure 5.3, for example, compare the two leaves extracted from differing zones in the series. Seen in isolation from the rest of the series, they are quite unlike. But let the observer work through the series both forward and backward, until it becomes a continuity, and glance again at the extracted forms. Viewed in the context of movement, the forms reveal what their stasis conceals, and they no longer seem unlike. In fact, the leaves may bear so strong a resemblance to each other that they seem to be *the same form*. Here is an intuited single form for the series, but it is a constant relation rather than a static particular.

We must now get over the linguistic difficulty I have myself created by my metaphor of movement, which conceals as much as it reveals. The movement under consideration is metamorphosis, which is not the outward alteration of one form into another but the differing outward expressions of an inward idea. What here appears as individual form is also, as *Bildung*, representative of the intuitive idea that is its intentional context. But if each sensible form is grasped as an expression of the idea, each is, qua sensible, an impossibly partial representation. As a result, the informing intuition cannot be quenched in the object, as is a grasp of the *Gestalt*, but overflows the particular with a sense of potentials. The idea is intuited in the object, as a felt potency of growth and, hence, "life." In the case of the plant, this impulse comes to appearance in the common identity of the plant's forms.

Fig. 5.3. Two leaves from the sequence of common-buttercup leaves in figure 5.2

This logic of becoming is something that Goethe understood very well, which is why he puts such emphasis on metamorphosis. He alone of all his scientific contemporaries seems to have realized in what manner the experience of life was rational and could be thought. Kant had entertained this possibility earlier but had retreated. It was his gesture, rather than Goethe's, that was representative of the age.[34]

Effort and Bildung

The notion that a single form underlay variation could hardly be attributed to Goethe—it was put forward by several other thinkers before Darwin, who was aware that Goethe had made such a proposal. Darwin, however, could not rid himself of the notion that the constant underlying organic form would itself be an individual shape, a specific *Gestalt*. Since this form was a particular, it could serve as the origin of multiple forms only by rooting their history. Darwin's work in the *Origin of Species* summed up the attempts to understand organic variation without departing from form as *Gestalt*. The departure into form as *Vernunft* was made by Goethe alone.

In any arena of inquiry, whether theoretical or practical, a problem must be recognized before it can be addressed. There is a difference between our experience of life and its scientific accounts, but the powers of our technologies can be advanced without a full illumination of appearances. In actuality, it is not our situations that define problems for us but our own thought. Only *our own demand* that immediate experience be raised to intelligibility can make the gap between phenomena and theory into a serious difficulty. Goethe came to the same conclusion, convinced that scientific problems arose from our own growth as thinking beings. When discussing his struggle toward a new organics he described the event as following from his nature:

> Impelled from the start by an inner need, I had striven unconsciously and incessantly toward primal image and prototype, and had even succeeded in building up a method of representing it which conformed to nature. Thus there was nothing further to prevent me from boldly embarking on this "adventure of reason" (as the Sage of Königsberg himself called it).[35]

The "Sage of Königsberg" is, of course, Kant, whose "adventure of reason," or Vernunft, is his ironic phrase for the attempt to grasp the living from the whole to the part, which he did not think possible.[36] Goethe's comments here argue that what he had already accomplished in botany demonstrated that Kant's limitation was mistaken.

Goethe's departure into "the adventure of *Vernunft*" was made without external support. By his own testimony, he was driven entirely by his inner need for a phenomenal world that was directly intelligible and a science "utterly identical with the object." As he added, however, "this enhancement of our mental powers belongs to a highly evolved age."

The age, Goethe admitted, is always a problem. It is the repository of habit—of whatever comes with greatest ease. Since the rise of modern science, our attention has focused on that which has already become—that is, come into manifestation as finished work—through the analytic style of thought that best treats it. This mode of cognition opened the inorganic realm to us. But while we are fully conscious of the fixed and dead, becoming enters perception more tacitly, on the edge of consciousness, and can be made explicit only though a greater intentional effort. Such an effort had become, for Goethe, a necessary step in his own *Bildung*, for he now saw Nature as the driving force in this ascent towards humanity.

The rise of scientific thought seems to have paralleled a devaluation of humanistic traditions.[37] It now appears that, with the turn towards the study of "the book of nature," the humanities relinquished the leadership they once exercised. Goethe was aware of this eclipse but, remarkably, did not bother to lament the event. He accepted the new situation, reasoning that if tradition had lost its guiding power through a turn towards Nature, then Nature must take the place of tradition. We are now in a position to understand what he meant.

In their deepest reading, the humanities contain traditions of what it means to be human and once took a leading role in the formation of culture, a role that Nature can assume only as a reflection of humanity. Nature cannot assume this role within present-day science. In a phenomenological science, however, phenomena are acts of knowledge and their immediate intelligibility is a human product. Perceptual experience is therefore an expression of human culture, which can no longer be separated from Nature—or at least, from Nature as it is presented in experience.

For such an outlook, a gap between experience and theory reveals a limit on our own development and a growing point. The somewhat drowsy acceptance of perception—and therefore phenomena—as fixed, merely to be explicated by theories that expand upon a Kantian or even Platonistic metaphysics of the imperceptible, cloaks a failure to grasp our human responsibility for the phenomenal world.

If we would assume this responsibility, Nature must be approached as the humanities are approached, not as a means to empower what we already are but as a means to grow beyond ourselves. Taken seriously, Nature in direct experience is a moving power, capable of forming human souls, for experience is more than memory:

> Whatever great, beautiful, or significant experiences have come our way must not be recalled again from without and recaptured, as it were; they must rather become part of the tissue of our inner life from the outset, creating a new and better self within us, continuing forever as active agents in our *Bildung*.[38]

We can find such "active agents" in perception only if we insist that experience be intelligible—that we be able to see directly into all its forms. For such an audience, Nature can be a most demanding teacher asking for a light that is within our faculty and moral responsibility to provide. If my argument is correct, this provision is a moral responsibility of *being human* in a scientific age. For some years, such considerations had been on Goethe's mind:

> For nearly a century now the humanities have ceased to permeate the people engaged in these studies as a living force. We have reason to feel happy over the fact that Nature has intervened and become the focus of interest, opening a new approach to *Humanität* for us from her angle.[39]

NOTES

1. Erik Nordenskiold, *The History of Biology: A Survey* (New York: Tudor, 1928), p. 282.

2. The practice of omitting Goethe's own discussion was not based on simple ignorance. Around the turn of the century, Rudolf Steiner published several commentaries that reviewed Goethe's reflections and indicated the actual

basis of Goethe's break with the science of his day. These seem to have been generally ignored as unreadable, and perhaps they were, given the prevailing mood. That mood, however, is changing—witness the independent and excellent discussion of just this aspect of Goethe's work in Dennis L. Sepper, *Goethe contra Newton* (New York: Cambridge University Press, 1988).

3. See Norwood Russel Hanson, *Patterns of Discovery* (New York: Cambridge University Press, Cambridge, 1958); Thomas S. Kuhn, *The Structure of Scientific Revolutions* (Chicago: University of Chicago Press, 1970).

4. The key publications in modern editions are Edmund Husserl, *Logical Investigations* (London: Routledge Kegan Paul, 1970), and Edmund Husserl *Ideas* (New York: Collier, 1962).

5. Immanuel Kant, *Critique of Judgement* (New York: Hafner, 1966).

6. Whether a living body or a cannonball, we can calculate the result of impressed forces as long as we know the weight, shape, velocity, air resistance, and so on, all of which can be abstracted from objects without regard for their identities.

7. See Kant, *Critique*, section 77, pp. 253–58.

8. Ibid., section 75, p. 248.

9. Ibid., section 78, pp. 258–64.

10. Ernst Haeckel, *The Riddle of the Universe* (New York: Harper and Row, 1900), p. 260.

11. The long title was used on the first printing in 1790. The text was reprinted as *The Metamorphosis of Plants*, which is the title used today. See Johann Wolfgang von Goethe, *Scientific Studies*, ed. and trans., Douglas Miller, Goethe Edition, vol. 12 (New York: Suhrkamp, 1988).

12. Johann Wolfgang von Goethe, *Goethe's Botanical Writings* (Honolulu: University of Hawaii Press, 1952), pp. 159–60.

13. Ibid. p. 160

14. Charles Darwin, *On the Origin of Species* (New York: Atheneum, 1972), p. 437.

15. J.W. Goethe, *Italian Journey* (New York: Shocken, 1968), p. 251.

16. Ibid. p. 305.

17. Goethe, "Fortunate Encounter," in *Scientific Studies*, p. 20.

18. Ibid., p. 5.

19. J. W. Goethe, *Goethe's Botanical Writings*, p. 235.

20. Goethe, *Scientific Studies*, p. 204.

21. Ibid., p. 115.

22. Goethe, "Maxims and Reflections," in *Scientific Studies*, p. 307.

23. Ibid., p. 307.

24. For commentary on his biology, see in particular Goethe, *Scientific Studies*, section II, pp. 57–69.

25. A stunning example of the resistance to Goethe can be found in Herman Ludwig von Helmhotz. In an 1853 lecture titled "On Goethe's scientific work," Helmholz admits that he finds Goethe's texts attractive, but then argues that this attraction must follow from their poetic rather than scientific value. He made this discovery by submitting the terms of the *Metamorphosis of Plants* to rigorous "scientific definition"—that is, fitting Goethe's ideas into the very terminology that Goethe had rejected. Once he completed this shift, Helmholz found that the texts seemed to say nothing at all and believed he had demonstrated that Goethe's claims could not be scientific. Hermann von Helmholz, *Vortrage und Reaten* (Braunschweig: Friedrich Vieweg und Sohn, 1896), pp. 36–37.

26. Goethe, *Scientific Studies*, p. 63.

27. Goethe, *Scientific Studies*, pp. 63–64.

28. See the discussion of *Bildung* in Hans-Georg Gadamer, *Truth and Method* (New York: Crossroad, 1975), pp. 10–19.

29. Stephen Edelglass, Georg Maier, Hans Gebert, John Davy, *Matter and Mind, Imaginative Participation in Science* (Hudson, N.Y.: Lindisfarne Press, 1992), p. 11.

30. I do not discuss the case of chemical phenomena—and self-organizing chemical structures—because these represent special cases of the mechanical. Change, in these cases, takes place within a whole—a solution—into which an unbalancing ingredient has been inserted, and evolves toward neutrality. Once the whole has become chemically neutral, however, no further change can occur unless introduced from without.

31. Goethe, "Maxims and Reflections," *Scientific Studies*, p. 308.

32. Goethe, *Scientific Studies*, p. 36.

33. I am speaking of law rather than fact. All the *potential* forms of the series are included in the continuous movement, but those that become *actual* or factual forms can be known only by observing a particular plant.

34. Although Immanuel Kant came to a halt before the organism, Georg Hegel did not, attempting instead to make the same penetration as Goethe. The two become friendly, but the degree of Hegel's success cannot be estimated here.

35. Goethe, "Judging through Intuitive Perception," *Scientific Studies*, pp. 31–32.

36. Kant, *Critique*, section 77, pp. 00.

37. See Anthony Grafton, *Defenders of the Text* (Cambridge, Mass.: Harvard University Press, 1991); Stephen Toulmin, *Cosmopolis* (New York: Free Press, 1990).

38. From a conversation reported by Johannes von Müller, November 4, 1823, and collected in J. W. Goethe, *Wisdom and Experience* (New York: Pantheon, 1949), p. 154.

39. Letter from Goethe to von Knebel, 1808, in J. W. Goethe, *Wisdom and Experience*, p. 157.

II

Doing Goethean Science

6

Jochen Bockemühl

Transformations in the Foliage Leaves of Higher Plants

One can approach the plant from two view points.[1] On one hand, the plant presents itself as a sophisticated whole that can be broken into a great number of individual parts and processes. On the other hand, the holistic quality of the plant suggests that it might be studied in terms of some higher unity, about which the individual parts and processes may give clues. Here, I call the sense of unity that a plant presents its *archetype*. As a way to examine archetype, I study leaf successions of several different plants. I argue that a complete series of fully developed foliage leaves mirrors the plant's development and says much about its archetype.[2] After F. J. N. Splechtner, I call these changes in form and pattern *transformations (Bildebewegungen)*.[3]

The reader must understand that a leaf's growth can be described in various ways. One common approach is to locate the leaf within the three dimensions of a Cartesian coordinate system, then to determine the leaf's length, breadth, and thickness as it grows. In contrast, following Goethe, what I try to do here is to describe the leaf appearances as much as possible in their own terms. I seek to avoid abstract scientific terminology and, rather, to emphasize descriptions that convey the qualities of the forms. In addition, my concern is not so much the individual leaf forms as the generative movements *between* them.

When we speak of "leaf apex," "petiole," "blade," and so forth, we see the plant as a material form. On the other hand, when we attend to

115

the process of transformation between the forms, we become aware of formative tendencies, or *activities* (*Tatigkeiten*). We make these activities our own when, in the process of studying one form's metamorphosing into another, we also bring a mobility and flow into our own thinking.

TRANSFORMATIONS IN FOLIAGE LEAVES

We begin with the transformations evidenced by individual leaves in the course of their development. Figure 6.1 shows the growth stages of the first leaf of *Cardamine hirsuta*, or Pennsylvania bittercress. First, a small tip, or apiculus, extends itself from the growing point. It continues to grow and differentiates, so that we soon recognize five distinct points. Between these, the leaf blade then begins to extend; the entire periphery of the blade is engaged in the growth of the green surface. Next, the leaf stalk, or petiole, extends itself. A shootlike "bundling" structure grows out in such a way that the leaf blade is borne away from the plant. At the same time, the tips continue to extend but become rounder and fuller until, finally, they round themselves out completely. The leaf blade, which previously took the form of several rounded but separate projections, or crenatures, is now uniformly round and differentiated from the stalk, which has become quite long.

This developmental sequence suggests that a leaf's growth involves four activities. As illustrated by the *far-left* drawing in the figure, the first activity can be called "shooting," when the leaf's apiculus extends away from the growing point. This tip continues to grow and begins to move in several different directions, as in the second drawing, and we can speak of "articulating." Third, the points of articulation begins to move away from each other, a situation that can be called "spreading" after the old West Germanic verb "spreiten."[4] Fourth, and in an analogous way, the stalk at the base of the leaf extends itself—a situation that can be described as "stemming."

I argue here that the contour of any individual leaf can be seen as a function of the intensity, timing, and duration of shooting, articulating, spreading, and stemming. In the development of *Glechoma hederacea*, or ground ivy, shown in figure 6.2, we see that the same four activities can interact to produce a substantially different form.[5] In looking at the sequence, one observes that shooting predominates initially, although articulating and spreading are also present.[6] Shooting and articulating continue at the base of the leaf through the fourth drawing but then stop. The rounded lobes of this fourth stage already announce the intensification of spreading, which continues but is "held back" at the top and at the base on both sides of each lobe, with the result that notches form

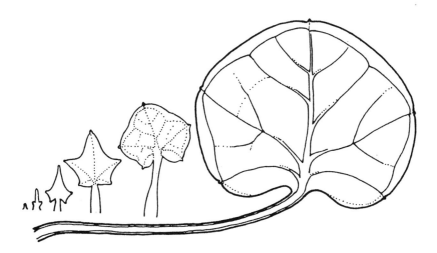

Fig. 6.1. Development of one of the first leaves of Pennsylvania bittercress (*Cardamine hirsuta*).

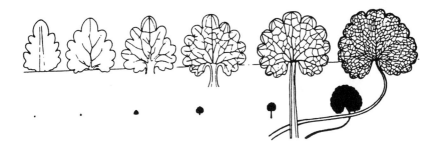

Fig. 6.2. Development of one of the first leaves of ground ivy (*Glechoma hederacea*). Each leaf scaled at the same size (actual size indicated by silhouette below).

where there were originally points. In the fully developed leaf, shooting and articulating have receded entirely, while the results of spreading and stemming are dominant.

TRANSFORMATIONS WITHIN LEAF SEQUENCES

We next need to apply the four interpenetrating activities to a *series* of fully developed foliage leaves. Earlier biologists attempting a Goethean approach to plants ran into problems by identifying a plant's archetype with a single, static form—the fully developed intermediate state of the

Fig. 6.3. Mature leaf sequence of corn salad (*Valerianella locusta*).

foliage leaf—which forced them in turn to see the higher and lower leaves merely as "suppressed" or "inhibited" manifestations of the archetype.[7] The four activities, on the other hand, provide a more flexible understanding of archetype, allowing one to follow its working through *all* stages of leaf development. We will find that this larger development reflects the sequence we followed in the individual leaf but reflects it as a *mirror image*.

This inversion of transformations (Gegenläufigkeit der Bildebewegungen) is most clearly seen within foliage leaves. Figure 6.3, for example, illustrates the sequence of forms for *Valerianella locusta*, a species of corn salad. Note that the leaves are arranged in "horseshoe" fashion, beginning at the lower left with the cotyledon and ending at the lower right with the last hypsophyll subtending the blossom.[8]

Studying figure 6.3, we note immediately that the earlier phase of development is marked by a lengthening separation of stem and blade. On the other hand, stem and blade fuse in the last stages of the sequence, while the intermediate stages indicate various degrees of interpenetration.

Though easy to summarize, the sequence is more difficult to interpret in terms of stemming, spreading, articulating, and shooting. These activities manifest themselves less in the phenomena—that is, in the individual leaf forms—and more in the movement *between* them. Looking again at figure 6.3, we can say that spreading and stemming predominate, although hints of articulating are suggested later by the points at the periphery of the leaves. In addition, shooting is suggested by the elongated leaves of the last stages.

In short, we can conclude that all four activities are present, although articulating and shooting are very nearly subsumed by spreading and stemming. When interpreting in this way, one should note that thinking must participate more actively in the leaf sequence—we must mentally contribute to constructing the experience. While remaining within the phenomena, we move a step closer toward apprehending something ideal.

The interplay of the four activities looks quite different when we return to the foliage leaves of our first example, *Cardamine hirsuta*, shown in figure 6.4. Again, stemming and spreading come initially to the fore. Then begins the process of articulating, which now manifests in such a thoroughgoing way that the stemming can carry into each of the separate "articulations"—each separate leaflet is carried away from the petiole, just as earlier the petiole carried the leaves away from the main stem. Stemming now appears *within* the spreading of each separate leaf. The "articulated" yet still rounded leaves now grow more slender as shooting finally appears. Comparing figure 6.1 with figure 6.4, we note that the foliage sequence is the inversion of the development of *Cardamine hirsuta's* individual leaf.

Figure 6.5 illustrates the foliage sequence for *Medicago sativa*, common alfalfa. Overall, one notes that the sequence involves a three-leaf pattern throughout; only the last leaf is undivided. All the parts, the pinnules as well as the leaf-like basal appendages, or stipulae, are initially round and coarse but later become more pointed and elongated. What is particularly striking here is the strong polarity between the first and last leaves in the sequence: apices form where there had originally been notches. We saw this same polarity for ground ivy (fig. 6.2); only here, in the development of the foliage leaves (fig. 6.5), we see the mirror image. All four activities appear in the developing foliage leaves of every plant, but their combinations of interactions are infinitely varied.

To what extent can these four activities be separated? The easiest distinction to understand is that between shooting and spreading: the former involves growth in one specific direction, while the latter refers to growth as it manifests through the extension of a surface. Because they are both connected with a change in length, the difference between shooting and stemming is more difficult to see. Shooting is characterized

Fig. 6.4. Mature leaf sequence of Pennsylvania bittercress, from seed leaf to flower

by growth at the apex, which extends itself away from the leaf; there is radiating movement from a center. In stemming, on the other hand, the leaf is pushed outward by intercalary growth primarily at the leaf base. The tendency in stemming is to "align" the radii—to draw them together into a stem or, in relation to the leaf blade, to allow the veins to run parallel along the length of the leaf.

The Full Development of Foliage Leaves

We next must consider the foliage leaves within the context of the leaf development in its entirety. To visualize such movement, we use the example of *Sisymbrian officinale*, or hedge mustard. Figure 6.6 illustrates the leaf sequences, arranged in concentric semi-lemniscates, for four mustard plants germinated at the same time and place but harvested

Fig. 6.5. Mature leaf sequence of alfalfa (*Medicago sativa*)

about a month apart. In the case of plants 2, 3, and 4, some leaves are missing because the earliest leaves withered away by the time of harvesting. Thus, plant 4 lacks most of its leaf forms; plant 3, about half; and plant 2, one or two leaves. These missing forms are no problem, however, because each of the outer series can be completed by adding with the mind's eye the forms from the next series in. Note that the *solid* arrows mark these transition points, while the *unfilled* arrows trace the development of a single plant's full life cycle.

This new level of complexity reveals a pattern not observable earlier: a regulative rhythm of separating, interpenetrating, and fusing that recapitulates itself not just in the foliage leaves but at every stage of leaf development as well. The unfilled arrows indicate the points where the transition from fusing to separating takes place. This pattern is repeated throughout the cycle: as a result of separating, the forms on the left half of each series are generally longer-stemmed and rounder; as a result of fusing, the forms on the right are shorter-stemmed and more pointed; yet again, forms in the middle show more evidence of articulating.

Again we see an inversion of the four generative activities: the embryonic sequence of shooting, articulating, spreading, and stemming—

Fig. 6.6. Developmental movement of all the leaves of the hedge mustard (*Sisymbrium officinale*). Mature leaf sequences from four plants grown simultaneously but picked and pressed at monthly intervals.

observed in figures 6.1 and 6.2—is mirrored in the fully developed forms of figure 6.6 by the sequence of stemming, spreading, articulating, and shooting. Yet careful observation of the development of a single plant (following the unfilled arrows) also suggests that the polarity between separating and fusing (and with it, the inverted sequence of activities as a whole) is much more pronounced in the lower leaves than in the higher. Note the unfilled arrows, each of which indicates the start of a new rhythm: the weakening in intensity becomes already quite evident in comparing the rhythms of plant 1 and plant 2.

We next turn to figure 6.7, which illustrates *Lapsana communis*, or nipplewort—a plant whose leaf series reveals a greater complexity than that of hedge mustard. Here, several plants, germinated and grown together, were harvested at weekly intervals and their leaves pressed. After thirteen weeks (the vertical dimension), leaf development had run its full course. Individual leaves are numbered from left to right; leaf forms drawn in outline are those that had withered away by the time of harvesting.

Reading the series from bottom to top, one observes that the inverse cycle is intense and full in the lower leaves but weakened in the upper: a

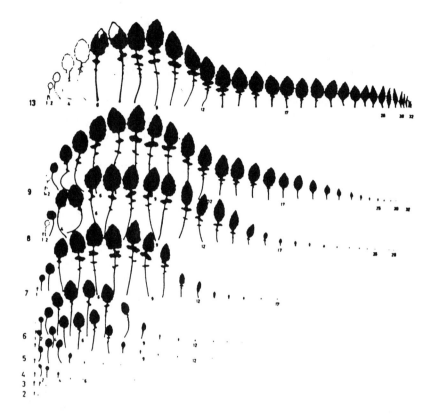

Fig. 6.7. Leaf series of nipplewort (*Lapsana communis*). Mature leaf sequences from several plants grown simultaneously but cut and pressed at weekly intervals for thirteen weeks. Individual leaves are numbered from left to right; leaf forms in outline had withered away by time of harvesting.

wavelike pattern moves to the right and exhibits a smaller relative amplitude as one moves vertically from series to series. The initial rhythm, full in the lower leaves, is hardly repeated in the upper series as they progress toward and through the stage of the blossom. Though the pattern is lost in the scale of the reproduction shown here, one also finds one very tiny "wave" just before the nipplewort blossom.

The nature of this weakening on the larger scale can be demonstrated better by looking at its mirror image on the smaller scale—the embryonic development of individual leaves, as shown in figure 6.8, which make a continuous series for nipplewort.[9] Each row represents the development of selected nipplewort leaves illustrated in figure 6.7 as undulating horizontal series. The numbers at the left of each row are those of the individual leaf's place within the entire foliar development, for example, number 1 in figure 6.8 is the first leaf after the cotyledons, while number 32 is the last of the blossom leaves.

Figure 6.8 strongly confirms the weakening of the inverse rhythm we observed within the larger development of nipplewort. Again, all four activities are at work in the formation of each of the leaves, with the possible exception of the first and the last, neither of which shows signs of articulating. Yet, the relative intensity of the four activities varies greatly from leaf to leaf. In the lower leaves illustrated in figure 6.8, all four activities are strongly engaged.

Look, for example, at leaf 2, in which the sequence of shooting, articulating, spreading and stemming manifests fully. By leaf 6, spreading is no longer able either to "round out" completely the apices created by articulating or to halt the multiplication of leaf forms. This tendency is accentuated even more strongly in, for example, leaf 12. By the time leaves 25 through 30 are reached, not only spreading but also articulating and stemming have nearly disappeared. Thus, leaf 32 represents the "confluence" of these two inverse streams, the place where the micro- and macro-developments intersect. The first activity of the embryonic sequence, shooting, manifests itself as the *last* predominant activity in the sequence of foliar development as a whole.

Figure 6.9 is an effort to make visible the interrelationships and interaction between these two inverse developments in the nipplewort. This figure returns to the form of the semi-lemniscate. Note, however, that the forms around the periphery represent the foliar development of a single plant beginning at the *lower left* and ending on the *lower right*. Curving radii extend from the crossing point of the lemniscate to the periphery. On these radii are the embryonic forms of the leaves at intervals proportional to their proximity to the shape of the fully developed leaf. These leaves are the same series that was arranged horizontally in figure 6.8.

Also note that there are straight radii that connect forms in which the four activities stand in approximately the same relationship to each other. One observes, for example, that in the leaf forms along the third and fourth straight radii counting clockwise, spreading clearly pre-dominates, while in the sixth radii, articulation is emphasized.

If the plant grew linearly, like a crystal, the growth of each leaf form would follow the straight radii. But the plant does not grow in this way. Rather, each form represents a nexus or confluence of complex growth rhythms. The first "gesture" of each leaf form is a step in the direction of the blossom, molded by shooting. But only the blossom itself carries this initial gesture through into its fully-developed form. All the other forms are, as it were, "bent back" around the circle counterclockwise by the inverse growth rhythm that moves through the fully developed leaves.

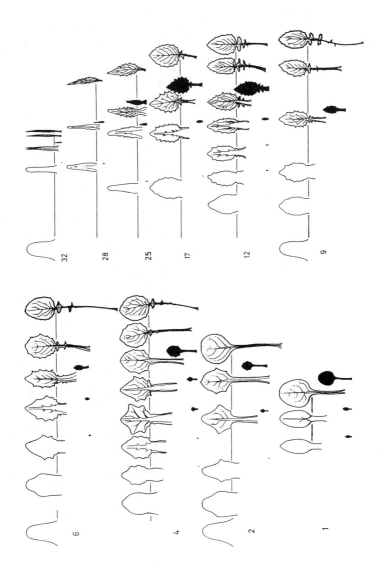

Fig. 6.8. The embryonic development of individual leaves for the nipplewort. Each row represents the development of a selected leaf. The numbers at the left of each row are those of the individual leaf's place within the entire foliar development. Only selected leaves are illustrated.

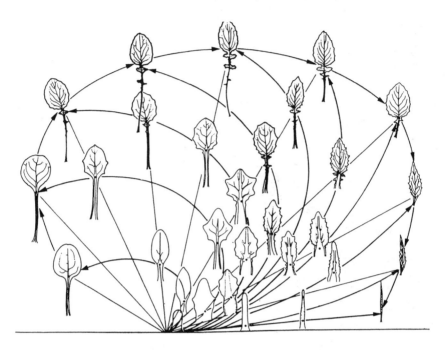

Fig. 6.9. Developmental movement of the leaves of nipplewort. The drawing shows the relation between the changes of form during the growth of individual leaves from growing point to mature leaf (arrows radiating counterclockwise from center) and the changes of form in the sequence of mature leaves from the seed leaf to the highest leaf (outermost arrows clockwise).

Take, for example, the embryonic sequence leading to leaf number 2, counting clockwise. All four activities are present in this full and intense rhythm—so much so that the original shooting has completely disappeared in the final rounded form. It is as though the inverse series of stemming, spreading, articulating, and shooting were working *backwards* through the finished leaf forms to counteract the initial embryonic activity. Again, we see that the full regulative cycle is most intense in the lowest leaves, while it manifests itself only weakly in the upper. We also see that each of the finished leaf forms is an image created by inverse rhythms flowing across one another.

PARTICIPATING MENTALLY IN THE PHENOMENON

Our study of plants suggests three levels of increasing ideality: the individual leaf forms, the four generative activities, and the regulative movements of separating/interpenetrating and fusing/inversion. It is crucial to emphasize that this increasing ideality is *not* an increasing abstraction. The greater ideality of the last two levels is not a function of their remoteness *from* the phenomena but, rather, of the *degree of intensity* with which we participate mentally in the phenomena.

These ideal activities, seen as moving through the empirically given, are Goethean "archetypal phenomena." Goethe pursued such essential patterns in full awareness of two possibilities of error: freezing oneself in abstraction or losing oneself in mystical reverie. To avoid these potential errors, observers must direct their gaze upon their own thinking activity as well as on the thing itself.[10] In this activity is revealed that which is not contained in the mere sense perceptions, yet that which binds them into a larger pattern of meaning.

As I have attempted to demonstrate, one must attain several intermediate levels of understanding before one can have a complete picture of archetype. By means of a shift in attention, one can reach a level of observation above and beyond the contemplation of individual formal elements—a level of recognition no longer accessible to sensory perception alone yet upon which the succession of form manifests itself in transformation. Led by sense perception, this way of thinking enacts (*vollzieht*) the transformation.

Yet, the more one understands the complexity of transformation, the more one sees that the archetype has not yielded up its full meaning in what we have done here. The regulative activities discussed earlier are thus only an indication of the higher plane upon which the archetype can reveal itself more completely. It is here also that one must seek the patterns that regulate the specific interpenetration of the various species. On the basis of what has been achieved so far, we note only that here something is both retained and released. In the multiplicity of the movements, we sense a wisdom-filled structure through which the archetype as a being first announces itself.

NOTES

1. This essay was originally translated by Frederick Amrine and then reedited by David Seamon, who drew heavily for clarification from Frederick Amrine's paraphrasing and interpretation of the article in his "Goethean Method in the Work of Jochen Bockemuhl," in *Goethe and the Sciences: A Re-Appraisal*, edited by F. Amrine, F. J. Zucker, and H. Wheeler (Dordrecht: Reidel, 1987), pp. 301–18. Sections drawn from this paraphrasing are used with the permission of Kluwer Academic Publishers. ©1987 by D. Reidel Publishing Company, Dordrecht, the Netherlands.

2. See Jochen Bockemühl, "Der Pflanzentypus als Bewegungsgestalt," *Elemente der Naturwissenschaft* 1 (1964):3–11.

3. F. J. N. Splechtner, "Goethes Gesetz der Metamorphose und die Regel von den sogenannten homologen Variationsserien," *Gaia-Sophia: Jahrbuch der naturwissenschaftlichen Sektion der Freien Hochschule für Geisteswissenschaft am Goetheanum Dornach* 5 (1930):118.

4. This description was first used by K. F. Schimper; see Wilhelm Troll, *Vergleichende Morphologie der hoheren Pflanzen: Band I: Vegetationsorgane* (Berlin: Gebruder Borntrager, 1935–1939), p. 1388.

5. Note that, in the top drawings of the figure, the blades of each leaf have been enlarged to the same size; the actual proportions are indicated in the silhouettes.

6. The rounding of the leaf apices in the first form is a distortion caused by the strong magnification.

7. Wilhelm Troll indicates that Wretschko has noted in a study of the leaves of *Umbelliferae* that "all the stem leaves through the umbel [flower cluster] represent in a way the extended developmental stages of a ground-leaf." See WilhelmTroll, *Vergleichende Morphologie*, p. 1388.

8. This arrangement should be understood not as a semicircle but, rather, as the top half of a lemniscate continuing down the left side through the blossom and up the right side through the fruit and seed. For further justification of this arrangement, see Jochen Bockemühl, *In Partnership with Nature* (Wyoming, R.I.: Bio-Dynamic Literature, 1991).

9. The mode of presentation is the same as in figure 2: blades of the leaves have all been enlarged to the same size, while actual proportions are indicated by the silhouette.

10. See Rudolf Steiner, *A Theory of Knowledge Based on Goethe's World Conception*, trans. Olin D. Wannamaker, 2nd ed. (New York: Anthroposophic Press, 1968).

7

Nigel Hoffmann

The Unity of Science and Art

Goethean Phenomenology as a New Ecological Discipline

In his own time, Goethe suffered from critics who could not understand that both science and art could be united in the work of one individual.[1] The same kind of criticism has continued over the years. Those who have regarded him as, above all, a poet have pronounced his science as either irrelevant or even detrimental to his poetic creativity. His scientific critics have likewise dismissed his experimental work as being much too influenced by his artistic sensibilities. Today there is abundant evidence of an awakening of interest in Goethe's methods of "nature study" yet a notable lack of commentary on the relationship of his science to his art, at least in the English-speaking world.[2] We may discuss Goethe's phenomenological method without adequately grasping what is unique about this method in terms of how it relates the artistic and the scientific. In fact, this link between art and science can provide a key to understanding Goethe's form of "nature study" as a new ecological discipline in our time.

One of the main tasks of this article is to present some results of my research into plants that are native to the area around Sydney. Prior to this presentation I set out, in four stages, the method used for this research, showing how it is derived from Goethe's indications. To give expression to my observations and insights, I use descriptive language of a standard scientific kind as well as painting and poems, the latter plainly taking me well away from orthodox scientific methodology. I consider it

unnecessary to characterize my work in advance as either primarily scientific or artistic; the word "phenomenology" is an inclusive term and has,
at the very least, the virtue of circumventing this dilemma. In the concluding section, I take up this question of the relationship of science and
art in Goethean phenomenology, especially as it pertains to contemporary ecological issues.

A Goethean Phenomenological
Method for Plant Study

There are many commentaries on the philosophical issues surrounding
Goethe's studies of natural phenomena and numerous descriptions of his
experiments. Not many authors, however, have focused on the question
of his experimental method. Fritz Heinemann is one who, earlier this
century, wrote specifically on that subject.[3] This philosopher draws from
Goethe's own descriptions of his method, which are by no means
systematic.[4] He explains:

> [Goethe's] method is genuinely phenomenological. It begins with
> phenomena, proceeds through them, and ends with them, returning at
> the last from the Ur-phenomenon (archetypal phenomenon) to the
> particulars whose claims have not at any point been abrogated.[5]

Goethe's germinal approach has been built on, more recently, by the
biologist Jochen Bockemühl, whose Goethean method will be used as the
basis for the work presented in this chapter.[6] What Bockemühl has done is
to mold Goethe's phenomenological method according to imagery related
to the four classical elements—earth, water, air, and fire—each element
indicating a discrete "observational mode."[7] Bockemühl adds to this an
initial stage, which he calls the "first impression." As shall be seen in what
follows, these stages correspond to, but expand upon, Goethe's own
division of his method into three stages—the "empirical phenomenon,"
the "scientific phenomenon," and the "pure phenomenon" (or archetypal
phenomenon), each stage representing the "self-distilling" process of
understanding.[8] The stages of this method are distinct but closely connected to one another. They are actually "moments" in the continuum
that is the research process.[9]

First Impression

The first impression is the crucial first step and probably the hardest to
describe. It is something that can be inferred from Goethe's approach. In

his nature study, he cultivated a contemplative approach that sought not to rush ahead of itself into all kinds of theorizing and categorizing but to rest content with taking in the thing on its own terms and in its own time. Goethe was well aware of how we tend to view things from a constricted view point, and he discussed this in "The Experiment As Mediator between Object and Subject." Here he suggests that, right from the beginning of research, there should be a calm openness and a willingness to let a thing speak on its own terms. He advises, "As a neutral, seemingly godlike being [the experimenter] must seek out and examine what is, not what pleases."[10]

The aim is to make conscious the moment of first contact with a phenomenon—a moment when one's sensibilities are most alive and open. Everyone has a first impression when experiencing something new, but this encounter is usually quickly forgotten as the thing becomes familiar and ordinary. It is like the moment of entering a foreign city for the first time and being immediately taken by its unusual sights, sounds, and smells. That initial encounter can be most telling, even if vague and generalized. Goethe's approach suggests that we can consciously carry this impression throughout the course of the research process and allow it to develop and become more clear.

This first impression is the intimation of a particular mood or quality that can be concisely recorded, verbally or pictorially. We cannot call this first impression a "knowing" in the full sense of the word. Knowledge is not just the "facts" that one arrives at in the end but the organic process of that knowing, beginning with the most rudimentary first impression.[11]

STAGE ONE: THE PHYSICAL/SENSORY INFORMATION/EARTH

The first stage of studying the phenomenon after the "first impression" corresponds to the transition from what Goethe called the "empirical phenomenon" to the "scientific phenomenon." The "empirical phenomenon" is, according to Goethe, that which "everyone finds in nature"—the world as we experience it immediately and directly.[12] This stage is the entry into what Goethe called the "experiment"—the process of exploring the phenomenon on progressively deeper levels of its being. In this phase of research, we are still at a preconceptual level and, in that sense, still close to the "first impression." We are dealing simply with what is grasped by the senses but, at this point, the senses are focused on the phenomenon in question. This is the stage where an exact description of the phenomenon is carried out with the aim to gather information from all the senses.

The methods employed at this stage are "empirical" according to the current scientific meaning of this term—that is, deriving from observation rather than from theory. Goethe considered this to be empiricism of a "lower" kind, the "higher" empirical evidence emerging at later stages of the experiment.[13] Every sense can be employed: sight, hearing, taste, touch, and smell.[14] For example, a flower generally has a characteristic fragrance, but so may the fruit, the seed, or leaf if rubbed between the fingers. Similarly, each different part of a plant may have a different taste. In keeping with Goethe's belief in the senses as "the greatest and most precise physical apparatus that can exist," Goethean method capitalizes on the senses' capacity to take in the phenomenon in every possible way.[15] In principle, there is no limit to the amount of information that can be obtained in this way but, in practice, a vast accumulation is not necessary.[16] Rather, the aim at this stage is to produce a description as precise and as systematic as possible.

Goethe's discussions of this phase of the research process highlight the need for precision of description and for remaining as open as possible to the phenomenon in question—something he had learned originally from the great empiricist philosopher Sir Francis Bacon. As opposed to the "natural way of seeing and judging things," Goethe explained that this descriptive phase is very difficult because we must attempt to see things clearly and in an unprejudiced way. He wrote, "We cannot exercise enough care, diligence, strictness, even pedantry, in collecting basic empirical evidence."[17] Thus, we can speak of the mental disciplines associated with this stage. One can cultivate the precision of one's approach by working from memory. One can, for example, make drawings without having the phenomenon before one, the next day or even weeks after the first observations. What is important at this stage is to use the exactitude of the drawing to assess the accuracy of one's memory.

This is the *earth* stage of the method. Here we have moved from an inchoate "first impression"—an overall mood—to an apprehension of the phenomenon that is immensely more "established" and firm. A plant, in the *earth* mode, is grasped only in so far as it is a solid object, seen in terms of its external "facts." Even its inner physical structure and anatomical features can only be known by making them *external*—that is, by dissecting the plant. To the extent that we perceive a living thing in this *earth* mode, we experience ourselves as separate from it as external observers. Only in this way can we stand back and see the thing as it is in itself, aside from our own needs, pleasures, or prejudices.

Stage Two: Time/Exact
Sensorial Imagination/Water

The second stage represents the conscious moving into another observational mode—in Goethe's terms, penetrating more deeply into the "scientific phenomenon." We move into an "inner" dimension of ourselves and the phenomenon in a gradually deepening journey of participation. First stage descriptions characterized the plant as something solid, objective, and having many qualities that could be apprehended by the senses. What did not come to light were the *relationships* among these qualities or characteristics. To enter this second stage of the research process is to open oneself to the dynamically relational character of the plant and to apprehend how one quality derives from the other, one part from another. The aim, in other words, is to experience the plant's time dimension and its growth process.

For example, we may focus on the relationship between a seed and a stem, or a stem and a calyx. These plant organs are not only contiguous in space but also in time, and it is with the latter relationship that we are now engaged. The dynamic relationships of growth are not "facts" in the manner of the data gathered in the first stage. In this second stage, we are not so much concerned with perceiving movements externally but "taking them within," perceiving them with our inner or artistic sense. The different physical parts of a plant are like frozen moments in a continuum of metamorphosis. The seed and the stem, the stem and the calyx, as contiguous organs of the plant, are related as the expressions of *one generative movement*, in which "imaginative" thinking can participate. Goethe called the process of cognitively participating in an organism's generative movements "exact sensorial imagination." The organs of a plant—for example, the flower, fruit, and seed—are not usually present at the same time, and Goethe relates how he proceeded to grasp the metamorphic process:

> If I look at the created object, inquire into its creation, and follow this process back as far as I can, I will find a series of steps. Since these are not actually seen together before me, I must visualise them in my memory so that they form a certain ideal whole. At first I will tend to think in terms of steps, yet nature leaves no gaps, and thus, in the end, I will have to see this progression of uninterrupted activity as a whole. I can do so by dissolving the particular without destroying the impression itself.[18]

This cognitive activity is the *water* stage of the research process. Water, the fluid element, has no definite form of its own but is forever taking on the form of that which it fills or surrounds and, in doing so, demonstrates its enormous sensitivity.[19] Water is therefore expressive of the movement of a form through time, and of imaginative cognition that is characterized by fluidity, sensitivity, and a capacity to experience these changes of living form. "Exact sensorial imagination" does this by molding itself to one form and then "flowing" to the next so that the particulars are "dissolved" into one fluid movement.

Up to this point we have been dealing first with impressions, moods, and then with precise descriptions of the phenomenon from the viewpoint of an external observer. In this *water* stage, we actually begin to relate ourselves to the organism in that we take up the dynamic character of the plant into ourselves—a relationship that fully realizes itself in the later *fire* stage as "creative action."

STAGE THREE: GESTURE /INSPIRATION/AIR

The third stage of Goethean method can be described as the further "intensification" or "distillation" of the phenomenon, so that we move even further into the "scientific phenomenon." Whatever results were obtained through the exercise of "exact sensorial imagination" in the water phase are deepened here through uncovering another orientation towards the phenomenon and another mode of observation. The metamorphic movements are now perceived in a way that brings them to light as formative *gestures*, which may also be called the plant's "formative life-principles." A gesture is not merely a movement but, rather, an action through which a definite *meaning* expresses itself. Here we are close to the dictionary definition of a gesture as an "indication of intention."[20] This is not to accord the plant a humanlike intelligence, but it is also not to deny that a certain intelligence works in nature's formative processes. Whatever "idea" lies behind the formative movements of a plant we begin to apprehend through an "airy cognition."

The method of working in this phase is, as in the *water* stage, both inner and outer. That is to say, this phase requires a deepening participation in the phenomenon through an inner or artistic faculty, and these inner perceptions are brought to outer expression as "gesture sketches" through a suitable medium, which may be visual, verbal, or even musical. Here, the less realistic, more expressive art forms become more appropriate. This is the phase of research when the "first impression," perhaps an overall mood, may become more meaningful and take a more organized expression. We have moved from this "first impression" to the solid, objective character of the plant, understood with a thinking related to the earth element. This is "dissolved" into the water element, a form of imaginative cognition that is able to live in the fluid growing processes of the plant. But this, too, requires a further "intensification."

Air, like water, is a fluid substance but without graspable materiality. The mode of cognition associated with this *air* phase is called "inspirational." One does not perceive the gestures of organic form as empirical facts or movements in time; instead, one takes them in as one takes in the moving gestures of music. In this sense, one *inspires* them with a kind of artistic cognition and so allows their meanings to come to light. Bockemühl calls air "the element of acquiescence."[21] By this he means that pure air has the character of not containing anything itself because it is transparent and insubstantial. We see things *through* the air but not the air itself, and this transparency or acquiescence needs to become the character of our cognitive mode.[22]

STAGE FOUR: CREATIVE POTENCY/INTUITION/FIRE

The fourth stage corresponds to what Goethe called the "pure phenomenon"; it is the "archetype" or "theory" of the organism as Goethe conceived it.[23] As already discussed, Goethe did not see the "pure phenomenon" as anything bounded or fixed. He recognized that, in the infinite depths of nature, there would always be higher principles under which one's axioms or theories could be subsumed. The third stage of Goethe's method was discussed in terms of the apprehension of the characteristic gestures of the plant. This fourth and last stage represents the further distillation of these gestures by means of another mode of observation—an intuitive mode. More precisely, Goethe spoke of *Anschauende Urteilskraft*, usually translated "intuitive judgment," as an exact mode of "seeing" a phenomenon that he considered to be a "higher" empiricism.

In terms of this Goethean method, the fourth stage represents the most inner way of experiencing the plant. Through intuitive perception, we apprehend what can be called the "creative potency" of the organism. This is the "theory" of the plant, but it cannot be formulated in any conventionally theoretical sense. Goethe talked about expressing the "archetypal phenomenon" in terms of "short, pregnant sentences" that he compared in their cogency and symbolic power to mathematical expressions.[24] We can extend this by saying that these intuitive perceptions could be brought to expression in any appropriate medium capable of transmitting "potent" or "pregnant" meanings. Intuitive perception is *intellectus archetypus*, thinking "from the whole to the parts"—from the formless to the formed.[25] The whole is nothing substantial or nothing actualized. It is pure potentiality or potency. Art is one means of suggesting this formative power of the whole.

In the Goethean method, this is the *fire* stage. Fire is related to air in that it is an insubstantial element. Yet, fire is not mere transparency; it does not have the character of acquiescence but of *intensity* and *self-generated activity*. These qualities may be experienced externally as warmth and inwardly as the immediate warmth of identification that one feels when he or she has made contact with a living being's "inner impulse." It is something of these qualities that needs to enter one's mode of cognition.[26] In my plant studies that follow, I employ poetry and painting as ways of actualizing this *fire* stage.

APPLYING GOETHEAN METHOD TO TWO PLANTS

The Sydney region of Australia contains numerous national parks and abounds in the unique native flora that so fascinated the botanist Sir Joseph Banks, who was aboard Captain James Cook's *Endeavour* when it first explored the east coast of Australia in 1770. My research focuses on a coastal bush area thirty kilometers north of Sydney, and here the two plants to be examined using the Goethean approach—*Banksia integrifolia* (Proteaceae) and *Kunzea ambigua* (Myrteaceae)—are found growing alongside each other. *Banksia integrifolia* is well known by locals, for it is very common in beach hinterlands and on headlands. The *Banksia* genus has become known to Australians through the children's stories of May Gibbs, in which the nasty "Banksia men" are personifications of the gnarled and "ugly" *Banksia* seed cone. As for *Kunzea ambigua*, the flowers of this plant exude a sweet perfume that fills the air on hot summer days. Many people recognize the characteristic fragrance of the Sydney bush without necessarily knowing that this is one of the plants responsible.

I selected these two plants for Goethean study for three reasons. First, the plants are both native to this locality; they have not been deliberately brought in from other regions of Australia or from other countries. Thus, they could be said to belong to this particular environment and brought forth by evolutionary processes.[27] Second, I chose these plants because each displayed all stages of their growth cycle during my period of research—January to August 1993. Last, these two plants contrast markedly in nature. Even the most cursory examination is sufficient to reveal differences in form and habit, the most obvious being that the *Banksia integrifolia* is a tree when mature whereas the mature *Kunzea ambigua* is a shrub.

I began this research by attempting to observe the plants as if for the first time. To begin with, I entered the selected environment and walked for an hour or so in silence, without referring to books or thinking too much. I tried to open my senses to the environment and to become aware of as much as I could. Most of the empirical work was done *in situ* or with a few cuttings or flowers taken home. I pursued my descriptions only as far as what the naked eye or a hand lens yielded. I did not pull the plants up to investigate their roots but was able to obtain seeds and grow seedlings and thereby study the root systems and germinal leaves.[28] In each case, I attempted to execute accurate drawings from memory, days or weeks after the first encounter.

I returned numerous times to the landscape but was able to carry out "exact sensorial imagination" almost anywhere—whenever a moment of stillness and concentration became possible. In this way I was connected to the plants and their environment over the period of the research. Within the *water* stage of the process, I experimented with different artistic ways to bring the plants to expression. In some of my drawings, I found that the lines became fluid and suggestive of movement, but then I also noticed a tendency to race ahead of myself and produce gesture sketches, which rightly belong to the *air* stage of the method. The illustrations that are presented in the *water* stage are the frozen moments of living processes that in nature and for the imagination are in flux.

I did not create the paintings and poems of the *air* and *fire* stages in the environment of the plants. I found that my work in the previous stages had enabled these plants to live in me in such a way that it was not difficult to inwardly distill them in the context of my studio. This distillation took place *through* the creation of the artworks. On the other hand, there were times when it was necessary to refer back to my previous empirical drawings and descriptions, and to the plants themselves. The total process was not a mechanical affair following hard and fast rules. It was truly experimental, trial and error in nature, and like an artist's palette, much messier than the finished work.

These experiments are not intended to be conclusive. I used this method to achieve an authentic understanding of the plants. But this does not mean that, on reaching the stage designated "intuitive cognition," anything more than an intimation or glimpse of the "theory" or "law" of the plant may have been obtained. Hence, the "theory" of these plants is not being presented in absolute terms. On the contrary, I approached these plants with the awareness that even the humblest of nature's phenomena, to use Goethe's words, "partakes of infinity."[29]

In most general terms, this investigation of two plants is primarily a study of plant morphology along the lines of Goethe's own morphological research. Goethe said that a living being comes forth out of itself, that it takes form out of its own generative "idea," yet he was quite aware that external factors play a shaping role.[30] Therefore, my empirical descriptions concentrate on the descriptions of the plants themselves, although the character of the environment in general is also taken into account. It is only in the *fire* stage that the "being" of the plant emerges as the expression of an environmental whole.[31]

As a final introductory note, it should be mentioned that neither of these plants shows a process of leaf metamorphosis such as Goethe observed in many of the plants he studied. He observed the change from rounded, germinal leaf forms to more differentiated forms farther up the stem, the leaves becoming progressively "cut away" and expanded upon longer petioles; finally, near the flower, the leaves reduced to narrow, pointed forms. For Goethe, this metamorphic sequence had an archetypal character because it gave him a particular insight into plant nature.[32]

Only one of the plants—*Banksia integrifolia*—demonstrates any significant leaf metamorphosis at all and, in this case, the leaf sequence would appear to be quite the opposite of Goethe's progression, moving as it does from more cutaway leaf forms in the young plant to more rounded, mature leaves. The fact that my two plants show either no leaf metamorphosis or an opposite progression does not mean that they, in any sense, go against Goethe's theory of plant development.[33] I have taken each plant as I found it, whatever progression (or lack thereof) it demonstrated, and interpreted the plant for what it is in itself.

1. *Kunzea Ambigua* ("Tick-Bush")

I encountered the Tick-Bush plants directly behind Bilgola Beach on the Barrenjoey Peninsula (fig. 7.1). Although there are numerous houses and roads nearby, some of the sand dunes and the beach's bushy hinterland have been preserved. This beach environment is found in a small valley that contains pockets of rainforest. The vegetation in the area where the Tick-Bush grows is dense and disturbed only in the places where there are tracks leading down to the beach. Nearby, there are open cleared areas more sparsely populated with shrubs and trees.

Kunzea ambigua belongs to the Myrteaceae family, which comprises about 80 genera and 3,000 species. This family is found mainly in the tropics and is concentrated in tropical America and Australia.[34] In Australia, the genera include—*Eucalyptus, Leptospermum,* and *Melaleuca*—all characterized by pellucid oil glands and an aromatic quality.[35] The family has economic importance, for example, the edible fruit of the guava (*Psidium*), spices such as the clove (dried flower buds of *Syzgium aromaticum*), and the allspice or unripe berry of *Pimenta dioica*, tea-tree oil (*Melaleuca*) and timber from *Eucalyptus*.

Fig. 7.1. Kunzea ambigua—Flowering branch. Photograph by J. Plaza and used with permission.

There is no observable reason why *Kunzea ambigua* has the common name Tick-Bush. The name *ambigua* comes from the Latin *ambiguus*— "going here and there," "uncertain." There are about twenty species of *Kunzea*, distributed in every state of Australia except the Northern Territory.[36] In the Sydney region there are five species, all shrubs.[37]

First Impression

A plant that at first does not stand out in the undergrowth yet has a pervading presence, for its perfume fills the environment. A mood of fragility and purity (fig. 7.2).

Stage One—Earth

The *root* on a 15-cm-high seedling is about 3 mm in diameter and has a reddish covering over a pale yellow interior (fig. 7.3). There is no detectable taste. The central root goes about 15 cm into the ground before lateral roots begin, these being about 0.5 mm in diameter.

The main *stems* are woody and dark brown in color; where the surface is peeled off they are light yellow (fig. 7.3 and fig. 7.4). There is a petiole every centimeter, arranged in a spiral around the central stem. Near the top of the plant, the new stems are not woody but pliable and reddish in color, with white hairs that turn pale yellow at the extremities.

Fig. 7.2. Kunzea ambigua—"First impression" Watercolor on paper, 40 x 55 cm, original in color.

Fig. 7.3. *Kunzea ambigua*—Three aspects of the plant. *Upper left*, lateral branch; *center*, stem with lateral branches; *lower right*, seedling. Pen and watercolor on paper, 40 x 55 cm, original in color.

The main stem of a mature plant is 30–50 mm in diameter and brownish white with slightly flaky bark. It has no detectable taste. The mature shrub is about 2 m high.

The *leaves* are yellow at their base and flattened where they connect with the stem (fig. 7.3 and fig. 7.5). They are about 1 to 2 mm wide and 5 to 8 mm long, slightly arched and covered with small, raised oil glands. The leaf is bitter to the taste and gives a honey aroma when rubbed between the fingers. Leaves are crowded in fivefold spirals along short, nonwoody lateral stems, which come off the central woody stems, also in fivefold spirals, at intervals of around 1 cm.

Fig. 7.4. *Kunzea ambigua*—Central stem of shrub

Fig. 7.5. *Kunzea ambigua*—View of branches (not in flower)

Fig. 7.6. *Kunzea ambigua*—Flower heads showing bunched structure
Pen and water color on paper, 25 x 25 cm, original in color.

The *flowers* appear along new shoots in the leaf axils (fig. 7.1 and fig. 7.6). The base of the flower is a greenish-yellow tube/cup covered with oil glands. The flowers also have a bitter taste. Around the rim of this cup are five roundish, pure white petals with little dots (oil glands) and between these are five pointed, leaflike shapes (sepals). Inside the cup and extending 4–5 mm beyond it are numerous shiny white threads with

Fig. 7.7. *Kunzea ambigua*—General view of shrub (not in flower)

yellow globular heads (filaments and anthers). At the center, and extending out as far as the threads, is a thicker stalk with a U-shaped yellow head (style and stigma). The plant flowers in spring to summer.

The *fruit and seed* appear on the plant when the floral tube has lost its petals and anthers (fig. 7.8). The tube becomes bright crimson around its rim. The fruit is a small capsule, 5 mm in diameter, with a leathery texture. It opens at the top to release seed. Each seed is about 0.5 mm long, a slightly bent, oval shape, and orange-brown in color when dry.

General features of the environment: The Tick-Bush was observed in a sand-dune habitat about 200 meters from the ocean and directly influenced by sea winds and salt (fig. 7.7). Growing behind a protective wall of Coast and Wallum Banksias (*Banksia integrifolia* and *Banksia serratifolia*) the Tick-Bush receives direct light most of the day. The plants are closely surrounded by other shrubs of a similar height, including Coast Tea-Tree (*Leptospermum laevigatum*) and Silky Spider-Flower (*Grevillea sericea*). This habitat grades rapidly into rainforest 100–200 m farther from the beach. The soil is sandy and made dark with organic matter.

Stage Two—Water

The Tick-Bush does not demonstrate any significant metamorphosis of leaf form. The movement from bud to flower, fruit, and seed

Fig. 7.8. *Kunzea ambigua*—Metamorphic sequence. *Upper left*, buds; *upper right*, flowers; *lower left*, unripe fruit; *lower right*, ripe gruit and seeds. Pen and watercolor on paper, original in color.

formation is the most readily apparent of this plant's metamorphic processes (fig. 7.8). I worked with this sequence by means of "exact sensorial imagination" to gather all the empirical information from stage one and allow it to dissolve into fluidity. This gave an inner picture of the whole plant as a living process or metamorphosis. The elongating of the stems and roots, the appearing of new shoots and leaves, the overall shaping of the plant in different phases of growth—all these became aspects of this inner picture. These movements became comprehensible in the next stage of the experimental process, when they were characterized as living *gestures*.

Stage Three—Air

Set forth here are "inspirations" of the Tick-Bush, emerging from a cognitive "breathing in"—an inner perception that allows the growth processes of the plant to become "expressive." At this point, what in the previous stage was perceived as *movement* becomes meaningful as *gesture* (fig. 7.9). I wrote:

> Tick-Bush—fragile, radiant plant. The shrub without flowers hardly stands out from the green mass of the vegetation. Its leaves are small and fine; they do not vary. Its branches are not prominent and blend with the overall texture of the plant. But in that inconspicuousness and sameness, there is a certain gesturing. This plant creates its space in an even way, its leaves finely divide the air in all directions.

> Veil of green,
> Filigree of earth-matter
> shaped by air,
> Blurred,
> Nothing asserted or
> separated out,
> Indefinite
> being of
> earth and air,
> Delicate whorling
> into the light.

> Yet here is potentialized
> a fine space,
> So refined,
> pure,
> That it shimmers green
> into radiant whiteness
> and honey pungency,
> Flowers
> which cluster and exude,
> still finely
> emanate.

Buds develop in groups along the outer branches; here there is no striving toward a terminal flower. The flowers collectively gesture—not inwardness—but full radiance:

Pervading
Crystalline light,
A light-space
not burning
as color,
Held like a torch,
But fine light,
white,
Honey light and
sweet,
Fragile
fragrant plant.

Stage Four—Fire

This landscape
lives finely,
outwardly,
Delicate and diffused,
As this plant
the landscape
lives so.
Speaks it,
Makes it present (fig. 7.10).

2. *Banksia Integrifolia* ("Coast Banksia")

The particular stand of Coast Banksias that I observed was in the same location as the Tick-Bush—behind Bilgola Beach north of Sydney. There is a considerable population of Coast Banksias here, with many immature shrubs growing in the more open disturbed areas, and mature trees growing amid thick vegetation, making a wall at the back of what would have been a sand dune but is now a car park (fig. 7.11).

Banksia integrifolia is a species belonging to the Proteaceae family, which comprises mainly woody shrubs and trees. This family is named after the Greek sea god Proteus, who could change his shape at will. Carl Linnaeus first used the name in 1735 to refer to South African plants in this family because he was impressed by their diversity.[38] There are seventy-three Proteaceae genera occurring in temperate to tropical environments, particularly in Africa, Australia, and South America, and there are more than 1,500 species. Australia has the greatest diversity, about 860 species. The family Proteaceae usually occurs in infertile soils and lateritic gravels; there are some rainforest species.[39]

Fig. 7.9. *Kunzea ambigua*—Gesture sketch. Charcoal on paper, 25 x 25 cm.

Fig. 7.10. *Kunzea ambigua*—Image of flower as plant "theory"
Watercolor on paper, 40 x 55 cm, original in color.

Fig. 7.11. *Banksia integrifolia*—Flowering branch of immature tree

There is a great deal of fossil evidence for the early existence of these plants, which are considered to be a very ancient family—some 80 million years old. It is possible that the *Dryandra* genus (growing only in Western Australia and belonging, along with *Banksia*, to the tribe Banksieae) was one of the first flowering plants on the planet. L. A. S. Johnson and B. G. Briggs believe that the family originated on the great southern continent Gondwanaland, which later broke up into Australia, Africa, South America, Antarctica, and India. The family may have first consisted of rainforest species, which later, as the continent dried out, became the hard-leaved specimens we know today.[40]

The genus *Banksia* was named after Sir Joseph Banks. There are seventy-five recognized species in Australia, most located in the south-western regions. Only one *Banksia* occurs naturally outside Australia— *Banksia dentata*—which is widespread in Northern Australia, Papua New Guinea, and Irian Jaya. No plants of this genus grow in the arid center of the country nor in the rainforests. Many *Banksias*, in both western and eastern Australia, grow in exposed coastal areas and on sand dunes and headlands; others are sand-plain species. In most cases the ground is well drained.[41]

Sir Joseph Banks first collected *Banksia integrifolia* when he landed in Botany Bay in 1770. It is found in coastal areas, from just north of

Brisbane right around into Victoria. In the northern part of its distribution, the plant grows on sand dunes, around tidal inlets, and on headlands. Its name comes from the Latin, *integer*, entire (i.e., smooth-edged) and *folium*, a leaf; this description refers to the entire margins of the mature leaves.[42]

First Impression

In this sea-blown atmosphere, the young trees are thin and silvery presences, tight, strong and drawing upward, as if crowded out. Yet, all around other plants are luxuriating. But the mature trees are rounded and full; now a mood of completeness, restfulness (fig. 7.12).

Stage one—Earth

The central *root* on the seedling has pale yellow woody interior and woody brown exterior (fig. 7.13). The root is about 3 mm in diameter with finer lateral roots appearing at irregular intervals. The roots have no detectable taste. I was not able to inspect the roots of the immature and mature trees.

The main *stem*, on the seedling, rises about 13 mm above ground before the first leaf (fig. 7.13). Here the stem has a diameter of about 3 mm with a rough, barky texture. Beyond the first leaves the stem is less woody, yellowish brown, and covered with brown hairs. On immature plants of 3 m in height, the stem at the base is around 8 cm in diameter; the bark is thin and has a shiny red color, with whitish knobs in places, and is easily pierced to reveal a green woody interior (fig. 7.14 and fig. 7.15). The bark has thin vertical creases. New shoots—diameter about 2 cm—are covered with dense short red hairs. The stems of these immature plants are extremely etiolated in places, with a meter or so between petioles. The lower trunk of the mature tree is around 30 cm in diameter with a very bumpy surface and a thick corklike texture (fig. 7.16). This trunk is blackish gray on the surface and, when peeled, reveals a yellow-ochre interior. Vertical creases cover the whole surface of the trunk, each crease around 5 cm wide. The lower branches of the tree bend out and downwards (fig. 7.17).

The *leaves* on very young plants stand on a 2 cm petiole (fig. 7.13 and fig. 7.18). Each leaf has an underside covered with dense silvery white hair, with a prominent yellowish green central vein. The immature leaves are around 5 cm long with a dark green-yellow upper surface and small yellow lateral veins forming reticulations. These leaves have spiky serrations and spiral around the stems in whorls of five. The leaves have no detectable taste.

On more mature trees the leaves—now 5 to 10 cm in length—are also silvery on the under surfaces and dark green on the upper surfaces.

Fig. 7.12. *Banksia integrifolia*—"First impression" Watercolor on paper, 40 x 55 cm, original in color.

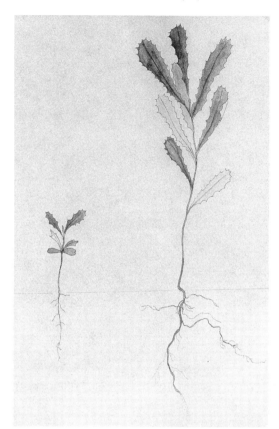

Fig. 7.13. *Banksia integrifolia*—seedling and slightly more advanced plant
Pen and water color on paper, 25 x 25 cm, original in color.

Here the leaf form is different on different parts of the plant: near the base of the tree, the leaves are serrated, less so in the middle, and entirely smooth edged on the uppermost branches (fig. 7.19 and fig. 7.21). All the leaves have a hard and brittle quality. No serrated leaves are present on the mature tree; here all are narrow obovate.

Flowers appear on immature trees from late summer to winter, the vertical spike generally appearing within the leaf whorl at the end of new shoots (fig. 7.11 and fig. 7.22). The spike grows to about 80 mm and is tubular in shape with a woody axis. On the flower spike, pale green flower buds appear in precise rows, in pairs, and surrounded by reddish flower bracts. One spike examined had an estimated 500 flower pairs.

On more developed spikes, a stalk of almost 1 mm diameter extends from each one of these pairs, with fine white hairs, and capped by a

Fig. 7.14. *Banksia integrifolia*—Bark of immature tree

paler, slightly pointed head. In even more advanced spikes, this thick stalk has split into a group of thin stalks, about 3 cm long, one, yellow and bent; the others, more red and grouped together, all held at the top by a grayish cap. In other cases, this cap has broken, and the thick stalk protrudes from the other stalks by about 4 cm, becoming a pointed filament with a reddish end. The other stalks remain 3 cm long, four in number, each with a gray cap (anther). The overall appearance of the flower spike when fully open is yellowish red, spiky, and cylindrical, with a radius of around 5 cm. The flowers of the mature tree are the same as those on immature plants.

Fruits and seeds appear on flower spikes that have lost all their colored filaments, have thickened, and become lumpy and conelike (fig. 7.22). Distributed unevenly around this form are half-moon-shaped follicles covered with short red hairs. These follicles are embedded in a cellular matrix, which is in regular rows where the cone is not swollen but becomes irregular where the red follicles have appeared. These cells are pale green-yellow, covered with short white hairs, with a darker center. In other cones observed, these follicles are very pronounced, do not have red hairs, and are woody and dark brown. Here, the moon-shaped follicles have opened and reveal a yellowish interior, each containing two seeds. The seeds are 1–2 cm long with a hard black center, surrounded by a white film and then by a brown-orange, winglike

Fig. 7.15. *Banksia integrifolia*—Immature tree

Fig. 7.16. *Banksia integrifolia*—Bark of mature tree

Fig. 7.17. Banksia integrifolia—General view of mature tree

Fig. 7.18. *Banksia integrifolia*—Leaf configuration of a very young tree

Fig. 7.19. *Banksia integrifolia*—Leaf whorl of immature tree

Fig. 7.20. *Banksia integrifolia*—General view of environment with immature trees

membrane. In other cases, the follicles are all open and without seeds; here, the whole cone has become very hard and dark.

General features of the environment are the same as for the Tick-Bush. Many immature Coast Banksias grow in the more open, cleared areas behind the wall of dense vegetation that is close to the beach and which contains most of the mature Banksias (fig. 7.20).

Stage Two—Water

Two metamorphic sequences of the Coast Banksia are here depicted—first, the changes of leaf shape from the immature to the mature plant (fig. 7.21). Not all of these stages can be observed on the same plant; the first three forms (*a, b, c*) belong to the seedling; the following four forms (*d, e, f, g*) were observed on an immature shrub, the serrated leaves appearing at the bottom of the plant, the entire leaves at the top. On the mature trees, only forms *f* and *g* in the sequence were observed.

Second, the "moments" of the development of the spike into the flower buds are depicted, from the budding and flowering stages to the production of fruit follicles and the release of the seed (fig. 7.22 *a–f*). Because of the time-frame involved, these "moments" of development could not be observed in relation to one particular flower spike. Consequently, the images are of flower spikes on the same tree which were in different stages of development—most immature and mature plants contain all stages.

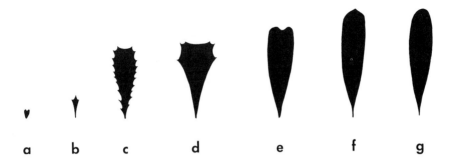

a   b   c   d   e   f   g

Fig. 7.21. *Banksia integrifolia*—Metamorphic sequence of leaves (a) germinal leaf; (b) first true leaf; (c) leaf of seedling; (d) leaf in lower parts of immature shrub; (e) leaf of higher parts of immature tree; (f) and (g) leaves of highest parts of immature tree

By means of "exact sensorial imagination," I worked with these sequences to perceive inwardly the metamorphic processes. As with the Tick-Bush, I imaginatively gathered all the empirical information from stage one and allowed it to dissolve into fluid form. In other words, I lived into the developmental journey of this plant—from seedling, to mature tree, to seed. These metamorphic movements, when further distilled, became comprehensible as *gestures* in the *air* stage of the experiment.

Stage Three—Air

Coast Banksia—ancient, commanding plant (fig. 7.23). These plants develop with great definiteness, leaves and stems stretched skyward. Close to the earth as the seedling, there is no naive, watery spreading of rounded leaf form so typical of other plants—no tentative feeling out into the world. Here, even the first leaves are serrated as if bringing a certain "knowledge" with them:[43]

> Sculpted leaves
> sharpened by ancient experience,
> Even as a seedling
> commanding a space.
> Cold chalices of leaves
> enclosed upon a red upthrusting,
> Leaves
> stiff and definite,
> Erect as a command,
> Only on high
> softening and rounding,
> Giving over all intensity
> to the flower.

Fig. 7.22. *Banksia integrifolia*—Metamorphic sequence. *Top*, spike with rows of paired flowers buds; *center*, opening flowers; *bottom*, open flowers.

Fig. 7.22 (cont.) *Banksia integrifolia*. *Top*, withered flowers; *center*, young follicle; *bottom*, mature follicle. Pen and watercolor on paper, original in color.

The young trees appear almost ghostly among the rich greens of their environment. Cold outwardly, but with a potent red axis and around it the rich green inner-leaf surfaces. This makes for a great focus of power—a containment, a holding inwards, concentrated and developed through tense fivefold whorls. A concentrated space so potentialized that something strong must come forth within it:

> The flower being,
> Held as focusing
> an immense space of light,
> A multiplicity folded,
> tightened into a spiralling rod,
> These many-as-one flower heads,
> Live in self-concentration,
> utter order,
> Until they burn,
> glow yellow.
>
> And die, lingering where they formed
> on the rounding, aging trees,
> Wizened presences, signs of the old
> alongside the new intensities,
> Ancient, potent plant.
>
> *Stage Four—Fire*
>
> Most potent sun space,
> Borne on high,
> Inwardness made visible,
> Galvanizing a
> multitudinous landscape,
> Giving it a moment
> when it is still,
> definite, incandescent,
> One (fig. 7.24).

TOWARD A PREGNANT POINT

My research began by gathering empirical data that I progressively distilled through the stages of the experiment. What eventually came to light were certain meanings that I called the "theories" of the plants (figs. 7.10 and 7.24). To make anything more of these meanings, we must stay within the process in which we have been engaged, within the sphere of

Fig. 7.23. *Banksia integrifolia*—Gesture sketch. Charcoal on paper, 40 x 55 cm.

Fig. 7.24. *Banksia integrifolia*—Image of flower as plant "theory." Watercolor on paper, 40 x 55 cm, original in color.

the phenomena themselves. We arrived at a "pregnant point"—a place of contraction or creative potency. Whatever may derive from the research needs to be born from this condition of potentiality.[44] This point is the threshold to a phase of creative expansion. Only in this way can we stay within the organic process of the experiment and avoid falling into abstraction, thus dividing the results of the research from their application, the theoretical from the practical.

In the *earth* stage of the research, I recognized that the two plants, which are found growing together in the landscape, are quite contrasting in their visible aspect—the aspect "everyone finds in nature." The factual descriptions at this *earth* stage, however, said nothing about why or how the plants *belong* together and to that environment. Indeed, that was not the initial concern; the research process began as a morphological study of two individual plants. The quality of *belongingness* is something that only came to light in the *fire* stage of the research, where the plants are invoked as expressions of the wholeness of the landscape. By dwelling within the descriptions of the *differences*, we came to an inner *identity* or *unity*, which is the landscape. In other words, the whole is encountered in the midst of the parts, by "stepping right into the parts."[45]

Thereby it was possible to say that the landscape gestures as a "radiant sweetness" in the form of the Tick-Bush. This plant lives in an *outward* gesture—delicate, almost fragile, and raying in all directions. In a quite contrasting manner, the landscape in the form of the Coast *Banksia* gestures *inwardly*—it "concentrates and commands." Those gestures express themselves most characteristically and subtly in the flower forms. The landscape "speaks" these meanings—*outwardness* and *inwardness*— like contrasting, yet related, movements of a musical work. Additional investigation of other neighboring plants would lead us to an even richer and more potent understanding of the "generative idea" of this unique landscape.

According to the philosopher Georg Hegel, an acquaintance of Goethe's:

> When nature is viewed by an alive and open mind, as it is in the apt and effectual manner we find so often in Goethe, this mind feels the life and the universal relatedness within nature; it has a presentiment of the universe as an organic whole.[46]

At such a moment, Hegel explained, "the spiritual eye stands immediately at the center of nature."[47] According to Johann Fichte, another of Goethe's philosopher acquaintances: "The mist of delusion clears away from before my sight! I receive a new organ, and a new world opens before me."[48] Goethe himself explained: "Every new object, clearly seen, opens up a new organ of perception in us."[49]

Either we dismiss with "a sigh or an ironic smile" all this talk of "spiritual organs of perception" as so much Romantic Age excess, or we ask just what it is to which these individuals refer.[50] The characteristic gesture or "theory" of the Tick-Bush and the Coast Banksia is not composed of abstract qualities but *creative actions* or *impulses*. To work with this phenomenology, we must rekindle in the words *theory, idea, whole* their fiery, creative character. A "spiritual organ" awakens when we "think" the phenomenon from its dimension of unity, from potentiality into actuality. This style of thinking is not abstract but has the character of an *action*.[51] Such a notion of thinking becomes more comprehensible when we realize that this is what an artist does to create a work—forming it from its generative idea. And this is exactly the capacity we are cultivating through a Goethean phenomenology—an artistic mode of cognition that enables us to realize the creative processes of nature, to actually experience an organism's or landscape's self-generated activity. We experience the creative gesturing of the wholeness of a place, which, according to Mark Riegner, "comes to expression *expansively* in the overall landscape and *focally* in the parts of the landscape."[52]

It follows that we may speak of the Tick-Bush and the Coast Banksia as organs *of* the landscape rather than as merely organisms *in* the landscape, and of the overall landscape as an *organized being*, each part or organ playing a particular role in relation to all others. Here the organs are spread out and visible rather than enclosed in a skin as they are in an animal or human individual.[53] My research into these two plants is just one aspect of a phenomenological ecology whose task it would be to find meaning in the overall organization of a landscape. To this end, the Goethean method I have used could be applied to the study of the animal, human, and other elements of a landscape. Goethe considered that the parts of a living being form themselves according to a lawfulness and so it is with landscape as a whole.

Again, we may better understand this way of seeing through referring to the work of the artist. A composer experiences a certain necessity in the arranging of all the elements of a work, and to live within this sense of necessity is the artistic struggle. It *has* to be this note; it *can't* be that one—this is the constant inner dialogue of the composer. It is this necessity, determined by the generative idea of the piece, that gives a created work its character of unity and authenticity. Just so, we experience the organized whole of a landscape as determined by an inner necessity, and we experience as aberrant certain alterations when they lack that character.

An artistic work can be considered as an *organ of the landscape* if it truly *belongs* to that landscape. It may seem unusual to speak of a poem or a painting thus, but Goethe's style of phenomenological orientation calls for it. Inasmuch as a work of art is a way of "knowing" nature (demonstrated in my method along the path towards intuitive or participatory cognition), then a work can be said to be organically connected to the landscape.[54] As Henri Bortoft suggests:

> Goethe . . . saw the knowledge of a phenomenon as being intimately related to the phenomenon itself, because for him the state of "being known" was to be understood as a further stage of the phenomenon itself. It is the stage which the phenomenon reaches in human consciousness. Consequently the knower is not an onlooker but a participant in nature's processes.[55]

Our creative productions, if they authentically allow the phenomena to speak, are embodiments *of the phenomena themselves* in a heightened and metamorphosed form. They are the landscape in a uniquely focalized condition. This suggests an extraordinary responsibility we have toward nature, something of which Goethe was well aware.[56] A building can thus function as an organ of a landscape, having a certain necessity of form determined *by the landscape itself*. If we call this "organic" architecture, it is not because the architecture simply imitates organic forms such as curves and spirals; it is because it may realize a *belongingness* in the manner described here, by bringing to presence the "wholeness" of a place. This is no vague exhortation but an exact requirement built on the kind of phenomenological research I have undertaken.[57] We can speak similarly of organic agriculture—of a farm as being an organ of a landscape, if it expresses this unity and inner necessity. The whole realm of human production that we call science and technology could involve the cultivation of this character.[58] These humanly created organs have a unique function in the landscape, serving as the link between human society and nature, the point where the evolution of nature and of human society is as one.

A New Ecological Discipline

Does this way of organically connecting art and science accord with current thinking on the subject? There is a considerable literature dealing with the relationship of science to art, much of which has been motivated by the need to heal the perceived rift between the two in modern times.[59] In general what is pointed to is the *complementarity* of science and art. The idea is that, while science may lay claim to the factual and to the objective aspect of things, art is vital in that it deals with the subjective dimension, with qualities rather than quantities, feelings rather than facts. It is argued that *both* science and art are necessary to obtain a full picture of reality or, in other words, that the two are in need of unification. Now, one might easily assume that such a unification or integration becomes possible through Goethe's investigatory approach, for we can distinguish aspects of his life's work that may be termed scientific and artistic. I suggest, however, that what he was essentially striving toward is a way of studying nature that emerges *out of* the unity of art and science, a "unity without unification."[60]

To explain better what is meant by this seeming contradiction, it is salutary to turn to Goethe's own thinking. Goethe was critical of tendencies around him to speak of both organisms and works of art as "compositions"—that is, composites of many parts. For him, "the individual parts of an organic whole . . . produce themselves with life, and are pervaded by a common soul." The work of art, he continues, "is a spiritual creation, in which the details, as well as the whole, are pervaded by *one* spirit, and by the breath of *one* life."[61] Such notions are entirely in keeping with his organic world view, which had a strongly Neo-Platonic basis. Goethe conceived of the universe as a dynamic, living whole and hence of the organic unity of nature and humanity.[62] Accordingly, he understood science and art as springing from *one* source, as pervaded by *one* spirit rather than being parts or aspects of human culture and personality that are in need of unification.

This perception of wholeness is difficult to grasp with our usual discursive way of thinking, which tends to confuse *unity* with the unification of parts into a *totality*. Such thinking leads us to speak of unity in the same sense as we speak, for example, of the "whole plant" or the "whole painting." The essential unity, however, is not the "whole thing" but the formative power or "breath of *one* life" that is reflected in all the parts. As I have already suggested, to *think* this unity we cannot remain discursive and abstract—our thinking needs to assume the character of a *doing*. It must become creative or intuitive (or fiery, in terms of the method I have used). It needs to *participate* in the creative emergence of the whole in the parts.[63]

Goethe was aware that, in his own time, it was this confusion in thinking that put his natural scientific work in danger of being misunderstood. The danger arises if this work is approached in a way that is too philosophically abstract or theoretical, that tries to understand unity from a detached view point without actually engaging in the phenomenological process and allowing the necessary organs of perception to awaken. It is hard not to feel that this danger of misunderstanding remains today—is perhaps even greater—so that, when a latter-day commentator on Goethe, L. L. Whyte, finds himself wanting to speak of Goethe's approach as one that unites or fuses different aspects of knowledge, he hears the spirit of Goethe whispering in his ear that he has made a mistake, telling him that "the unity is there to discover, and always has been." Whyte explains:

> That warning from Goethe is needed. Owing to the limitations of language, nearly all the finest Goethe critics have suggested that he sought to integrate knowledge or personality. That is wrong. If either nature or man is composed of ultimately separate parts man cannot integrate anything. But if nature and man are ultimately one—in some sense still to be understood—then man can learn to recognize and make effective that fundamental unity.[64]

We are now in a position to see Goethe's phenomenological approach in its true light. He sought a form of nature study that is living, creative, and thus commensurate with the living nature that he wished to understand: "[T]hrough an intuitive perception of eternally creative nature we may become worthy of participating spiritually in its creative processes."[65] For Goethe, only a knowing that strives toward the level of intuitive judgment is capable of apprehending and continuing nature's inherent creative impulses and so enhancing rather than degrading nature. Goethe's phenomenological approach helps us enter the currents of creative forces in nature and so become the voice of the "pure phenomenon" or the phenomenon's dimension of unity; science and art can be understood as each representing a different "speaking" of that unity.[66]

While Goethe's approach can usefully be compared to modern forms of ecological and phenomenological thought, I believe that it would be a mistake to view it merely as a historical curiosity. To do so would prevent us from discovering what is unique and valuable about Goethe's phenomenology, from realizing its potential to become a new ecological discipline in our time.

NOTES

1. According to the biographer J. G. Robertson, "To many of us to whom Goethe is, above all things, the great poet, there is a dark side to Goethe's scientific pursuits. Did they not place hindrances in the way of his poetic activity? It may have been that he only turned to science when poetic inspiration left him in the lurch; but it may also have been that science was at times responsible for that failing inspiration and led to his neglect of that function for which he was supremely gifted." From Goethe, *The Life and Work of Goethe* (London: George Routledge and Sons, 1932), p. 312.

2. An extensive bibliography up to the mid-1980s is provided in *Goethe and the Sciences: A Reappraisal*, eds. F. Amrine, F. Zucker, and H. Wheeler

(Dordrecht: D. Reidel, 1987). I have listed more recent references in my "Beyond Constructivism: A Goethean Environmental Education," *Australian Journal of Environmental Education* 10 (1994):71–90.

3. Fritz Heinmann, "Goethe's Phenomenological Method," in *Philosophy* 9 (1934):67–81.

4. The essay, "The Experiment As Mediator between Object and Subject," provides a relatively comprehensive account of his methodology. See J. W. von Goethe, *Scientific Studies* (New York: Suhrkamp Publishers, 1988), pp. 11–17.

5. Heinmann, "Goethe's Phenomonological Method," p. 79.

6. See Jochen Bockemühl, "Elements and Ethers: Modes of Observing the World," in *Towards a Phenomenology of the Etheric World*, edited by J. Bockemühl (New York: Anthroposophic Press, 1985), pp. 1–67; and J. Bockemühl, *Dying Forests. A Crisis in Consciousness* (Stroud: Hawthorn Press, 1986). See also E. Marti, *The Four Ethers* (Roselle: Schaumburg, 1984); also, see G. Maier, "Die Elemente als Stufen der Naturbetrachtung," in *Elemente der Naturwissenschaft* 13 (1970):1–9.

7. Bockemühl calls the fourth element "warmth," but for my purposes I will abide by the traditional terminology.

8. Goethe discusses these stages in his essay, "Empirical Observation and Science," in Goethe, *Scientific Studies*, pp. 24–25.

9. Traditionally, the four elements were the means of expressing the correspondence between the psyche and elemental substances. For example, when water was discussed, what was meant was not only just the physical substance, but also a fluid state of awareness and cognition. *Nous*, or mind, for Aristotle and Thales before him, resembles water; it is fluid because it can run through and take on the form of all things. See D. A. Hyland, *The Origins of Philosophy* (New York: Capricorn, 1973), p. 100. In terms of the traditional understanding of consciousness, each level of awareness corresponds to a particular element. These traditions recognize that different levels (or "organs") of consciousness need to be *cultivated* by means of the experimental process. In other words, scientific research has an ontological as well as epistemological basis; it is not only considered to be about *knowing* more, but also about *being* more.

10. Goethe, *Scientific Studies*, p. 11.

11. Martin Heidegger considered that the mood evoked by the first encounter with a phenomenon has a definite ontological function and is not "merely subjective." As M. E. Zimmerman describes: ". . . moods are not merely psychological 'colorations' projected onto things; instead, moods articulate humanity's openness for the being of entities." See M. E. Zimmerman, *Heidegger's Confrontation with Modernity* (Bloomington: University Press, 1990), p. 141. According to Heidegger himself, "All knowing is only an appropriation and a form of realization of something which is already discovered by other primary comportments" (Zimmerman, *Heidegger's confrontation*, p. 141).

12. Goethe, *Scientific Studies*, p. 25.

13. See Goethe, *Scientific Studies*, pp. 24–25.

27. There is always the possibility that, in some past millennium, these plants were deliberately brought to this area by native Australians, though this possibility is most unlikely because the Aborigines were hunters and gatherers. The ecology of the environment could, however, have been determined to some extent by the tendency of the Aborigines to use bush fires as part of their way of hunting. See S. J. Pyne, *Burning Bush: A Fire History of Australia* (Sydney: Allen and Unwin, 1991).

28. Goethe felt disinclined to study the roots of plants. See his "An Unreasonable Demand," in Goethe, *Scientific Studies*, p. 98.

29. Goethe, *Scientific Studies*, p. 9.

30. For Goethe's thoughts on the self-generation of organisms, see Goethe, *Scientific Studies*, p. 8. Some of his ideas relating to the broader environmental influences upon organic development can be found in Goethe, *Scientific Studies*, p. 79 and pp. 53–56.

31. In Goethe's time, there were only the beginnings of what we would now call "ecological understanding"—that is, the apprehension of an organism within the whole pattern of relationships that make up an environment. Goethe, however, did recognize that the form of plant organs reflects environmental conditions as a whole, and he writes about this connection, for example, in "Toward a General Comparative Theory" (Goethe, *Scientific Studies*, pp. 53–56). It was Goethe's colleague, Alexander von Humboldt, who developed the ideas that became the basis for modern ecological biology.

32. For a detailed discussion, see Bockemühl, "Elements and Ethers: Modes of Observing the World," pp. 131–61.

33. Mark Riegner clarifies this point, referring to Goethe's archetypal sequence as a "critical phenomenon": "The configuration of such a critical phenomenon need not be the most frequent motif observed; commonality is not a criterion for its important status. Rather, its value lies in its being a particularly clear window through which to behold the pattern of a natural principle." See M. Riegner, "Toward a Holistic Understanding of Place: Reading a Landscape Through its Flora and Fauna," in *Dwelling, Seeing and Designing: Toward a Phenomenological Ecology*, edited by D. Seamon (Albany: State University of New York Press, 1993), p. 187.

34. G. H. M. Lawrence, *Taxonomy of Vascular Plants* (New York: Macmillan, 1951), p. 634.

35. N. C. W. Beadle, O. D. Evans, and R. C. Carolin, *Flora of the Sydney Region* (Sydney: Reed, 1972), p. 306.

36. See Nuri Mass, *Australian Wildflower Magic* (Summer Hill: The Writers' Press, 1967), p. 120.

37. Beadle et al., *Flora of the Sydney Region*, p. 344.

38. J. W. Wrigley and M. Fagg, *Banksias, Waratahs and Grevilleas and All Other Plants in the Australian Proteaceae Family* (Sydney: Collins, 1989), p. 15.

39. Ibid., p. 16.

14. In the case of plant research, a larger part of the information come through sight rather than hearing. This emphasis on vision, however, might not be the case if my research also included the animals and human beings of the landscape.

15. Quoted in G. Altner, "Goethe as a Forerunner of Modern Science," in *Goethe and the Sciences: A Reappraisal*, edited by F. Amrine, F. Zucker, and H. Wheeler, pp. 341–50.

16. Goethe wrote, "It is like trying to drink the sea dry if we try to stay with the individual aspect of the phenomenon, observe it, measure it, weigh it, and describe it." See Goethe, *Scientific Studies*, p. 24.

17. Ibid., p. 17.

18. Ibid., p. 75.

19. For a comprehensive description of the various characteristics of water from the point of view of Goethean phenomenology, see Theodor Schwenk, *Sensitive Chaos* (London: Rudolf Steiner Press, 1965).

20. *Collins Concise Dictionary*, 2nd edition, s.v. "gesture."

21. J. Bockemühl, "Elements and Ethers: Modes of Observing the World," p. 25.

22. This idea of acquiescence can be related to Heidegger's elucidation of truth as *aletheia*. He shows that *Aletheia* is more essential than factual truth. It arises out of an engaged knowing, and signifies an act of "unconcealing," a gesture of acquiescence which allows an entity to come forth and stand in the light of its truth, to "show itself from itself." We could say that, while in the *earth* stage the truth we sought was *factual* truth (accurate correspondence of the description to the object), the truth we seek in this *air* stage is truth as *aletheia*. See M. Heidegger, *Being and Time* (Oxford: Blackwell, 1992), pp. 256–73; and M. Heidegger, *Poetry, Language, Thought* (New York: Harper and Row, 1971), pp. 51–57.

23. This notion of theory is connected to the original meaning of the Greek word *theoria*, "to behold something." The theory is not a mental abstraction; rather, it is "seen" in the phenomenon with the cultivated "spiritual organs" of perception. Goethe wrote: "Let us not seek for something behind the phenomena— they themselves are the theory." (Goethe, *Scientific Studies*, p. 307).

24. See H. Hegge, "Theory of Science in the Light of Goethe's Science of Nature," in *Goethe and the Sciences: A Reappraisal*, edited by F. Amrine, F. Zucker, and H. Wheeler, p. 202.

25. Goethe discusses the *intellectus archetypus*, an expression he derives from Kant, in his essay "Judgment through Intuitive Perception" (Goethe, *Scientific Studies*, pp. 31–32).

26. Bockemühl relates this *fire* stage of the method to the stage of seed formation in a plant. Here, the external material form of the plant is "burned up" and its living impulse, or "idea," returns from a condition of maximum exteriority in the flower to maximum interiority in the seed. Thus, the seed represents a center of creative possibility and potency, a "pregnant" point. See Bockemühl, "Elements and Ethers: Modes of Observing the World," pp. 28–31.

40. See L. A. S. Johnson and B. G. Briggs, "On the Proteaceae—The Evolution and Classification of a Southern Family," in *Botanical Journal of the Linnean Society* 70 (1975): pp. 83–182.

41. Wrigley and Fagg, *Banksias, Waratahs and Grevilleas and All Other Plants in the Australian Proteaceae Family*, p. 80.

42. Ibid., p. 99.

43. According to Nuri Mass: "Banksias, even when they are quite young, make you feel as if they have lived a long, long time and know a great many things and are extremely wise. They sit up, very straight and dignified, among their hard, stiff leaves, and there is no nonsense about them whatever." From Nuri Mass, *Australian Wildflower Magic*, p. 36. Such a statement, coming from a source totally unrelated to Goethean phenomenology, would typically be considered subjective and fanciful. In the way I am studying these plants, however, I believe this description to be an authentic insight and a statement that supports my own discoveries.

44. In regard to his method, Goethe wrote that he always persisted until he found "a pregnant point from which several things may be derived" (Goethe, *Scientific Studies*, p. 41). The polarity of contraction and expansion was for Goethe a "primal phenomenon"—an archetypal creative principle. In any organic process, the point of contraction is the point of greatest potentiality, like a seed, in the development of a plant (see Goethe, *Scientific Studies*, pp. 76–97). In the *fire* stage of the method, one's cognitive attitude corresponds to this seed condition.

45. See the discussion of parts and wholes in Henri Bortoft, "Counterfeit and Authentic Wholes: Finding a Means for Dwelling in Nature," in *Dwelling, Place and Environment: Towards a Phenomenology of Person and World*, edited by D. Seamon and R. Mugerauer (New York: Columbia University Press, 1985), pp. 281–302; reprinted as chapter 12 in this volume. The "unity" that is typically referred to in biological science is abstract, created through numerical taxonomic processes whereby plant characters are grouped according to degrees of similarity or difference. In this way, plants are "unified" into families, genera and so forth.

46. Georg W. F. Hegel, *Philosophy of Nature*, vol. 1, (London: George Allen and Unwin, 1970), p. 202.

47. Ibid., p. 199.

48. Johann G. Fichte, *The Vocation of Man* (New York: Liberal Arts Press, 1956), p. 116.

49. Goethe, *Scientific Studies*, p. 39.

50. I borrow "a sigh or an ironic smile" from the philosopher John Passmore, who used it in his *Man's Responsibility for Nature* (London: Duckworth, 1974), p. 34, in reference to idealistic notions of Fichte.

51. Goethe wrote: "[A]t [the] higher level we cannot *know* but must *act*" (*Scientific Studies*, p. 305). He used the word *Handeln* to signify this "activity," which is the unity of concept and experience. Peter Salm comments: "The nature of such activity, difficult to define, is nevertheless so central to Goethe's outlook

that it comes close to being an analogy to life itself." See P. Salm, *The Poem as Plant* (Cleveland: Case Western University Press, 1971), p. 16.

52. Riegner, "Toward a Holistic Understanding of Place: Reading a Landscape Through its Flora and Fauna," p. 204.

53. For a more detailed discussion of these ideas, see J. Bockemühl "Landscape as Organism and the Way it Comes to Expression through the Kingdoms of Nature," in *Awakening to Landscape*, edited by J. Bockemühl, (Dornach: Allgemeine Anthroposophische, 1992), pp. 200–68.

54. This idea can be compared to Martin Heidegger's understanding of art as the "clearing" in nature where truth "sets-into-work." Notably, Heidegger doesn't talk about art in terms of *representation* or of *correspondence* to the entities of nature. See M. Heidegger, "The Origin of the Work of Art," in *Poetry, Language, Thought* (New York: Harper and Row, 1971).

55. Henri Bortoft, *Goethe's Scientific Consciousness* (Nottingham: Russell Press, 1986), p. 66.

56. Many references could be given that attest to Goethe's concern that his "way of knowing" was not destructive to nature. He talked about "defending the rights of nature" (*Scientific Studies*, p. 30). Goethe explains, "The phenomena must be freed once and for all from their grim torture chamber of empiricism, mechanism, and dogmatism" (p. 309).

57. For an example of the development of organic architecture using the same Goethean method I have employed, see the unpublished paper by M. Colquhoun and C. Day, *Study and Development of Place: An Exercise in the Use of Goethean Science as a Tool for Environmental Planning*, 1992, School of Life Science, Kirkbridge Cottage, Humbie, East Lothian, EH36 5PA, Scotland.

58. This idea can be related to Martin Heidegger's views on authentic technology and science; see M. Heidegger, "The Question Concerning Technology," in *The Question Concerning Technology and Other Essays* (New York: Harper and Row, 1977). Michael Zimmerman has presented Heidegger's views on how nature (*physis*) expresses itself uniquely through human existence as productivity of every kind (including art and technology). See Zimmerman, *Heidegger's Confrontation with Modernity*, pp. 229–37.

59. See, for example, H. G. Cassidy, *The Sciences and the Arts: A New Alliance* (New York: Harper and Row, 1962); R. Arnheim, "Beyond the Double Truth," in *New Ideas in Psychology* 9, 1 (1991):1–8; E. Laszlo "The Unity of the Arts and Sciences," in *Main Currents in Modern Thought* 24, no. 3 (1968):75–81; A. Ross, ed., *Art vs. Science: A Collection of Essays* (London: Methuen, 1967).

60. An expression used by Henri Bortoft in his *Goethe's Scientific Consciousness*, pp. 26–29.

61. Johann Wolfgang von Goethe, *Conversations with Eckermann* (Washington: M. Walter Dunne, 1901), p. 377.

62. For a general discussion of the historical background of Goethe's world view, see H. B. Nisbet, *Goethe and the Scientific Tradition* (London: Institute for Germanic Studies, 1972).

63. See Bortoft, "Counterfeit and Authentic Wholes," p. 287.

64. L. L. Whyte, "Goethe's Single View of Nature and Man," in *German Life and Letters* 2 (1949):296.

65. Goethe, *Scientific Studies*, p. 31.

66. As Rudolf Steiner explains: "Goethe, in fact, wanted neither science nor art: *he wanted the idea* (pure or archetypal phenomenon). And he expresses or represents the idea . . . through the medium of art or of science as required." Steiner further explains that the scientist seeks to express the archetypal phenomenon in terms of thoughts whereas the artist seeks to imbue his or her medium with the power of the archetypal phenomenon. See Rudolf Steiner, *Goethean Science* (Spring Valley, N.Y.: Mercury, 1988), pp. 98–103.

8

Mark Riegner

Horns, Hooves, Spots, and Stripes: Form and Pattern in Mammals

The world of mammals boasts a fascinating array of forms, color patterns, and behaviors.[1] Consider the blue whale (*Balaenoptera musculus*), which plunges to the depths of the world's oceans; the tiny masked shrew (*Sorex cinereus*), which probes nervously along the forest floor for insects and worms to satisfy its ravenous appetite, its heart beating about one thousand times per minute; the tropical American two-toed sloth (*Choloepus didactylus*), which spends most of its life hanging upside down from branches, and moves with an almost imperceptible slowness; the handsomely spotted cheetah (*Acinonyx jubatus*), which is capable of startling bursts of speed up to seventy miles per hour; and the elegant giraffe (*Giraffa camelopardalis*), the tallest living land animal. Despite their variety, these animals share essential anatomical and physiological characteristics that unite them in the class Mammalia. To many nonscientists, the diversity of features within this class may seem bewildering, numbering 4,629 living and recently extinct species.[2]

Taxonomists have brought reasonable order to this multiplicity by arranging mammals in hierarchical categories based on the system of classification developed by Carl Linnaeus (1707–1778), the "father of taxonomy." In a biological classification, members of each category (e.g., class, order, family) share key structural features and other characteristics. For example, the familial category Felidae includes jaguars

177

(*Panthera onca*), tigers (*Panthera tigris*), and domestic cats (*Felis catus*), while the family Canidae includes gray wolves (*Canis lupus*), red foxes (*Vulpes vulpes*), and domestic dogs (*Canis familiaris*). In turn, the ordinal category Carnivora contains the Felidae, Canidae, and other families that share properties designated for that particular order.

This system of classifying biological phenomena gained new significance in 1859 with the publication of Charles Darwin's *Origin of Species* and the scientific revolution it precipitated. From an evolutionary perspective, members of a Linnaean category were seen not only as sharing certain features, but also as related by a common line of descent, which explained their similarities. Modern taxonomic classifications thus often reflect phylogeny, the presumed evolutionary history of a group of organisms.

When classifying organisms on the basis of their similarities, however, taxonomists are often faced with a perplexing problem: remarkable resemblances appear in many animals that are only distantly related.[3] In mammals, for example, the fur pattern of longitudinal rows of spots and stripes typical of the cat family is also seen in the paca (*Agouti paca*), a relatively large, heavy-bodied rodent inhabiting tropical forests from central Mexico to southern Brazil. The same pattern also appears in the young of most species of wild pigs of the Old World, as well as in the majority of fawns and many adult deer throughout the world.

How do taxonomists account for such similarities among disparate groups? They do so by assuming that the corresponding features originated independently and converged to resemble each other superficially by evolving under similar external conditions. In other words, the argument is made that such correlations are the result of like responses to like environments.

There is, however, an alternative approach by which these correlations are regarded as the results of the working of an *inherent* biological process. In other words, resemblances among distantly related organisms are the expression of a common organic principle. Such a notion, if affirmed, would have far-reaching implications for our understanding of biological organization. Indeed, the meaning of the word "organism" would be modified so that an animal, for example, would be viewed as a product not only of multiple responses to external conditions, but also of an intrinsic organizing principle with which these external conditions interact to bring about that animal's particular configuration.[4]

Wolfgang Schad subscribes to this latter approach and demonstrates that, through an understanding of the implied principle, one can recognize an order embracing phenomena previously thought to be unrelated.[5] Schad, a biologist and educator at the Institute for Evolutionary Biology and Morphology of the University of Witten/Herdecke,

Germany, bases his methods on Goethe's scientific work and on further contributions made by the Austrian philosopher and scientist Rudolf Steiner (1861–1925), who spent much of his life developing and elaborating Goethe's ideas.[6]

GOETHE'S PRINCIPLE OF POLARITY

Although few question Goethe's credentials as a master poet and great literary figure, his scientific work is typically viewed as a historical curiosity and often regarded unfavorably by the scientific establishment. This state of affairs is somewhat ironic because Goethe, in his later years, hoped to be remembered more for his science than for his poetry. Despite the general disregard of his scientific endeavors, to date over 10,000 studies have been published that were inspired directly by Goethe's original research on chromatics, meteorology, morphology, and a host of other subjects.[7] The aspect that has generated much of this interest is not so much Goethe's particular discoveries (e.g., his discovery of the inter-maxillary bone in the human skull), which he himself never emphasized, but rather his unique way of science.

Goethe maintained that through unbiased, keen observations within the sphere of phenomena, the secrets of nature would declare themselves. His approach, which deals with qualitative considerations, led to the recognition that the principle fundamental to the organization of natural phenomena was that of polarity. All phenomena presented themselves to him as fluctuating between opposing tendencies: light and dark, diastole and systole, contraction and expansion, inhalation and exhalation. To Goethe, nature's creations were engaged in ceaseless motion as they metamorphosed between polarities. Pursuing this line of thought, Rudolf Steiner asserted that from the dichotomy of polarity a mediating, third property emerges. The polar interplay between inhalation and exhalation, for example, produces a third element—rhythm—and a threefold association is established. Steiner applied the principle of polarity with its emergent central property to a wealth of organic systems, including aspects of the human physical and psychological organizations.

Schad applies Goethe's principle of polarity, with its inherent threefold structure as developed by Steiner, to a study of mammalian diversity.[8] His method of classification is compatible with conventional schemes but superimposes upon them a supplementary interpretation. In what follows, I hope to give the reader an introduction to Schad's extensive work and some appreciation of the opportunity it provides to deepen our understanding of the intrinsic organic order within the world of mammals.

As we proceed, our methodology will be Goethean in that we will remain within the realm of phenomena and concentrate on form, color pattern, and behavior, which for us will remain unabstracted qualities readily apprehended through our senses. We will then contrast and interrelate these phenomena as they appear in different mammals, bearing in mind that each mammal we study is a totality of interwoven qualitative elements.[9]

The Principle of Threefoldness in Mammalian Dentition

To discover an expression of threefoldness within the mammals, we may begin by observing their teeth. An inspection of a mammal's teeth can reveal much about the structure of its jaw, the form of its skull, and even its ecology. Mammalian dentition is remarkable in its variety of specialized formations. To illustrate the threefold structure of mammalian teeth, however, we need to examine an unspecialized dentition. For this purpose, we can direct our attention inside our own mouths and have the benefit of a convenient reference. But here we find an interesting contrast in morphology between humans and other mammals, one that warrants a brief digression.

The most striking difference between human and animal morphology is the relative structural specialization found in the latter. For instance, hooves, claws, flippers, and wings are evolved "tools," each adapted to a restricted range of activities. The human hand, in contrast, has remained in a generalized condition resembling the presumed ancestral form of mammalian appendages. Consequently, the hand is not limited to a narrow scope of movements, but can perform a host of actions from wielding a hammer to fingering a violin. The Dutch anatomist Louis Bolk (1866–1930) noted that certain early morphological features of human and animal embryos bear a close resemblance, but as development progresses, the animal forms depart dramatically from the human one, which, quite remarkably, changes only slightly.[10] In fact, Bolk maintained that a unique attribute of human development is its high degree of morphological retardation; the adult human departs relatively little from its generalized, fetal condition while other mammals, for example, show accelerated development with accompanying morphological specializations.[11] Bolk's observations have stimulated more recent questions about the nature of human developmental rates and timing.[12]

Schad acknowledges the unspecialized, "underdeveloped" condition of the human form and offers an explanation. Following suggestions of Goethe and Steiner, he asserts that the human form is the central, unifying figure among the mammals. Human morphology maintains a delicate balance among qualities that appear in one-sided development in the various other mammals. The equilibrium seen in the human body can only be found in the other mammals when the class is taken as a whole.

To understand what he means, we return to the human dentition, which will help to construct a key for understanding threefoldness as expressed among the mammals. Significant for our study are the forms of the teeth and their positions in the jaws (fig. 8.1). The relatively delicate incisors are flattened front to back, forming a single cutting edge, and occupy the frontmost position in the jaw, near the midline (i.e., median position). At the back of the mouth are the relatively massive molars or cheekteeth, boxlike in form with a grinding surface; these are situated backmost and laterally, that is, farthest from the jaw's midline.[13] The canines occupy an intermediate position, lying between the incisors and molars, and lateral to the incisors but not as far to the sides as the molars. In form, the conical, pointed canines show likewise an intermediate state between those of the flattened incisors and the boxlike molars.

Despite their differences in form, human teeth show a harmonious balance in the mouth; incisors, canines, and molars are not exaggerated relative to each other. The peculiar feature of human teeth is their relatively unspecialized condition. A survey of the mammals, however, reveals three major groups, each of which accentuates one type of tooth: rodents have exaggerated incisors; carnivores, exaggerated canines; and ungulates (hoofed mammals), exaggerated molars (fig. 8.1). If we apply the tooth relationships found in the human mouth to their respective mammalian groups, we can say that rodents are polar to ungulates, with carnivores occupying an intermediate position. These groups form the foundation of Schad's threefold classification and provide clues to guide us in a more detailed investigation of mammalian characteristics.

THE RODENTS AS NERVE-SENSE MAMMALS

Next, we must direct our attention to the specific motifs expressed in each group. We turn first to the order Rodentia, whose members constitute over 40 percent of living mammal species and are found virtually worldwide in a range of diverse habitats. Rodents have, in each jaw, one pair of exceedingly lengthened incisors that grow throughout life; canines are absent and a gap (*diastema*) exists between the incisors and molars (fig. 8.1). Most rodents survive on a high-protein, vegetarian diet consisting mainly of grains, seeds, and nuts, although many are also insectivorous. In contrast to the specialized teeth and associated jaw/skull

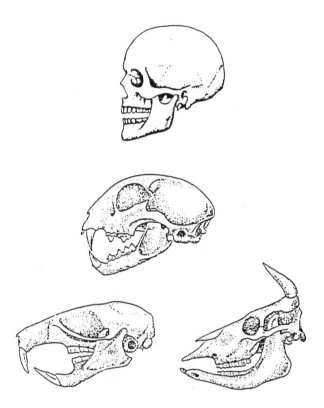

Fig. 8.1. *Top*, skulls of human; *center*, carnivore; *lower left*; rodent; *lower right*, ungulate. Drawings by F. A. Reid, with permission.

modifications, the body and limbs have remained in an unspecialized condition, although exceptions do occur; the forelimbs usually have five digits, the hind limbs from three to five. As a rule, rodents are born after a brief gestation in large litters and in an extremely immature (*altricial*) state; newborns are hairless and helpless, with eyelids and nostrils closed.

To enhance further our image of rodent qualities, we will place before us for reference a representative animal—in other words, an animal that illustrates the characteristics most typical of this group. A thorough study of the order Rodentia would find one such animal to be the Old World harvest mouse (*Micromys minutus*) (fig. 8.2). Common and widespread from western Europe through Asia, this tiny mouse prefers habitats of tall grass along roadsides, fields, and streams. In form, it shows a rather undistinguished head with small ears and a greater substantiality in its hindquarters, further accentuated by a long tail. This

Fig. 8.2. Representative mammals: *Top*, leopard—a carnivore; *lower left*, harvest mouse—a rodent; *lower right*, bison—an ungulate. Based on line drawings by F. A. Reid, with permission.

mammal's rear or posterior pole seems exaggerated relative to its front or anterior pole, a motif seen in varying degrees in all rodents. The fur color pattern also exhibits a motif typical of rodents: a dark back contrasted with a lighter underside. Although the actual colors vary markedly among rodents, the contrasting pattern of dark dorsal (back) and light ventral (underside) fur is prevalent in this order.

In behavior, too, this nimble-footed mouse reveals typical rodent qualities. Whether foraging for food, manipulating seeds, weaving a grass nest, or running through the underbrush, the harvest mouse shows a restless, almost frantic, activity. Its movements are rapid, jerky, and perhaps epitomized in the twitching of its nose and facial whiskers, or in the blurred, forwards-backwards gnawing motions of its lower jaw. These animals give the impression of living intensely in their nervous and sensory systems; in fact, rodents in general require frequent periods of sleep daily to avoid nervous exhaustion. In this sense, rodents appear to be animals oriented primarily to their nervous and sensory systems, with the anterior pole of the body—the head—as the major center for these organic systems.

THE UNGULATES AS METABOLIC-LIMB MAMMALS

What qualities are expressed in those mammals that emphasize the molars or cheekteeth—the ungulates? This group consists of the odd-toed Perissodactyla, such as horses, and the even-toed Artiodactyla, such as pigs, cattle, and deer. The ungulates' molariform teeth have evolved into massive grinders used to masticate plant matter high in cellulose. Canines are often absent, and upper incisors are lacking in some species (fig. 8.1). A cellulose-rich, protein-poor diet necessitates an elaborate, highly specialized digestive-metabolic system, which is developed to the extreme in the ruminant ungulates—cud-chewers like cattle and deer, which ferment fiber in a forechamber of the stomach called the "rumen." In addition, the ungulates show the highest degree of limb specialization of all mammals. Not only have the limbs elongated considerably, but also a marked reduction in toes has occurred from the ancestral five-toed condition. In a sense, horses run on the tips of their middle toes, which are encased in hooves. Unlike rodents, ungulates are born after a long gestation, usually singly, in a well-developed (*precocial*) condition. Sense organs are functional, and many newborns are able to stand and even run shortly after birth. Here, as with rodents, a representative animal will serve to develop a graphic picture of the order. One example is the American bison (*Bison bison*), sixty million of which once roamed the North American prairies and woodlands. Bison were saved from the brink of extinction in the late nineteenth century, and some 140,000 wander in well-protected national parks today.[14]

Contemplating the bison's form, we discover motifs polarly opposite those of the harvest mouse (fig. 8.2). The bulk of the bison's mass is concentrated at the anterior pole, exaggerated by a high shoulder hump. The thick, dense coat is restricted to the forequarters and to the large, weighted head, whose bearded chin adds further emphasis to this part of its body. Moreover, the anterior pole is crowned with an additional feature unique to ungulates: horns. The function of these cranial out-growths has been debated vigorously among biologists, but for our purposes we need only regard horns as anterior enhancements of the ungulate's morphology. The significance of their presence or absence among ungulate species and of variations in their position and composition will be considered later.

Compared with the tail of the harvest mouse, the bison's tail is considerably shorter in proportion to its body length. In concert with the radical limb specialization, the ungulate's tail is endowed with a limblike function familiar to anyone who has watched how domestic cattle respond to pestering flies. Unlike the distinctly bicolored pelage of the harvest mouse, the bison's dorsal and ventral coats are more or less uniform in color.[15] A dark, unpatterned coat is a common trait within the ungulate group. Behaviorally, the gregarious bison presents a contrast to the predominantly solitary harvest mouse, the ungulate preferring open grassland habitats, the rodent, closed, sheltered habitats. Powerful and generally imperturbable, these magnificent grazers drift placidly across the open plains like cumulus clouds floating across the prairie sky. This image of tranquility, however, can be shattered when a herd stampedes in unison and the earth rumbles under thundering hooves.

The bison's temperament as a ruminant is revealed especially when it is reclining, leisurely chewing the cud, with its lower jaw moving lazily from side to side, a dreamy gaze in its eyes. During those times, the beast's awareness appears to be withdrawn into the depths of its organism—a sharp contrast to the harvest mouse, which regularly seems to have its attention directed outward to its surroundings.[16] The bison's highly developed ability to digest and metabolize coarse, fibrous plant matter (with the aid of symbiotic microorganisms) and its extreme limb specialization suggest that bison specifically, and ungulates in general, are oriented to their limbs and metabolism.[17] Accordingly, the posterior pole, which accommodates the bulk of digestive and metabolic organs, is the functional pole characteristic of this group.

A comparison of rodents with ungulates shows polarities both within and between groups: the rodent's form is exaggerated in its posterior pole while its characteristic functional systems (nerve and sense) are situated chiefly anteriorly; the ungulate's form is accentuated in its anterior pole while its distinguishing functional systems (metabolic and limb) are located predominantly posteriorly. Thus, form and function interweave in a reciprocal relationship: where one dominates, the other is de-emphasized.

When we direct an aesthetic eye to our representative mammals, a herd of grazing or ruminating bison presents a scene of harmonious serenity, a contentment in digesting nature. In contrast, the trembling, frenetic harvest mouse, often in an alarmed state, emanates an anxiety of being digested by nature, that is, a fear of being eaten. The animals to which the harvest mouse fears it will fall prey are the carnivores, the group we examine next.

THE CARNIVORES AS RHYTHMIC MAMMALS

Worldwide in distribution, the mammalian carnivores occupy a broad spectrum of environments ranging from lush tropical forests and grasslands to barren arctic tundra and marine ecosystems. Although most members are indeed meat eaters, as their name denotes, many are omnivorous, and some, like the giant panda (*Ailuropoda melanoleuca*) of China, are almost exclusively vegetarian. Carnivore dentition typically includes three pairs of small incisors and one pair of elongated canines in each jaw; molars (and premolars) vary in number and often express a canine quality, being pointed and sharply ridged for shearing (so-called carnassials) (fig. 8.1). Whereas a rodent's lower jaw moves forwards and backwards, and an ungulate's side to side, a carnivore's jaw is limited to vertical movements. The limbs usually have four to five digits as in most rodents, but only the toes contact the ground (i.e., digitigrade), thereby approaching the condition of ungulates (i.e., unguligrade).[18] Among carnivores, the condition at birth varies from altricial to precocial, but the extreme states evident in rodents and ungulates are foreign to this order. Likewise, carnivores exhibit intermediate gestation periods and litter sizes, and in overall body dimensions fall between the other two groups. In many respects, as will be discussed below, carnivores occupy a central position between the polarly opposite rodents and ungulates.

At this point, we pause to recall the specific attributes of a threefold structure and the singular properties of the middle position. Within such an organization, two elements stand conspicuously as extreme opposite tendencies. The middle constituent is more difficult to identify because it arises from an interplay between polarities and is perpetually in flux as it mediates between them. Thus, the dynamic properties of the carnivores are more challenging to grasp than those of the rodents and ungulates. Again, a representative species can indicate phenomenologically the motifs that typify the order. Here, we consider the Felidae as the central family within the Carnivora, and the leopard (*Panthera pardus*) as the species that perhaps best depicts the felids (fig. 8.2). The most widely distributed of big cats, leopards are found in habitats ranging from dense forests to open grasslands, in Africa and Asia. Adhering to our qualitative approach, we must "read" the features of the leopard and interrelate them with those of our other group representatives.

The leopard's powerful musculature is molded into graceful contours and gentle outlines that suggest both strength and suppleness. A study of the big cat's form shows this mammal to be situated between the extremes of harvest mouse and bison. Neither fore nor hindquarters are accentuated. The tail is smaller in proportion to the length of the body than in the harvest mouse but greater than in the bison. The alternating, spotted pattern of the leopard's fur—a common motif among carnivores, especially felids—can likewise be seen as lying between the simple, light-dark contrasting pelage pattern of the harvest mouse and the uniform, dark color of the bison. And here, in the markings of the leopard's plush fur, is expressed externally and spatially the *temporal* qualities of those organic systems that predominate internally—the circulatory and respiratory systems. These organic systems are characterized by rhythm, that is, a patterning in time. In the heart, rhythm arises from movement between systole and diastole; in the lungs, between inhalation and exhalation. These organs are located in the middle region of the body, where even the enclosing structure of the ribcage reveals a rhythmic design in the alternation of ribs with intercostal spaces. Although recent theoretical studies[19] have identified a pattern-formation mechanism presumably responsible for determining coat marking such as those seen in the leopard, the threefold principle addresses the context in which these phenomena occur and thus offers an explanation as to why spots, for example, are expected to covary with other characteristics.

Standing between the rodents, in which an outward sensitivity predominates, and the ungulates, which are governed by the inner processes of digestion and metabolism, the carnivores typify the quality of rhythm. An inkling of this connection can be discerned by observing the leopard's behavior, which is characterized by a remarkable ability to swing between extremes. For example, the image of a hunting leopard crouching silently on a branch, muscles tensed, a penetrating gaze focused on its approaching quarry, and that of a gorged leopard sprawled leisurely in the fork of an acacia tree, peacefully digesting a meal, illustrate polarly opposite behavioral states. In the former, the animal is intensely alert, concentrating outwardly on its environment; in the latter, the big cat's awareness is apparently withdrawn into its organism, into the digestive and metabolic processes. In the leopard perhaps more than in any other mammal, the dynamic movement between these behavioral extremes is clearly evident, and it is in this activity that a significant quality of rhythm is manifested.

The leopard bespeaks its relationship to the middle organic systems not only in its rhythmic color pattern, balanced form, and characteristic behaviors, but also in its carnivorous diet rich in blood—the pulsating liquid of the circulatory system. Furthermore, the mediating, balancing properties of the carnivores are suggested in their ecological role; as predators, carnivores are often responsible for helping to regulate prey abundance and thus to balance prey density with the carrying capacity of their environment.

We could go further in relating features among the three mammalian groups, but my aim has been to establish some foundation for understanding the threefold classification. Certainly, many questions have been raised thus far, the most obvious being: What about all the anomalies, the animals with qualities that fail to conform to our group motifs? What about certain pelage patterns, for instance? Beavers (*Castor canadensis*) have no contrasting dorsal-ventral colors as indicated for rodents, and carnivorous least weasels (*Mustela nivalis*) are unstriped and unspotted, while many deer do show longitudinal rows of spots. Do examples such as these undermine the validity of classification within their respective groups? It is just here, in addressing such questions, that one sees the wisdom underlying the threefold system of classification. In fact, the so-called exceptions are not exceptions at all. When viewed holistically, in relation to the totality of phenomena, they fit soundly into a meaningful pattern.

To demonstrate how the threefold classification embraces apparent anomalies, we need only pursue its application in greater detail. We may turn, for instance, to the ungulates, bearing in mind the characteristic qualities of our representative mammals: harvest mouse (nerve-sense), leopard (rhythmic), and bison (metabolic-limb). As examples of ungulates, animals such as horses, pigs, and camels deviate considerably from the motifs found in the bison. As we shall discover, however, the interrelationships of their discrepancies reveal an inherent order when illuminated by the threefold principle.

As previously noted, ungulates, the metabolic-oriented mammals, consist of two orders: the odd-toed Perissodactyla and the even-toed Artiodactyla. The latter order, however, exhibits a significant natural division between the ruminants (cud-chewers) and nonruminants (e.g., swine). Thus, adhering to standard mammalian taxonomy, we recognize the ungulates as quite naturally partitioned into three categories: odd-toed (e.g., horses), even-toed nonruminant (e.g., swine), and even-toed ruminant (e.g., cattle). How do these groups interrelate with respect to the threefold principle? Visualize a horse—highly specialized limbs, ears pricked attentively, sensitive, agile, fleet; a dairy cow—highly specialized digestion and metabolism, dull, plodding, sluggish; and a pig—limbs not as specialized as those of a horse, digestion and metabolism not as developed as those of a dairy cow. Thus, we can outline the following scheme as a preliminary step toward an organic classification: perissodactyls—sense orientation; nonruminant artiodactyls—central orientation; ruminant artiodactyls—metabolic orientation. To elaborate this basic scheme, it is necessary to survey and interrelate the various families nested within each of these three ungulate groups.

THE PERISSODACTYLS AS NERVE-SENSE UNGULATES

In the sense-oriented Perissodactyla, taxonomists recognize three families: horses (including zebras and asses), tapirs, and rhinoceroses. That exactly three distinct families occur in this group is of no consequence to taxonomists but is significant from our standpoint. Accordingly, we ask: Do

Fig. 8.3. Perissodactyls: *Top*, Brazilian tapir; *lower left,* African wild ass; *lower right,* rhinoceros. African Wild ass drawn by author. Other renderings based on drawings by F. A. Reid, with permission.

parallels exist between each of these three families and the motifs expressed by each of our three representative mammals, the harvest mouse, leopard, and bison? Applying Goethean methodology, we can answer yes. Horses show alertness, sensitivity, and agility, which are typical rodent qualities. Moreover, this ungulate has well-developed, chisel-like incisors reminiscent of rodent dentition. And in body color, many wild species show undersides lighter in shading than upper parts, such as in the African wild ass (*Equus asinus*), which sports a gray coat with a white belly (fig. 8.3). This is apparent even among zebras, for in Burchell's zebra (*Equus burchelli*), the black stripes taper toward the belly, and in Grevy's zebra (*Equus grevyi*), the dark stripes actually terminate on the flanks above a white underside.[20] We can conclude that, in their expression of "rodent" qualities, horses are the sense-oriented perissodactyls.

Next, consider the rhinoceroses of Africa and Asia: their massive bulk; heavy, pendulous head; uniform, dull color; ponderous gait; and, of course, their conspicuous snout adornments—horns (fig. 8.3). No doubt these are metabolic-oriented perissodactyls and thus offer a polar contrast to the horses. Compared with those of horses, incisors and canines are reduced in number and even absent in some rhino species. Whereas in horses the head—the nerve-sense pole—is distanced from the metabolic pole by a sleek neck, in rhinos the head is, in effect, drawn in toward the metabolic pole; hence, perhaps, the dull temperament of these creatures.

We begin to glimpse the dynamic, mobile character of the threefold classification. Rather than rigidly assigning animals to static pigeonholes, our cognition sways like a pendulum to and fro among the mammals, interrelating while aesthetically appreciating their qualities. Regarding the position of the rhinoceros, we sway first toward the generally metabolic-oriented mammals (ungulates), then we reverse our motion to the sense-oriented perissodactyls, and then we swing back again to the metabolic-oriented position within the perissodactyls. We could even apply the threefold classification to the rhinoceros family itself and interrelate the various species: the largest—the white rhinoceros (*Ceratotherium simum*)—has the greatest accentuation of the anterior pole, with a huge, low-hanging head and formidable horns, while the smallest—the Sumatran rhinoceros (*Dicerorhinus sumatrensis*)—has a smaller head relative to its body length and even slightly accentuates the hindquarters.

And what about the piglike tapirs (fig. 8.3)? Is this family positioned centrally within the perissodactyls? These timid, retiring mammals inhabit dense forest environments in tropical America and Asia. The tapir's unspecialized form shows a slight middorsal arch; neither the anterior nor posterior pole is accentuated. Its limb structure is generalized, too, retaining four toes on the forefeet and three on the hind feet. Although almost exclusively vegetarian, tapirs have accentuated canines. The above features incline us toward classifying tapirs as central perissodactyls, and an additional characteristic lends further support to this choice. Mature tapirs have a uniform, dark coloring (except the Asiatic tapir [*Tapirus indicus*]), but the young of all species exhibit a variant pattern, namely, longitudinal rows of spots and stripes—a motif typical of central carnivores. Granted, the juvenile color pattern may give these mammals an adaptive advantage by rendering them less conspicuous to predators in their forest habitat, but the threefold classification reveals just why this particular fur pattern might be expected in this central family.

THE NONRUMINANT ARTIODACTYLS AS RHYTHMIC UNGULATES

The nonruminant artiodactyls comprise the middle ungulate group. Besides having well-developed molars, these mammals have a rather balanced form and accentuated canines. The following families are recognized in this group: peccaries, swine, and hippopotamuses. Again, to taxonomists it remains a fortuitous fact that exactly three families are distinguished in this group; the threefold classification, however, finds significance in this partitioning.

Peccaries, also called javelinas in the American Southwest, are active, nervous mammals, much smaller than most swine, and have two functional hooves on each of the fore- and hind feet (fig. 8.4). These gregarious, fast-running mammals are found in a variety of habitats from desert scrubland to rain forest, from the southwestern United States to Argentina. Their bodies are slightly compressed laterally and covered

Fig. 8.4. Nonruminant artiodactyls: *Top*, wild boar; *lower left*, white-lipped peccary; *lower right*, hippopotamus. Based on drawings by F. A. Reid, with permission. Reprinted from *A Field Guide to Mammals Coloring Book*, by permission of Houghton Mifflin Co. © 1987 by Houghton Mifflin.

with a bristly pelage highlighted with a white collar in one species, a white "chin" in another, and both a white collar and chin in a third species. Peccary dentition includes a full complement of chisel-like incisors used to nip off food in rodent fashion; canines form moderately long tusks with sharp edges; molars are not as specialized as in most other ungulates. Their omnivorous diet consists mainly of vegetable matter. Within the central ungulate group, peccaries appear to be dominated by the nerve-sense system.

The hippopotamus (*Hippopotamus amphibius*) presents a striking contrast to the peccary, although both share many features (fig. 8.4). The leviathan of African waterways, the hippo is unquestionably the metabolic-oriented member of the central nonruminants as attested by its massive dimensions; huge, weighted head exaggerating the body's anterior pole; uniform, dark color; laterally flattened tail; protein-poor, herbivorous diet; elaborate digestive and metabolic systems (e.g., three-chambered, but nonruminating, stomach); gregarious behavior; and life in aquatic habitats. Additionally, the hippo's relationship to the central group of ungulates is affirmed by its enormous, persistently growing canine tusks—incongruous teeth for a strict vegetarian! With the hippopotamus,

Fig. 8.5. Pygmy hippopotamus

we have a metabolic-oriented mammal within a middle group that lies nested within the most metabolic-oriented of mammalian groups, the ungulates. Interestingly, the pygmy hippopotamus (*Choeropsis liberiensis*), compared to its gargantuan cousin, has a smaller head relative to its body length (thus de-emphasizing the anterior pole), is less aquatic, and also much less gregarious (fig. 8.5). Therefore, in morphology and behavior, the pygmy hippo is the more nerve-sense oriented of the two.

Not surprisingly, the swine are positioned centrally between the peccaries and hippos (fig. 8.4). The balanced form of these Old World inhabitants is reminiscent of the tapirs. Ever-growing canines are often lengthened into tusks that may extend far beyond the jaws, providing formidable weapons. Besides eating leaves, roots, and fruits, swine exhibit carnivorous tendencies by taking small animals and birds' eggs. As with young tapirs, juveniles of almost all wild pig species have longitudinal rows of stripes—an unmistakable "rhythmic" quality. Notably, the young of sense-oriented peccaries lack this color pattern (fig. 8.4).

THE RUMINANT ARTIODACTYLS AS
METABOLIC UNGULATES

Next, we direct our attention to the extreme metabolic-oriented group of hoofed mammals: the ruminant artiodactyls. This group contains the camel and chevrotain families, both characterized by a primitive, three-chambered, ruminating stomach; and the pecorans (infraorder Pecora), which possess an advanced, four-chambered, ruminating stomach, and head protuberances (i.e., horns and antlers). Pecorans encompass a variety of families, such as giraffe, deer, and cattle, and include our representative ungulate, the bison. The bison's qualities are repeated quite faithfully in many other pecorans. The powerfully built yak (*Bos grunniens*), for example, which roams the mountains and plateaus of central Asia, exhibits a radical exaggeration of the anterior pole, with high withers, a pendulous head, and spectacular horns (fig. 8.6). Its dense, shaggy fur is a uniform brownish black and serves as an effective insulator against the frigid temperatures of high elevations. The enormous bulk of this ungulate is nourished on a high-fiber diet of grasses, sedges, and lichens with which only an advanced digestion and metabolism could cope.

Next, we ask how camels and chevrotains relate to the metabolically advanced pecorans. Among camels, the South American species most closely resemble the ancestral humpless forms. The swift, nimble, alert guanaco (*Lama guanicoe*) has a small head atop a long, slender neck, indicating a marked separation between sense and metabolic poles (fig. 8.6), even more so than in horses (which is expected because camels are ruminants). Its hindquarters are slightly accentuated, and the beautiful, dense fur is contrasted tawny orange above and white on the underside. And remarkably, the closely related vicuna (*Vicugna vicugna*) is unique among artiodactyls in having ever-growing, rodent-like incisors! Clearly, nerve-sense qualities predominate in this family, in which the humped forms, such as the Bactrian camel (*Camelus bactrianus*), are secondarily metabolic-oriented (fig. 8.7).

Some of the smallest of hoofed mammals, the secretive, nocturnal chevrotains, are found in dense vegetation near water in Africa and Asia (fig. 8.6). These tiny ungulates have many primitive features. Their limbs are less advanced than those of camels, and their digestive and metabolic organization (e.g., three-chambered stomach) is more primitive than that of the so-called true ruminants that have four-chambered stomachs. Upper canines of males are elongated into pointed tusks, which protrude downwards and curve backwards. Although basically vegetarian, chevrotains eat meat readily. Moreover, the brown fur of most species is adorned with rows of spots on the back and stripes on the flanks. These "carnivorous" qualities are indicative of the chevrotain's central position within the ruminant artiodactyls.[21]

Before we apply the threefold classification to partition the pecorans, we will ask an apparently naive question: Why are a rhino's horns positioned on its snout and a dairy cow's horns located high on its skull? To answer this question, we must also examine the head protuberances

Fig. 8.6. Ruminant artiodactyls: *Top*, chevrotain; *lower left*, guanaco; *lower right*, yak. Based on drawings by F. A. Reid, with permission.

Fig. 8.7. Bactrian camel

of pigs, their so-called facial warts. Our examples will be the black rhinoceros (*Diceros bicornis*), wart hog (*Phacochoerus aethiopicus*), and Scottish highland cattle (*Bos taurus*), which are, respectively, perisso-dactyl (sense-oriented), nonruminant artiodactyl (rhythmic-oriented), and ruminant artiodactyl (metabolic-oriented) ungulates (fig. 8.8).

Fig. 8.8. *Left*, black rhinoceros; *center*, wart hog; and *right*, Scottish highland cattle. Drawings by F. A. Reid, with permission.

Contemplating the positions of their head protuberances, and keeping in mind the relative positions of the three representative tooth types (incisors, canines, and molars), we discover surprising parallels. The rhino's horns, like incisors, are located anteriorly and medially; the wart hog's facial projections are midway along the length of the skull and midway down the side of the head, as in the relative position of canines in the jaw; and cattle horns, like molars, are situated posteriorly and laterally. Furthermore, the rhino's horns originate from epidermis, the exterior skin layer; the wart hog's "warts" arise from dermis, the middle skin layer; and cattle horns have a bony core, which originates subcutaneously, that is, below the skin. By proceeding from the whole to its parts, the threefold classification illuminates intrinsic relationships among these phenomena previously thought to be unrelated.

THE HORN AND ANTLER-BEARING RUMINANTS

We turn next to those ruminant mammals that possess a four-chambered stomach and frontal appendages: the pecorans. Here again three groups

Fig. 8.9. Giraffe

can be delineated based on morphology and behavior. Recalling two previously mentioned groups characterized by being metabolic forms with secondary nerve-sense orientation—horses and camels—it would follow that a nerve-sense oriented pecoran would exhibit a further development of the motif expressed in those groups. Both horses and camels have long necks, which serve to distance the head from the digestive pole; as ruminants, camels take this gesture further than horses. Accordingly, we would expect an advanced ruminant to continue this morphological trend. This is indeed the case, for the giraffe (*Giraffa camelopardalis*) exaggerates this tendency to perhaps the limits of morphological possibilities (fig. 8.9).

The tallest of all living land mammals, giraffes are found in sub-Saharan Africa. Their long eyelashes, narrow snout, extensible tongue, and overall acute senses bespeak the sensitivity, grace, and alertness typical of these towering ungulates. Two to four peg-like horns grow from the head in both sexes and occasionally an additional ossification occurs medially, that is, between the eyes, which is in keeping with the nerve-sense qualities of this mammal.

In the central, rhythmic group of pecorans, we would expect to find balanced forms and carnivorelike characteristics. In the deer family, this pattern is, in fact, borne out. Standing between giraffes and bovids (e.g., cattle), the stateliness of the deer is perhaps attributable to its harmonious form (fig. 8.10). Moreover, adults of many species have spotted coats (as do most fawns), possess canines, are capable of barking or roaring, and, in general, display aggressive tendencies. The deer's central position is also suggested by the fact that most species are found in mid-latitude forest ecotones, that is, the habitat between closed forest and open grassland. Regarding diet, deer are woodland browsers and thus are relatively intolerant of the exceptionally high-fiber foods of grazers and, under experimental conditions, are less efficient than cattle at digesting a moderately high-fiber diet.[21]

Those deer species that lack antlers are most similar to the ancestral forms, and, like their prehistoric antecedents, have large canine fangs to compensate for the absence of cranial appendages. Males of most living species, however, display impressive antlers, the products of a season's growth and "the most rapidly growing structures in the animal kingdom."[22] Females lack antlers, with the exception of the metabolically oriented caribou (*Rangifer tarandus*), which lives in large herds on open tundra and feeds on crude plant matter (e.g., lichens and forbs).

Informed by the threefold principle, it is instructive to examine variation in antler morphology. As a general rule, antlers of the smaller species—often the more nerve-sense oriented forms—tend to be stunted, often unbranched, positioned close together on the skull, and directed almost straight upward (e.g., in brocket deer, *Mazama* spp.). The larger species, in contrast, sport massive, multibranched (i.e., multitined) antlers that expand laterally to a considerable extent. Accordingly, the antlers of the large, metabolic species mimic the relative position of molars, as is most evident in the moose (*Alces alces*). Called the elk in Europe, the moose—the largest living deer—exemplifies metabolic qualities within the deer family, not only in its staggering size and enormous laterally extended antlers, but also in its body form and color pattern: large shoulder hump, mane, heavy head with blunt, drooping muzzle, dewlap, and mostly uniform dark coat (fig. 8.11). Interestingly, moose calves are unspotted.

The Bovid Ruminants as Extreme Metabolic Ungulates

The third major group of ruminant mammals that possess frontal appendages—in this case, horns—is the family Bovidae, the most meta-

Top: Fig. 8.10. *Left*, White-tailed deer fawn; *right*, buck.
Bottom: Fig. 8.11. *Left*, Moose calf; *right*, bull.
Based on line drawings by F. A. Reid, with permission. Reprinted from *A Field Guide to Mammals Coloring Book*, by permission of Houghton Mifflin Co. © by Houghton Mifflin, 1987.

bolically oriented of all mammals. The 140-odd living species exhibit a panoply of morphologies, color patterns, and behaviors as variations on the theme of a large, gregarious, cloven-hoofed mammal with an anterior accentuation and uniform coloration, as exemplified in the previously discussed bison. These variations, however, parallel the general pattern of relationships identified earlier among rodents, carnivores, and ungulates. For example, P. Jarman described for African bovids a general trend in which preference for open habitats and group size both increase with larger body sizes.[24] Accordingly, small bovids are more nerve-sense oriented with respect to their relative diminutive size, accentuated hind-quarters, tendency to be found in closed, forested habitats, and solitary or small- group habits. In addition, within a taxonomic assemblage, the ability to digest forage—that is, cellulose—increases with body size.[25] Overall, "small herbivores tend to be selective feeders on succulent vege-tation, living in closed habitats such as forests, whereas larger herbivores tend to feed less selectively on more fibrous vegetation and may be found in more open grassland habitats."[26] What follows is an overview of three groups that comprise the bovids.

Wakefulness, agility, and contrasting coloration are several charac-teristics expected in the nerve-sense oriented bovids, and, within this family, the antelopes typify these qualities. Consider the gazelle (*Gazella thomsoni*), impala (*Aepyceros melampus*), and gemsbok (*Oryx gazella*). Each is wary, boldly patterned, and adorned with slender, sharply pointed, upwardly reaching horns (fig. 8.12). As nerve-sense members of the most metabolic group, however, the antelopes exhibit high species diversity with concomitant morphological variation, and many species, therefore, are exceptions to the general pattern. The anomalies them-selves, however, support the threefold relationship, which is made evident, for example, by a comparison of the gazelle with the black wildebeest (*Connochaetes gnou*), a metabolically oriented antelope (fig. 8.12). Compared to the gazelle, the wildebeest, or gnu, is substantially larger, overall darkly colored, has high withers accentuated by a mane, a bearded muzzle, and broad, heavy horns that flair outward to the sides. Once again, elements of form and coloration can be seen to covary predictably when viewed from the threefold perspective.

If space permitted, a detailed analysis of the antelopes could be undertaken to reveal underlying patterns of form, color, and behavior. Central to such a study would be an examination and comparison of the morphology, size, and position of the horns, features that would be consistent with the character of each species. As seen previously, every detail of an organism, when viewed holistically, is consistent with the organism's overall character. From horn to hoof, the traits of each antelope species disclose both the uniqueness and relatedness of each

Fig. 8.12. *Left,* comparison of gazelle with *right,* black wildebeest

animal examined. Even the quality of the antelope's dung is revealing: hardened, compacted pellets reminiscent of the fecal pellets of the nerve-sense-oriented rodents, in contrast, for example, to the amorphous mass of cow patties.

Before leaving the antelopes, it is useful to observe a rather anomalous species, the pronghorn (*Antilocapra americana*), which is placed in its own family (Antilocapridae) by some researchers (fig. 8.13). The swiftest land mammal in North America, the pronghorn can sprint up to fifty miles per hour on level terrain in its desert and grassland habitats. This tan-colored ungulate, with contrasting white underparts, has a unique feature among horned mammals: it sheds the keratinous sheath of its horns annually. Only deer among ungulates shed their frontal appendages, antlers; in contrast, the bovids retain their horns throughout life. Interestingly, as Schad points out, in the pronghorn, the branched horns resemble antlers and, through shedding, even "behave" like antlers.[27]

Between the sense-oriented antelopes and the extreme metabolically oriented cattle-like bovids are the goats and sheep (fig. 8.14). Their middle position is most evident in their behavior: they are not as "awake" as antelopes nor as "dreamy" as cattle. The horns of goats grow straight out of the skull and arc gently backwards while those of sheep tend to spiral out toward the sides. Moreover, "the goat is a comparatively selective feeder and is inferior to cattle and sheep as a digester of fiber"[28]—an observation indicating that goats are more nerve-sense oriented than sheep. Goats are also exceptionally agile and can maintain their footing on precarious high-mountain crags; some can even climb trees. Sheep, in contrast, are more typical of lower elevations, such as mountain pastures and valleys. A closely related species, the muskox (*Ovibos moschatus*), clearly represents exaggerated metabolic qualities in this group: massive size, high withers, more or less uniformly dark coat, and heavyset horns that grow laterally (fig. 8.15). To maintain its huge

Top: Fig. 8.13. Pronghorn.
Middle: Fig. 8.14. *Left*, Mountain goat (*Oreamnos americanus*); *right*, bighorn sheep (*Ovis canadensis*).
Bottom: Fig. 8.15. Muskox.
Based on line drawings by J. A. Reid, with permission. Reprinted from *A Field Guide to Mammals Coloring Book*, by permission of Houghton Mifflin Co. © 1987 by Houghton Mifflin.

bulk, the muskox feeds during the coldest months on frozen plants beneath the snow, and thus must possess a powerful metabolism to digest and assimilate such poor-quality forage.

Finally, our investigation leads us to the most metabolically oriented of all mammals, the grass and roughage eaters: the oxen, bison, buffalo, and related bovines (fig. 8.16). Ponderous size, accentuated shoulder hump, uniformly dark coat, and formidable, laterally extended horns are the signatures of this group. Behaviorally, these mammals are typically highly gregarious, stolid grazers, but, when threatened by predators or by intraspecific male rivals, some can display sudden bursts of aggressive behavior. Typical members of this group include the earlier discussed bison, the African buffalo (*Syncerus caffer*), the Asian water buffalo (*Bubalus bubalis*), the banteng (*Bos javanicus*), and the various breeds of domestic cattle (Bos taurus), the latter thought to be derived 8,000 years ago from a presently extinct beast called the "aurochs." Thus, with an examination of these formidable animals, our classification of hoofed mammals, based on the threefold principle, is complete. Figure 8.17 schematically illustrates the threefold relationships among the ungulates.

THE THREEFOLD PRINCIPLE IN RODENTS AND CARNIVORES

It is important to realize that a detailed application of the threefold principle, as was done here for ungulates, can be undertaken for the other two major mammalian orders, the rodents and carnivores, as well as for additional groups of mammals. Although interested readers are referred to Schad for in-depth treatments of these groups, the following examples can serve as highlights for a demonstration of the broad applicability of the threefold perspective.[29]

For instance, by reviewing the qualities of an earlier-mentioned rodent, the beaver, its relationship among the rodents becomes apparent (fig. 8.18). Its relatively large size, mostly uniformly dark pelage, broad, flattened tail, and ability to digest exceptionally coarse material—tree bark and twigs—are indicative of its metabolic position within this group of mammals.[30] Similarly, the world's largest rodent, the capybara (*Hydrochaeris hydrochaeris*), can be considered cattle-like by virtue of its gregariousness, short tail, uniform fur coloration, squared off, blunt snout, and, for a rodent, rather dull temperament (fig. 8.19). Furthermore, the threefold principle helps shed light on the configuration of characteristics of another previously mentioned rodent, the paca; its generalized form, spotted and striped pelage, solitary habits, and most

Fig. 8.16. Water buffalo

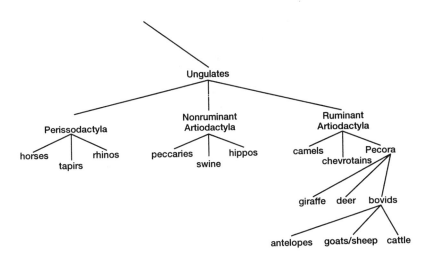

Fig. 8.17. Threefold relationships among ungulates

unusual (for a rodent) ability to roar (due to specialized cranial resonating chambers) bespeak its position as a central, rhythmic rodent (fig. 8.20).

The least weasel, which was mentioned earlier as a nonconforming carnivore and consequently as a potential contradiction to the threefold principle, can now be viewed in a broader context. Its small size, sharply contrasting fur pattern, ability to sit upright on its haunches, and quick, nervous movements clearly identify this mammal as a nerve-sense

Fig. 8.18. Beaver. Based on line drawing by F. A. Reid, with permission. Reprinted from *A Field Guide to Mammals Coloring Book*, by permission of Houghton Mifflin. © 1987 by Houghton Mifflin.

Fig. 8.19. Capybara

Fig. 8.20. Paca

Fig. 8.21. Least weasel. Based on line drawing by J. A. Reid, with permission. Reprinted from *A Field Guide to Mammals Coloring Book*, by permission of Houghton Mifflin. © 1987 by Houghton Mifflin.

Fig. 8.22. Lion

oriented carnivore (fig. 8.21). The closely related martens (*Martes* spp.) are larger, heavier bodied, less nervous in their movements, and lack the weasel's white belly, their highlighted underparts restricted to the chest and throat.

Regarding the earlier characterization of carnivores in general and the cat family specifically, the African lion (*Panthera leo*) may at first appear as a contradiction (fig. 8.22). Closer examination, however, reveals this big cat as not so much an exception as yet another example of the interweaving pattern among the mammals. Its large size, more or less uniformly tawny fur (in adults), and impressive anterior accentuation in males (i.e., the mane) constitute a suite of metabolic qualities. Moreover, unlike all other cats, the lion is a highly social animal, hence a metabolically oriented carnivore.

The pinnipeds—seals, sea lions, and walrus—are closely allied to the carnivores and in fact considered by some taxonomists to be a suborder within the Carnivora. These marine mammals can be considered members of the middle group that have become secondarily metabolically oriented as evidenced by numerous characteristics: large size, uniformly dark fur, and sociability (fig. 8.23).[31] Moreover, many species, especially the males, exhibit an accentuated anterior pole and shift of center of gravity toward the head in that they possess significantly thickened, robust necks (often covered with dense fur) as well as, in some species, an inflatable proboscis—for example, northern elephant seal (*Mirounga angustirostris*) and hooded seal (*Cystophora cristata*). The most extreme swing toward the metabolic pole is observed in the walrus (*Odobenus rosmarus*), whose tremendous size, exaggerated forequarters, blunt muzzle, and herding behavior are further complemented not by horns but by ever-growing upper canine tusks (fig. 8.24). Like submarine cattle, herds of walrus "graze" the ocean floor for benthic invertebrates.

THE THREEFOLD PRINCIPLE IN PRIMATES

As a final example of the application of the threefold principle to mammalian diversity, consider the primates. Although, according to Schad, members of this group have not fully differentiated their threefold organic systems relative to rodents, carnivores, and ungulates (for reasons that cannot be discussed here due to space considerations), one can still identify formative tendencies among the various species that are consistent with the threefold pattern.[32] For instance, the form, coloration, and behavior of the anthropoid apes patently distinguish these as the metabolically oriented primates. Gorillas (*Gorilla gorilla*) of equatorial Africa are huge, lumbering mammals with a high cranial crest (accentuating the head pole), longer forelimbs than hind limbs, absence of a tail, uniformly black fur (except in older males that develop "silverbacks"), and a well-developed social system (fig. 8.25). In addition, their diet is almost exclusively vegetarian, and they are known to regurgitate semi-digested food and then reingest it, an image of rumination. The orangutan (*Pongo pygmaeus*), of Borneo and Sumatra, is also a metabolic form as evidenced especially in the male's frontal accentuation through the presence of huge cheek pads and a beard.

Shifting toward the nerve-sense pole of the primates, we encounter species with rodent-like qualities. The Neotropical marmosets and

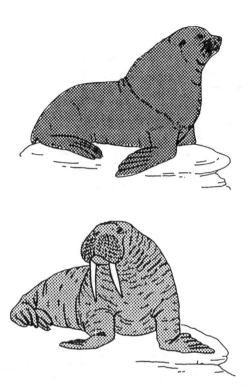

Top: Fig. 8.23. Steller sea lion (*Eumetopias jubatus*).
Bottom: Fig. 8.24. Walrus.
Based on line drawings by J. A. Reid, with permission. Reprinted from *A Field Guide to Mammals Coloring Book*, by permission of Houghton Mifflin. © 1987 by Houghton Mifflin.

Fig. 8.25. *Left*, Comparison of gorilla with *right*, cotton-top marmoset

tamarins are some of the world's smallest primates, about the size of a squirrel, and provide a striking contrast to the great apes (fig. 8.25). They have hind limbs longer than forelimbs, a tail often as long as or longer than the body, and they travel quickly and nervously through the forest canopy, moving jerkily emitting high-pitched chattering vocalizations. Moreover, some species, such as the cotton-top marmoset (*Saguinus oedipus*), are boldly patterned. Again, the threefold principle makes sense of this diversity of forms, and it is evident why one would not expect a primate in the form of a marmoset to grow to the size of a gorilla, nor the converse. Between the extremes of the metabolic apes and the nerve-sense oriented marmosets is a spectrum of intermediate forms comprised of the New World and Old World monkeys. The baboons form a curious offshoot that leans toward the metabolic pole and embodies dog-like qualities.

A Formative Principle

In this essay, I have sought to demonstrate that an application of the threefold classification based on the Goethean principle of polarity can uncover an inherent organic order within mammalian diversity as exemplified by the work of Wolfgang Schad.[33] The patterns among the mammals provide a plausible argument for the existence of a formative principle whose elements may manifest repeatedly as similar motifs in different families of mammals. The individual organism may be seen as a composite of qualities woven together according to the laws of this principle. Although one cannot claim to have identified this principle, the threefold classification can indicate its existence by enabling one to apprehend its mode of expression, that is, to read its signature in phenomena. Its signature, however, becomes intelligible only when the *relationships among phenomena* are grasped in their wholeness. Just as it is fruitless to search for meaning in the isolated letters of a word, so do isolated phenomena yield only a fragment of their full significance.[34]

The analytic and quantitative methods of contemporary biology have led to major advances in our understanding of the natural world, but for all their achievements, a coherent, comprehensive grasp of the organism is lacking. Why? Perhaps a reason lies in the limitations of the methods themselves. By probing ever deeper into the organism, segregating parts and uncovering detail upon detail, the whole is lost from view—an ironic twist, considering that the very nature of "organism" is wholeness. Should the analytic and quantitative methods be abandoned? Certainly not. What is necessary, however, is a recognition and application of their counterparts—methods that are synthetic and qualitative—through which one can relate details to one another without losing sight of the context of relationships to which they belong. This study focused on details of mammalian form, color pattern, and behavior but always compared and contrasted these details as they appear in different animals. Indeed, it was only through interrelating qualities that the inherent order within the mammals emerged. Synthetic, qualitative, and holistic, the threefold classification provides a useful complement to conventional analytic and quantitative taxonomy. When applied jointly, the two approaches sustain a union that promises to broaden and deepen scientific study.

NOTES

1. This essay is a revised and expanded version of an article originally published in *Orion Nature Quarterly* 4 no. 4 (autumn 1985): 22–35. The author and editors wish to thank the publisher for permission to draw on this earlier work.

2. D. E. Wilson, and D. Reeder, eds. *Mammal Species of the World: A Taxonomic and Geographic Reference*, 2nd ed. (Washington, D.C.: Smithsonian Institution Press, 1993).

3. These resemblances also appear in many plants, though I will not discuss the topic here. See M. Riegner, "Toward a Holistic Understanding of Place: Reading a Landscape Through its Flora and Fauna," in *Dwelling, Seeing, and Designing: Toward a Phenomenological Ecology*, edited by David Seamon (Albany: State University of New York Press., 1993), pp. 181–215.

4. For a discussion of this phenomenon in plants, animals, and landscapes, see Riegner, "Toward a Holistic Understanding of Place."

5. Wolfgang Schad, *Man and Mammals: Toward a Biology of Form* (Garden City, N.Y.: Waldorf Press, 1977).

6. See, for example, Rudolf Steiner, *Goethe's World View*, trans. W. Lindeman (Spring Valley, N.Y.: Mercury Press, 1985; originally published 1918); and Rudolf Steiner, *Goethean Science*, trans. W. Lindeman (Spring Valley, N.Y.: Mercury Press, 1988; originally published as introductions to Goethe's natural-scientific works and edited by Rudolf Steiner, 1883–1897).

7. Goethe's scientific writings can be found in Goethe, *Goethe: Scientific Studies*, ed. and trans. Douglas Miller (New York: Suhrkamp, 1988). For a useful cross section of professional reactions to Goethean science, see F. Amrine, F. J. Zucker, and H. Wheeler, eds., *Goethe and the Sciences: A Reappraisal* (Dordrecht: D. Reidel, 1987).

8. Schad, *Man and Mammals*.

9. I draw the information for my interpretation of mammals in this essay from two books: D. Macdonald, ed., *The Encyclopedia of Mammals* (New York: Facts on File, 1984); and R. Nowak, *Walker's Mammals of the World. 5th ed.* (Baltimore, Md.: Johns Hopkins Press, 1991). I used these texts throughout to

corroborate factual material and will not, therefore, cite them each time a new mammal is discussed.

10. Louis Bolk, "On the Problem of Anthropogenesis," *Proc. Section Sciences Kon. Akad. Wetens. Amsterdam* 29 (1926): 465–75.

11. Ibid.

12. For reviews, see S. J. Gould, *Ontogeny and Phylogeny* (Cambridge, Mass.: Harvard University Press, 1977); M. McKinney, ed., *Heterochrony in Evolution* (New York: Plenum, 1988); M. McKinney and K. McNamara, *Heterochrony: The Evolution of Ontogeny* (New York: Plenum, 1991); B. Shea, "Heterochrony in Human Evolution: the Case for Neoteny Reconsidered," *Yearbook of Physical Anthropology* 32 (1989): 69–101; and J. Verhulst, "Speech and the Retardation of the Human Mandible: A Bolkian View," *Journal of Social and Evolutionary Systems* 17, no. 3 (1994): 307–37.

13. Because of their similarity to molars in form and function, premolars are not considered separately.

14. J. Berger and C. Cunningham, *Bison: Mating and Conservation in Small Populations* (New York: Columbia University Press, 1994).

15. Ibid., p. 11.

16. Remarkably, a ruminating animal's brain waves are similar to those measured in sleeping nonruminants; see R. H. Bell, "A Grazing Ecosystem in the Serengeti," *Scientific American* 224 (1971): 86–93.

17. "Metabolism" is used here unconventionally to denote the activity of vital organs. The whole animal is seen as an embodiment of powerful processes that cope with the breakdown and assimilation of crude plant matter. Conventionally, the word is usually associated with cellular activities.

18. Exceptions include bears (*Ursidae*) and raccoons (*Procyonidae*), in which the heel and sole of the foot meet the earth (i.e., plantigrade).

19. See J. Murray, "How the Leopard Gets its Spots," *Scientific American* 258, 3 (1988): 80–87; and B. Sleeper, "And Stripes on the Tail: The Mathematics of Animal Coat Patterns," *Pacific Discovery* 46, no. 2 (1993): 8–16.

20. Interestingly, within the horse family, zebras can be seen to occupy the central position; hence the "carnivorous" stripes associated with their more pointed canines and untamable, aggressive nature.

21. See Schad, *Man and Mammals*, 1977, pp. 186–87, for a discussion of the chevrotain's small size.

22. On deer as woodland browsers, see P. Van Soest, *Nutritional Ecology of the Ruminant*, 2nd ed. (Ithaca, N.Y.: Cornell University Press, 1994); on the relative digestive efficiency of browsers in relation to grazers, see J. Huston, B. Rector, W. Ellis, and M. Allen, "Dynamics of Digestion in Cattle, Sheep, Goats and Deer," *Journal of Animal Science* 62 (1986): 208–15.

23. R. Goss, *Deer Antlers: Regeneration, Function, and Evolution* (New York: Academic Press, 1983), p. 3.

24. P. Jarman, "The Social Organization of Antelope in Relation to their

Ecology," *Behaviour* 48 (1990): 213–67.

25. Van Soest, *Nutritional Ecology.*

26. C. Janis, "Correlation of Reproductive and Digestive Strategies in the Evolution of Cranial Appendages," in *Horns, Pronghorns, and Antlers: Evolution, Morphology, Physiology, and Social Significance,* edited by G. Bubenik and A. Bubenik (New York: Springer-Verlag, 1990), p. 116.

27. Schad, *Man and Mammals,* p. 149.

28. Van Soest, *Nutritional Ecology,* p. 28.

29. Schad, *Man and Mammals,* p. 101.

30. In the Pleistocene, there existed a beaver the size of a present-day black bear!

31. The Baikal seal (*Phoca sibirica*), found in Lake Baikal, is an exception to the pinnipeds' habit of living in marine environments. In regard to fur patterns, some species, such as the ringed seal (*Phoca hispida*), retain an echo of spots in the form of blotches.

32. Schad, *Man and Mammals,* pp. 242–44.

33. The threefold classification, with modifications, can also be applied to other groups of organisms. Space permits only brief mention here. The extraordinary diversity among birds, for example, reveals many of the motifs described above. Large metabolic forms, such as the ratites (ostrich, emu, cassowaries, rheas), have a head (nerve-sense pole) significantly distanced from their digestive organs (metabolic pole) correlated with a wakefulness that typifies birds as a class; in addition, specialized limbs (e.g., the ostrich has only two toes on each foot), exaggerated head growths (e.g., casques and wattles in the cassowaries), and precocial young are found among ratites. Some of these features are also apparent in other groups. Among herons (Ardeidae), the taller species (e.g., great blue heron, *Ardea herodias*) have proportionately longer necks relative to their body size compared with the smaller species (e.g., green heron, *Butorides virescens*), the latter typically being relatively stout, chunky birds. The small species of woodpeckers (Picidae) are, like rodents, compact-bodied with very short necks (e.g., downy woodpecker, *Picoides pubescens*), whereas the larger species (e.g., pileated woodpecker, *Dryocopus pileatus*) have relatively elongated necks and exaggerated crests on their crown. Among waterfowl (Anatidae), the large swans have the longest relative neck lengths, geese are intermediate, and ducks have relatively compacted bodies.

The motif of spots and stripes—typical of mammalian carnivores—is also evident in many birds of prey. The plumages of numerous hawks, eagles, falcons, and owls are often streaked, spotted, banded, or barred. The nerve-sense oriented passerines (perching birds) typically have small, compact bodies and often display striking color contrasts in their plumage (e.g., wood warblers); crows and ravens are among the largest of passerines and exhibit more metabolic qualities in their overall size, uniform dark plumage, and gregarious nature. The few examples mentioned here, however, cannot do justice to the complex diversity of avian plumages and morphologies; interested readers are encouraged to discover patterns within this diversity.

As a final example of how the threefold classification can illuminate details of avian morphology, I turn to a species that perhaps has the most powerful metabolic/digestive capabilities among birds. The South American hoatzin (*Opisthocomus hoazin*) has a digestive system similar to that of mammalian ruminants in that it ferments plant fiber in a foregut, in this case a modified esophagus and crop (A. Grajal et al., "Foregut Fermentation in the Hoatzin, a Neotropical Leaf-eating Bird," *Science* 245 [1989]: 1236–38). Accordingly, the hoatzin's diet is composed mainly of green leaves—very unusual for a bird! Correlated with its highly developed metabolic physiology are the following features we've come to know among secondarily metabolically oriented mammals: gregariousness, preference for watery environments (river and lake margins), and anterior accentuation, here in the form of elongated, upstanding crest feathers. Furthermore, just as in mammals where a highly developed metabolism is often accompanied by limb specialization, the young hoatzin is the only bird that has functional wing claws, a remarkable specialization for a bird. Thus, in form, behavior, and physiology, the hoatzin is a metabolic bird par excellence.

34. See H. Bortoft, "Counterfeit and Authentic Wholes: Finding a Means for Dwelling in Nature," in *Dwelling, Place, and Environment: Towards a Phenomenology of Person and World*, edited by D. Seamon and R. Mugerauer (New York: Columbia University Press, 1985), pp. 281–302; reprinted as chapter 12 in this volume.

9

Craig Holdrege

Seeing The Animal Whole

The Example of the Horse and Lion

*Hence we conceive of the individual animal as a small
world, existing for its own sake, by its own means. Every
creature is its own reason to be. All its parts have a direct
effect on one another, a relationship to one another,
thereby constantly renewing the circle of life; thus we are
justified in considering every animal physiologically
perfect. Viewed from within, no part of the animal is a
useless or arbitrary product of the formative impulse (as so
often thought). Externally, some parts may seem useless
because the inner coherence of animal nature has given
them this form without regard to outer circumstance.
Thus, in the future, members such as the canine teeth of
the* Sus babirussa *[fig. 9.1] will not elicit the question,
What are they for? but rather, Where do they come from?
We will not claim that a bull has been given horns so that
he can butt; instead, we will try to discover how he might
have developed the horns he uses for butting.*

—Goethe, *Scientific Studies*

These thoughts of Goethe have become a leitmotif for a growing body of
research that studies the animal as a creature with "its own reason to
be."[1] Practicing Goethe's method entails overcoming ingrained habits of
thought regarding the understanding of organisms. In the first sections of
this essay, therefore, I address the nature of the Goethean approach to
animals in light of contemporary Neo-Darwinian thought. I then present
two animals—the horse and the lion—to give the reader an impression of
a concrete application of Goethe's method.

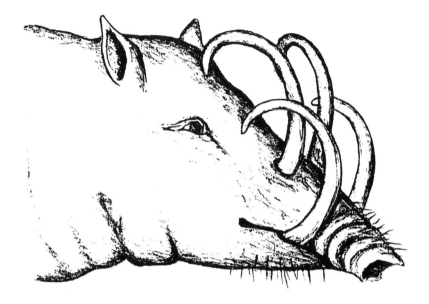

Fig. 9.1. *Sus babirusa* (*Babyrousa babirussa*). The four tusks are canine teeth. (Author's drawing based on H. W. Flower and R. Lydekker, *An Introduction to the Study of Mammals Living and Exitnct* [London: Adam and Charles Black, 1891]).

Why the horse and lion? I have studied them for a long time, and, through comparison, have found them increasingly to illuminate each other. As a large herbivore and a large carnivore, respectively, the horse and lion in many respects represent a polarity, in terms of which the one appears more clearly in light of the other.

THE NEO-DARWINIAN EXPLANATION

"What is it for?" This question arises automatically as an expression of the human desire to understand. Because they appear to our minds as a riddle, we ask why a bull has horns. The answer—"the bull has horns so that it can butt"—imbues the horns with meaning. Through this explanation, the horns are no longer isolated facts but can be seen in a larger context as useful instruments. Whether this answer—which may satisfy us as human beings—has much to do with the bull and its horns is another matter. If we observe the bull using its horns as a weapon, then we know that horns do actually have this function. This discovery does not preclude the likely possibility that the horns have additional functions that we have not yet observed. To discover a function of an organic structure adds to our knowledge of the organism. From a

Goethean viewpoint, however, it is crucial to emphasize that function does not explain form. Instead, form and function can be regarded as two different ways of looking at the same thing.

If, however, one keeps the horn qua form and structure separate in the mind from the horn qua function, then the functional description can be felt to be an explanation, but an explanation that reduces one phenomenon to another. The riddle posed by the horn is thus solved by the answer "butting." The horn no longer puzzles us but, rather, comes to rest in its defined, "explanatory" function.

In this way, Neo-Darwinian explanations reduce organic structure to particular functions that are purported to increase the survival value of the given organism or species. The bull's horns serve as weapons; its large molars are good for grinding grass; the eyes, positioned on the sides of the head, provide a large field of vision, enabling it to flee predators. In this approach, the organism disintegrates into a conglomeration of parts, each of which has "reason to be" outside itself in the purported selective value of its function. In this conventional perspective, the organism has no inner coherence. It is nothing in and of itself but, rather, the product of outer "causes", that is, natural selection.

The horns, of course, must come from somewhere and, in Neo-Darwinian theory, the origin of characteristics is the mutation, recombination, and expression of genes. Mutations are usually thought to be spontaneous, chance occurrences. Mutated genes are arranged in new combinations through sexual reproduction. New mutant traits, if they arise, may or may not increase the survival value of the organism. The horn is thus "explained" in two different ways. First, it has arisen through the accumulation of mutations that gradually, through eons, lead from a small bony protrusion on the frontal bone to a fully developed horn. Second, the preceding "almost-horn" stages and the horn itself exist by virtue of usefulness, contributing to the survival of the evolving species.

DWELLING WITHIN THE ORGANISM

It is certainly possible to consider organisms from this Neo-Darwinian perspective, which in fact dominates most thinking on animal form and function today.[2] From a Goethean viewpoint the problem with this perspective is that one does not gain an understanding of the organism as a *coherent whole*. The Neo-Darwininan framework forces us to leave the organism to explain it, to search for an answer outside the animal itself. The organism qua organism becomes an abstraction. Goethe clearly recognized that life is lost through the process of abstraction and reduction. He revolted against teleological as well as materialistic reduction of the organism to something other than itself. In other words, Goethe's approach has to do with finding a way between the Scylla and Charybdis of anthropomorphic and mechanistic explanations to begin to dwell within the organism as an entity in its own right.

Goethe's endeavor is to understand the unity of the organism—in the present case, the horse in the horse, the lion in the lion. Every part can reveal something of the whole organism. But one can also lose the organism in the study of its parts. It is a strenuous task to keep alive the intention of seeing the whole, while delving into the world of details that the organism presents. If, in moving through the structures and functions, the researcher can hold this intention present, then the whole can begin to form in the mind. One catches a glimpse of the animal, and a living understanding emerges. This understanding is a picture of the whole, however elementary. It is a picture that can grow richer and richer, revealing ever more dimensions of the animal.

Goethe clearly recognized the monumental task he set for himself and future science: "There is a delicate empiricism which makes itself utterly identical with the object, thereby becoming true theory. But this enhancement of our mental powers belongs to a highly evolved age."[3] This task is difficult because we must gradually change our way of thinking. Instead of adapting the organism to our preferred thinking, we must attempt to adapt ourselves to the organism. If we can follow it, the organism becomes a teacher and along the way begins to reveal itself. In this sense, one can say that the language of the animal slowly becomes decipherable. As Henri Bortoft writes, "when the point is reached where the animal discloses itself, the animal becomes its own language. In this moment, the animal is language."[4]

The Animal and Its Environment

Goethe's intention to view the animal as "a small world, existing for its own sake" might appear at first to separate and isolate the animal from its environment. In fact, Goethe sought to hold the animal and its world in intimate relationship and to understand the organism in the context of its environment. According to Goethe:

> The statement "The fish exists for the water" seems to me to say far less than "The fish exists in the water and by means of the water." The latter expresses more clearly what is obscured in the former; i.e., the existence of a creature we call "fish" is only possible under the conditions of an element we call "water," so that the creature not only exists in that element, but may also evolve there.[5]

To say that a fish is adapted to water is to say very little—so, for example, are sponge, starfish, squid, and crab. It is a question of *how* the fish relates to the element of water. This we learn by studying its characteristics in water.

Analogously, the lions that live in the African savannah share their surroundings with elephants, giraffes, rhinoceroses, monkeys, hyenas, zebras, and many other mammals. Two animals may have the same surroundings, but they do not live in the same environment, which is, rather, the *actual relationship* between an organism and its surroundings. In this sense, the fruit of a tree belong as little to the lion's environment as the flesh of a zebra does to the elephant's. The same watering hole is a very different environment for a lion (primarily a place where prey are stalked) than it is for the elephant (primarily a place to bathe). The environment *as lived* cannot be seen. It is a relationship and, therefore, cannot be described directly.

In describing *how* the lion stalks, feeds, sleeps and so forth, we form a picture of the lion *and* its environment. The environment is revealed through the animal, and the animal is revealed in its relationship to the environment. This mutuality lies at the heart of contextual understanding. As Goethe explained:

> We will see the entire plant world, for example, as a vast sea which is as necessary to the existence of individual insects as the oceans and rivers are to the existence of individual fish, and we will observe that an enormous number of living creatures are born and nourished in this ocean of plants. Ultimately we will see the whole world of animals as a great element in which one species is created, or a least sustained, by and through another. We will no longer think of connections and relationships in terms of purpose or intention. This is the only road to progress in understanding how nature expresses itself from all quarters and in all directions as it goes about its work of creation.[6]

THE HORSE AND LION IN THEIR WORLDS

Imagine a grazing horse. Long, gracile legs carry the large yet smooth and tight trunk, which extends into the long neck and elongated head tapering toward the snout. Like other grazing animals, the horse lives in its food. The lowered head moves over and through grasses and wildflowers. Lips, nostrils, and jaws move constantly as the front teeth nip off plants. In the recesses of the mouth, the food is thoroughly ground between the cheek teeth in a rhythmical, circling motion of the jaws. The horse eats and grinds for hours on end, but—unlike cattle or sheep—does not ruminate—that is, it has neither a four-chambered stomach nor does it egest initially digested food back up into the mouth and chew cud. The horse's digestive organ comparable in function to the rumen is an enlarged portion of the large intestine—the cecum—which is situated in the rear part of the trunk.

As it eats, the horse stands or slowly walks. In fact, the horse will stand approximately twenty hours of the twenty-four hour day and will also sleep while standing. The horse is an animal of endurance not only in feeding and standing but also in running. It can gallop for up to four miles (eight minutes) and trot for twenty miles (one hour).[7] When it stops, it does not collapse in exhaustion but remains on its legs. With its head held above the body, the horse also has an awareness of its environment on all sides. Its ears are mobile and can be turned in all directions. The eyes lie on the side of the head, giving the horse a very wide field of vision.

The lion is another world. If we imagine it in grass, then it is not grass for grazing but grass as a realm in which to stalk prey. The lion crouches, muscles tensed and eyes oriented to the front and focused on its prey. The lion attends to what is before it. A sudden thrust of activity follows as the lion sprints for its prey and lunges for the nape or throat, which it pierces with its canines. The forelegs grasp the prey and pull it down. The lion may open its gaping jaws and close on the muzzle of the prey, suffocating it. The lion proceeds to chomp into the flesh and shear off chunks with jagged cheek teeth. It swallows without any chewing. An adult lion may devour from twenty to fifty pounds of meat at one feeding so that to speak of gorging is to use a descriptive and not a derogatory term. A pride of lions feeding on one zebra can devour the entire carcass in thirty minutes.[8]

The lion then retreats to a secluded spot and rests, sleeps, and digests for many hours. Most of the lion's day is spent resting, as Anne Morrow Lindbergh says, "poured out like honey in the sun."[9] Such utter relaxation alternates with periods of moving from place to place and the occasional burst of power and wakefulness in the hunt. The lion has no endurance. It embodies immense strength, tension and speed for short spurts, but then its power is spent. Extended periods of rest follow.

THE HORSE AND LION IN THEIR LIMBS

From this first impression of horse and lion in their specific environments, we can turn towards a more detailed consideration of their contrasting body structures. Since the horse is a horse and a lion is a lion in each of their parts, each part must reveal the whole. Morphology in a

Goethean sense is an endeavor to view anatomical details with an eye towards the whole. They become transparent when grasped as an expression of the whole.

The skeleton is my point of departure in considering the whole through its parts. The skeleton is the most definitively formed structure in an animal. It resists decomposition when the animal dies and can then be studied as a clearly formed memory of the whole. In penetrating this memory, the whole can come to life in us. I focus primarily on the limbs and skull—those parts of the body through which the animal, in movement and perception, relates most directly to its surroundings, thereby meeting and making its environment.

As figures 9.2 and 9.4 illustrate, the horse rests upon long, stable columns of bone. The upper parts of the legs are muscular but this muscularity is embedded in the trunk. The bones that are comparable to our human elbows and knees do not extend beyond the horse's trunk. The lower part of the legs below the trunk (comparable to our lower arms and legs, hands and feet) has few muscles. Long tendons extend from the upper muscles down into the lower legs and feet. Tendons permeate many of these muscles, a telling characteristic of the horse anatomy.[10] Tendons are tougher and not as flexible as muscle so that when tendon permeates muscle, the muscle becomes less elastic but has more stability. The tendency toward hardening increases in the lower portion of the limbs; the tendons, for example, are exceedingly tough, almost like bone in their consistency.

The upper limb muscles in the trunk move the horse's leg. As a result, there is no finely differentiated movement of the limb. In a sense, the horse's limbs become living architecture. This structure of bone, ligaments and tendons has its own stability by virtue of which the horse can stand with no muscular effort.[11] Its muscles can relax in sleep but the horse does not collapse. The stability of the horse limb is connected with the strength of the bones but also with their form and the fact that the limb has fewer bones and joints than the limb of other land mammals. Figure 9.4 shows the bony structure of the horse's forelimbs, which carry about 70 percent of the body weight. We human beings can rotate our lower arm around its axis; this is only possible because we have two bones—ulna and radius—that allow this movement. In the horse, these bones are fused to form one straight, stable bone, which is the longest in the horse's body. Below it a "wrist" is formed by eight thick, compressed bones, or carpals. As figure 9.5 illustrates, these carpals have horizontal surfaces that rest upon one another and provide stability but little flexibility.

The columnar tendency of the horse extends into the elongated but stout bones of the feet. The horse does not stand upon feet with five toes

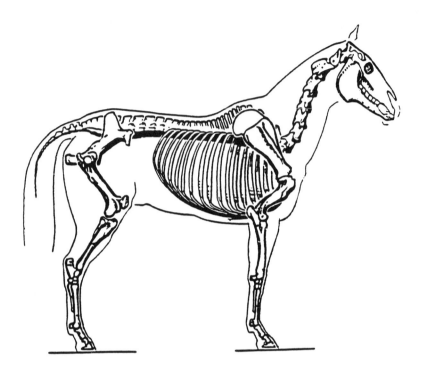

Fig. 9.2. Skeleton of the horse. Based on W. Tank, *Tieranatomie für Künstler* (Favensburg, Germany: Otto Maier, 1984), p. 108. Reprinted, by permission of Mrs. Ingeborg Tank.

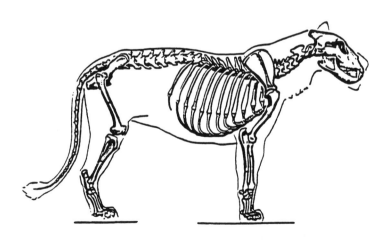

Fig. 9.3. Skeleton of the lion. Based on W. Tank, *Tieranatomie für Künstler* (Favensburg, Germany: Otto Maier, 1984), p. 90. Reprinted, by permission of Mrs. Ingeborg Tank.

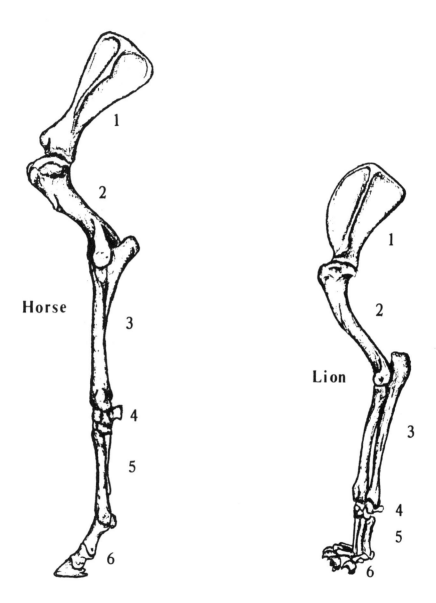

Fig. 9.4. Forelimb of horse and lion: (1) scapula, (2) humerus, (3) radius and ulna, (4) carpals, (5) metacarpals, (6) phalanges (toes). Author 's drawings based on information in W. Ellenberger, H. Dittrich, and H. Baum, *An Atlas of Animal Anatomy for Artists* (New York: Dover, 1947).

but, rather, upon one enlarged toe that ends in the thick, horned sheath of the hoof. Through bone fusion and bone reduction, the horse's limb becomes a stable column. The fewer bones mean fewer joints; the fewer the joints, the fewer the muscles. The flexibility the horse thereby loses in the leg is compensated for by the stability and strength it gains through its bone structure. The horse can stand, walk, trot, and gallop with great endurance but cannot crouch to the ground or scratch an ear with its hoof.

We now turn to the lion, which has the possibility of supple and agile yet forceful movement. As figures 9.3 and 9.4 show, there are many joints in the lion's limbs, and the bones are not so tightly connected as in the horse. The wrist bones, for example, have rounded surfaces—the gesture of mobility. They do not possess in themselves the stable architecture of the firmly set, horizontally placed carpals of the horse (fig. 9.5). The ulna and radius are two separate bones, allowing rotation of the forelimb, which comes into play, for example, when the lion grasps its prey or cleans itself with its paws. Compared to those of the horse, the lion's limbs are short and stocky, embedded in an array of muscles.

The lion's front feet have five toes, the back feet four. The body's weight is carried by the pads beneath the joints between the last toe bones, so that the lion's characteristic softness and buoyancy in motion extends even into these outermost members. The other element of lion movement—the powerful forward thrust culminating in the leap for prey—also comes to expression in the feet, namely, in the claws. Held hidden in the paw, they lash out, gash into the prey, and then retract. The activity of the claws in this hunting sequence vividly reveals the way of the lion as a whole—springing forward, penetrating, and withdrawing into inactivity.

Overall, one can say that the lion's stance and movement are directed and modulated at every moment by muscle. By living in the medium of muscle, the lion is capable of utmost force and complete relaxation. Moreover, every movement is characterized by a polarity of tension and restraint, power and suppleness.

FROM NECK TO TAIL

Another way to see the contrast between the horse and lion is to study the vertebral columns of the two animals. The neck is the anterior part of the vertebral column. With two exceptions—the manatee and three-toed sloth—every mammal's neck consists of seven vertebrae. This means that the elongation of the horse's neck is realized through the elongation of the individual vertebrae (fig. 9.2). In contrast, the lion's neck, like its limbs, is short and stout (fig. 9.3).

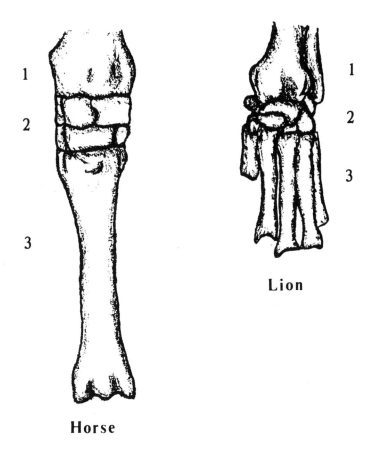

Lion

Horse

Fig. 9.5. Detail of the lower forelimb of horse and lion, illustrating the carpals' different forms: (1) distal end of radius and ulna (fused in horse), (2) carpals, (3) metacarpals. Author's drawing based on information in W. Ellenberger, H. Dittrich, and H. Baum, *An Atlas of Animal Anatomy for Artists* (New York: Dover, 1947).

The horse's spine—the middle part of the vertebral column—is fairly rigid, although it consists of more vertebrae than the lion's. As in the legs, interlocking surfaces and strong ligaments make the spine a stable, horizontal axis supporting the body through its very structure. This spine keeps essentially the same form under all conditions, whether the horse is galloping or lying. In contrast, the lion's spine is much more mobile; its capacity to flex, extend, and bend laterally is much greater. When a lion sprints, the spine rhythmically oscillates between concavity in expansion and arching convexity in contraction. And lying at rest, the lion can stretch out lengthwise or curl up. Because of this flexibility, the body can follow, in its form, any irregularities of the surface upon which the lion lies.

The vertebral column has its continuation in the tail, which can be said to be the animal's characteristic extension into the world behind it. The horse's streaming, long-haired tail emphasizes its vertical aspect. The tail hangs down, is blown by the wind, but also swishes to and fro. The muscular, bony core of the tail extends only into its upper half, while the rest consists of long strands of hair, a substance in which the animal no longer lives. In contrast, the lion lives in its muscular tail out to the very tip. The lion always holds its tail actively and never lets it hang down or drag. Perhaps more than any other organ, the tail with its fine undulating movements expresses the lion's momentary state and the inner direction of its alertness. In broadest terms, one can conclude that the horse's tail is an organ that is moved, while the lion's tail is informed by movement.

THE HEADS OF THE HORSE AND LION

As figure 9.6 suggests, the horse's head is striking in its length. Just as with the limbs, the part of the head farthest from the body proper is elongated. This distal portion of the skull is formed by long, tapering bony plates. The snout is not muscular and its form thus reveals the underlying bone structure in the same way the lower limbs appear as "skin and bone."

The head's high, broad rear portion is embedded in the neck and jaw muscles. The latter insert into the massive rear section of the lower part of the jaw. The center of gravity is therefore at the rear of the head, just as the rear of the horse is its most bulky aspect, as one can see from above (fig. 9.8).

The horse's organs for perceiving what is around and behind it are the nose, eyes, and ears. The eyes are positioned not only sidewards but quite far back in the skull. The horse cannot focus on what is directly before it, for example, the grass, which is not prey and, therefore, is not a point to be focused on but, rather, a surface to be grazed calmly. Moreover, in times of danger, the horse typically flees by means of its swift, enduring gallop; it does not attack like the lion. Fleeing involves no aim before the animal, no focal point; the direction is only "away from." Because of its wide field of vision, however, what is behind the horse remains part of its world. The contrast with the lion's aggressive, focal relation to its surroundings could hardly be greater.

As figure 9.6 illustrates, the horse's jaw is dominated by long rows of large cheek teeth. Each row forms one uniform surface that meets with its counterpart in grinding. The image of persistent grinding in which surface meets surface is paralleled by the image of the horse standing or running with its hard hooves striking the surface of the earth.

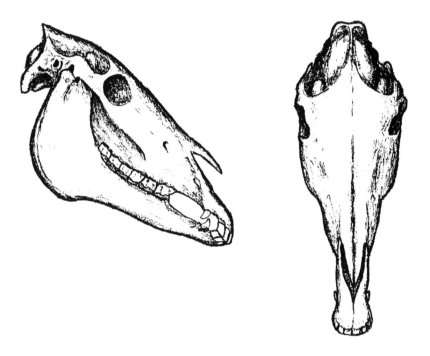

Fig. 9.6. Skull of horse. Author's drawings based on information in W. Ellenberger, H. Dittrich, and H. Baum, *An Atlas of Animal Anatomy for Artists* (New York: Dover, 1947).

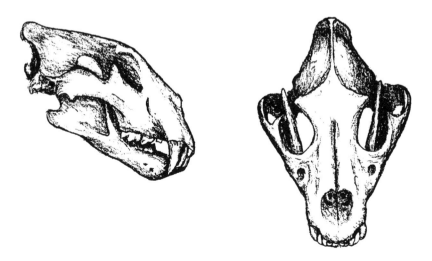

Fig. 9.7. Skull of lion. Author's drawings based on information in W. Ellenberger, H. Dittrich, and H. Baum, An Atlas of Animal Anatomy for Artists (New York: Dover, 1947).

Like the cheek teeth, the front teeth, or incisors, form uniform rows. All these teeth end evenly and the horse can easily tear grass. Characteristically, the one tooth type in mammals that is pointed and never forms surfaces that meet—the canine—is present in the horse only in a rudimentary form and, in mares, is missing altogether. Thus, the tendency toward the formation of unified, hard surfaces—in the horn of the hoof, in the tightly fit, stout bones, and in the rows of teeth—dominates in the horse. This important aspect of the language of the horse, revealed in its anatomy, corresponds to the constancy observable in its activity—standing, running, and grinding.

Figure 9.7 shows the lion's broad, compact skull—it is almost as wide as the shoulders and hips shown in figure 9.8. The back half of the skull is surrounded by a thick layer of muscles. The space between the broad arcs of the cheek bones and the cranium are filled with the massive jaw muscles. The skull ends at the front in the powerful gesture of the enormous canine teeth.

The lion's canines are as deeply rooted in the upper jaw as they protrude from it. The form of the canines—pointed and conical—dominates the structure of the other teeth as well. In great contrast to those of the horse, the lion's incisors are not broad and spatula-like; rather, they are small and have the form of short spikes. The cheek teeth do not form flat surfaces but possess pointed cusps that give them a jagged appearance. When the jaw clamps down (the jaw can only move vertically and there is little lateral movement), the surfaces pass by one another, forming shears that pierce and cut the flesh of the prey.

It is as though the forward thrusting movement of the lion has become frozen in the form of the canines. As we have seen, the same is true in the claws. There is a further accentuation of this tendency in the frontal positioning of the eyes, which lie quite far forward in the short skull. The gaze holds the prey, as it were, before it is grasped in claw and tooth. The male's mane is a majestic image of the forward thrust, which comes more to realization in the activity of the female, who is the dominant hunter among lions.

THE HORSE AND LION AS CONTRASTING WHOLES

I now want to present a condensed picture of the various qualities through which the horse and lion come to expression as unique wholes. The horse lives on the basis of its robust bone structure. Bone is life-compressed into solid, enduring form. The horse stands upon the ground in the same way that it stably rests upon its own limb bones. The hooves hit the ground when running; the teeth grind grass between their hard

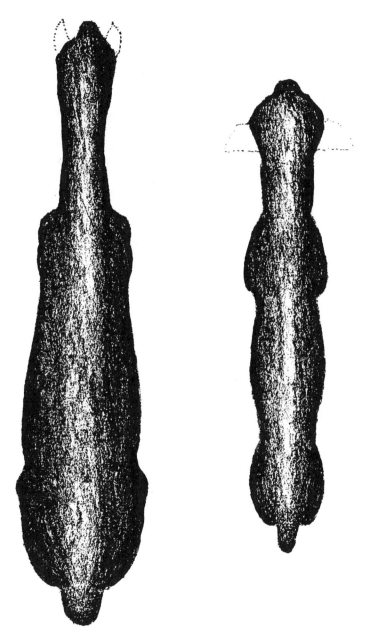

Fig. 9.8. Silhouette of horse and lion, viewed from above. Author's drawings based on information in W. Ellenberger, H. Dittrich, and H. Baum, *An Atlas of Animal Anatomy for Artists* (New York: Dover, 1947).

surfaces. The horse meets its world in activity through hard, compact surfaces. In addition, the horse shows stamina in all its activities—standing, running, grazing, grinding, digesting. Such stamina is the physiological and behavioral expression of the same stability revealed in the skeletal anatomy.

Nonetheless, the horse's bone structure is not overly encumbered by gravity; the long legs and neck elevate the horse in its surroundings. Despite its size, the horse's movements are graceful and light. Moreover, with its head held high, the horse is acutely aware in the breadth of the world around it. In contrast, other more bulky and compact hoofed grazing mammals—for example, the rhinoceros and bison—hold their heads below the body proper, as if pulled down by gravity.

In contrast to the horse, the lion lives in its muscles, which function through an interplay between tension and relaxation. The life of a lion oscillates between extremes—focused, powerful action in the hunt, followed by complete relaxation and lassitude.

Stocky limbs and skull express in form the predominance of muscle in the lion. Since its legs are bent when stalking, the lion must draw on enormous strength to hold its body close to the ground. This concentrated tonicity pours forth into the sheer might of its sinewy being when the lion surges, pulls its prey to the ground, and sinks its teeth into the flesh. The lion feeds ravenously upon the element in which it lives—muscle.

Only an animal that lives to such a degree in the power and tension of muscularity is capable of such complete relaxation. A lion can sleep curled up and entwined with the bodies of its kin, but it could never sleep while standing. It would collapse the moment its muscles relaxed. When the rested lion rises, it stretches every sinew.

Lion activity is not a matter of either force or relaxation. In the smoothness, softness, and agile muscular modulation of a moving lion, we can observe the interpenetration of tension and relaxation. The paws roll softly over the ground, and the tail undulates. As seen in the muscular fluidity of body movement, flexibility through joints—and not bony stability—predominates in the lion. This quality also manifests in behavior, for example, play between members of a pride often involves chasing, hitting, and biting. Lion play is a form of "relaxed tension" and, inasmuch, a reflection of the lion's way of life as a whole.

BEYOND HORSE AND LION

When we begin to discern the qualities that dominate in the horse and lion, we enter into an exploration of specific expressions of animalness.

The course I have taken here can be expanded in at least two directions. First, much of what I have suggested concerning the horse is also valid for the zebra, just as what I have said about the lion can be related to the tiger or leopard. A next step of differentiation would be to grasp the specific qualities of the species within its respective genus. As Adolf Portmann points out, the skeletons of the lion and tiger are very similar, yet their outer appearance is significantly and clearly distinct.[12] To begin to differentiate between these two species, therefore, we would need to consider such features as the color and pattern of the coat, differences in habitat, the fact that lions are the only species of cats that live in groups, and so forth.

Second, we can broaden our view to include other groups of mammals. The unique qualities of the giraffe stand vividly before the mind's eye when one has begun to penetrate the horse. The tendency towards elongation is carried to an extreme in a very particular way in the giraffe.[13] The giraffe does not merely have a long neck. Rather, this length is mirrored in the formation of the rest of its body, especially in the very long legs. The forelegs are longer than the hind legs and the giraffe must spread its forelegs to reach the ground with its mouth. In addition, the giraffe's snout is extremely long and the even longer tongue extends from the mouth to embrace and tear tree leaves. In contrast to the horse's trunk, however, the giraffe's trunk remains proportionately short.

Through a Goethean approach, each animal begins to reveal its unique way of being-in-the-world. Each animal is one-sided, and yet, in its one-sidedness, points beyond itself to a greater whole that encompasses all animals. By dwelling within particular animals and moving from one to the next, we see the broader concept "animal" gradually become filled with living content. Goethe's previously quoted words take on more concrete meaning: "Ultimately we will see the whole world of animals as a great element in which one species is created, or a least sustained, by and through another." This statement can be understood not only in external ecological terms (e.g., prey-predator relationships), but also in terms of the principles of animal formation (e.g., the dominance of a particular aspect—bone in the horse, muscle in the lion). To achieve Goethe's dynamic picture of animals, we begin with an open interest in the animal as a creature with its "own reason to be." We attend to the phenomena of animal life and picture each aspect of the animal exactly and vividly. We then must draw upon our capacity to recreate, as it were, the particular animal in our mind. The imagination begins to weave among the parts, and a picture of underlying patterns emerges. This is a demanding task because it involves, as Goethe says, "dissolving the particular without destroying the impression itself."[14] It calls for the faculty that Goethe called "exact imagination," which only develops through practice.[15] We must try again and again to gain the necessary inner flexibility to form a living picture of the animal. This way of knowing has a fluid quality, and its results cannot be fixed in any narrowly circumscribed definition.

At the same time, we must cultivate an inner tension that keeps us open for the new and does not let us become overly enamored with the knowledge already gained. As Goethe says:

> For here at this pass, this transition from empirical evidence to judgment, cognition to application, all the inner enemies of man lie in wait: imagination, which sweeps him away on its wings before he knows his feet have left the ground; impatience; haste; self-satisfaction; rigidity; formalistic thought; prejudice; ease; frivolity; fickleness—this whole throng and its retinue. Here they lie in ambush and surprise not only the active observer but also the contemplative one who appears safe from all passion.[16]

Through Goethe's method, we begin to enter into the life of nature because we are on the way to grasping the whole that lives in every part. This approach is even more timely today than it was in Goethe's day, when the external manipulation of life was only in its advent. Genetic engineering, for example, considers and manipulates organisms as complicated mechanisms for human purposes. Its practical power is unquestionable and growing. But such manipulative power is not based on knowledge of the organism qua organism.

When rat-sized transgenic mice are "produced" in a laboratory, the question of the mouse's size as an essential quality of its wholeness is not raised. But if the mouse becomes so heavy that it would break the plant stem it would need to climb to gather seeds, then one has—by manipulating a part—radically changed the whole animal and its relationship to its environment. Such manipulation is performed with little awareness of the implications for the organism, because the living organism per se has never been taken into consideration. In this respect the ignorance of the life of organisms in our day is staggering, and Goethe's approach is more needed than ever.

NOTES

1. Some examples of this research include: Jochen Bockemühl, "Die Bewegung des Tieres als Ausdruck seiner Innerlichkeit," in *Elemente der Naturwissenschaft*, no. 27 (1977): pp. 32–45; Brian Goodwin, *How The Leopard*

Changed Its Spots (New York: Charles Scribner's Sons, 1994); Frits H. Julius, *Das Tier zwischen Mensch und Kosmos* (Stuttgart: Freies Geistesleben, 1970); Friedrich A. Kipp, "Bezahnung und Bildungsidee des Organismus," in *Goetheanistische Naturwissenschaft*, edited by Wolfgang Schad, Bd. 3 (Stuttgart: Freies Geistesleben, 1983), pp. 167–79; Ernst Michael Kranich, *Von der Gewissheit zur Freies Wissenschaft der Evolution* (Stuttgart: Freis Geistesleben, 1989), pp. 37–49; Ernst Michael Kranich, "Der Loewe," in *Erziehungskunst*, Heft 10 (Oktober 1993): pp. 195–202; Mark Riegner, "Toward a Holistic Understanding of Place: Reading a Landscape through its Flora and Fauna," in *Dwelling, Seeing, and Designing: Toward a Phenomenological Ecology*, edited by David Seamon (Albany: State University of New York Press, 1993), pp. 181–215; Wolfgang Schad, *Man and Mammals: Toward a Biology of Form.* (Garden City, N.Y.: Waldorf Press, 1977).

2. Work illustrating the Neo-Darwinian perspective includes: John Maynard Smith, *The Theory of Evolution* (New York: Penguin, 1975); Ernst Mayr, *Population, Species, and Evolution* (Cambridge, Mass.: Belknap Press, 1970); A. S. Romer, *Vertebrate Paleontology* (Chicago: University of Chicago Press, 1966); George G. Simpson, *Horses* (New York: Oxford University Press, 1951); George G. Simpson, *The Meaning of Evolution* (New Haven, Conn.: Yale University Press, 1976); J. Z. Young, *The Life of Vertebrates* (London: Oxford University Press, 1973).

3. Goethe, *Scientific Studies*, p. 307.

4. Henri Bortoft, "Counterfeit and Authentic Wholes: Finding a Way to Dwell In Nature," in *Dwelling, Place and Environment*, edited by David Seamon and Robert Mugerauer (New York: Columbia University Press, 1985), p. 299. This article is reprinted as chapter 12 in this volume.

5. Goethe, *Scientific Studies*, p. 54.

6. Ibid., p. 55.

7. James Gray, *Animal Locomotion* (London: Weidenfeld and Nicolson, 1968), p. 279.

8. George Schaller, *The Serengeti Lion* (Chicago: University of Chicago Press, 1972), p. 268.

9. Quoted in Schaller, *The Serengeti Lion*, p. 120.

10. R. Nickel et al., *Lehrbuch der Anatomie der Haustiere, Bd. I: Bewegungsapparat* (Berlin and Hamburg: Paul Parey Verlag, 1968), p. 402.

11. Gray, *Animal Locomotion*, p. 250f.

12. Adolf Portmann, *Die Tiergestalt* (Basel: Verlag Friedrich Reinhardt AG, 1960), p. 33ff.; also see Adolf Portmann, *Animal Forms and Patterns* (New York: Schocken, 1967).

13. Ernst Michael Kranich, *Von der Gewissheit zur Wissenschaft der Evolution* (Stuttgart: Freies Geistesleben, 1989), p. 44f.

14. Goethe, *Scientific Studies*, p. 75.

15. Ibid., p. 46.
16. Ibid., p. 14.

10

Mark Riegner and John Wilkes

Flowforms and the Language of Water

Goethe met his world with the insight of an artist and the discerning mind of a scientist.[1] He produced masterful works of literature and also made significant scientific contributions to botany, animal morphology, chromatics, and meteorology.[2] To Goethe, nature could be comprehended through an artistic reading: "He to whom nature begins to reveal her open secrets will feel an irresistible yearning for her most worthy interpreter: Art."[3]

In this essay, we describe a Goethean phenomenological approach to understanding water. For such study, one must develop appropriate interpretive faculties because water speaks a language of movement. What follows, therefore, is an exploration of one way in which this language of movement can be interpreted intuitively and then put to practical use. Our focus is *Flowforms*—sculpted vessels by means of which streaming water is brought into rhythmic movement. First, we review the Goethean research on the movement of water and then illustrate how this understanding became the foundation for Flowform design.

A GOETHEAN APPROACH TO NATURE

Understanding a language of movement requires a reorientation in the way we observe natural phenomena. Goethe pioneered a dynamic,

233

participatory approach to the observation of nature. To Goethe, an isolated phenomenon held little value; only when it was interrelated with other forms did its significance emerge as one element of a larger progression, or "metamorphosis," as he called it.

Goethe's method was to search for an invariant principle amid a family of diverse phenomena—in other words, to apprehend the unifying movement among changing forms, the unity within diversity.[4] By meticulously observing and interrelating the anatomical structures of plants, for example, he believed that a unifying principle would emerge—the universal within the particular. He called this ideal element the "archetypal plant," or common "idea" that comes forth through the metamorphosing forms. Goethe's archetypal plant was neither a static blueprint nor a fixed notion but came to presence through an active cognitive effort that bears little resemblance to our ordinary static mental representations.[5]

Rudolf Steiner (1861–1925), the Austrian philosopher, scientist, and educator, was one thinker who further elaborated the methods of observation initiated by Goethe. Steiner built a philosophical yet practical foundation for developing the latent possibilities of cognition explored by his predecessor.[6] Steiner argued that, by training one's observational skills and by becoming increasingly aware of one's cognizing activity, the student would be led toward an experience of "the idea within reality."[7] Moreover, Steiner maintained that if artists could school themselves to apprehend the inherent principles manifesting in, and giving order to, natural phenomena, they could create forms with an inherent consistency. The result, he argued, would not be naturalism— that is, a copying of nature—but a free expression of the underlying formative principles working in nature.

THE WATER RESEARCH OF
THEODOR SCHWENK

Inspired by both Goethe and Steiner, Theodor Schwenk (1910–1986), while director of the Institute for Flow Sciences in Herrischried, Germany, investigated the metamorphic potential of water as manifested in fluid dynamics.[8] Underlying Schwenk's research was a recognition of water's close affinity to living processes in that the existence of all life depends on water, and all organisms undergo a highly fluid phase during their development. Vertebrates, for example, pass through a mostly fluid state during their early embryogenesis, while many unicellular aquatic organisms never fully "solidify" out of their watery environment and often bear resemblances to fluid forms, such as the vortex.[9]

Schwenk maintained that a dedicated, comprehensive study of water would provide a schooling of observation and thinking necessary to guide the researcher in unravelling the secrets of the living world:

> Through watching water . . . with unprejudiced eyes, our way of thinking becomes changed and more suited to the understanding of what is alive. This transformation of our way of thinking is . . . a decisive step that must be taken in the present day.[10]

Schwenk's approach, based on Goethean phenomenology, provides a path whereby one can enter holistically into a thoughtful, dynamic relationship with natural phenomena. By acquainting ourselves with water in the way initiated by Schwenk, we may gain an appreciation for this fluid upon which all life depends. In regard to water's metamorphic potential—whether in a falling raindrop, meandering stream, curling wave, tumbling cascade, or swirling vortex—water adopts a host of forms, while always remaining the same, undifferentiated substance. Schwenk observed that, at times, the forms of water showed a remarkable degree of order as if it had a life and intention of its own.

This quality of consistency is most easily observed in a laboratory demonstration. If a brush is drawn in a straight line through a shallow tray of standing water into which glycerin has been thoroughly mixed, an orderly train of vortices appears. These spiralling patterns can be made visible by prior dusting of the water surface with lycopodium powder (fig. 10.1). The overall form bears a resemblance to the developmental process seen in living forms such as the sequence of leaves from the base to the apex of many herbaceous plants (fig. 10.2).

Working in the field of projective geometry, mathematician George Adams (1894–1963), who was also inspired by Goethe and Steiner, undertook a geometrical study of organic forms in which he discovered that many living organisms exhibit a tendency to build surfaces on the basis of movements that can be described mathematically as "path curves" or lines of flow.[11] Adams also became interested in the possible relationship between such ideal surfaces and water's life-supporting capacities. This latter topic led to his collaborating in research with hydrologist Schwenk. In the 1950s, the two men founded the Institute for Flow Sciences, of which Schwenk became director. A major aim of the Institute was to study the rhythmic qualities of water and its relation to life and natural forms.[12]

THE RHYTHMS OF WATER

Working as research assistant to George Adams in the early 1960s, sculptor John Wilkes pondered this resemblance of the forms of moving

Fig. 10.1. A train of vortices produced when a brush is drawn in a straight line through a shallow tray of standing water mixed with glycerin. Photograph © John Wilkes, used with permission.

Fig. 10.2. Leaf metamorphosis in the Small Scabious (*Scabiosa columbaria*). Note the changing forms of the leaves from bottom to top and compare with the changing pattern of the vortex train in fig. 10.1. From a plant pressing by John Wilkes, used with permission.

water to those of the organic world. He observed that the formative processes underlying organic growth are essentially of a fluid nature. For example, many organisms undergo a continuous metamorphic change from stage to stage as they develop; there is an underlying continuity of movement—a kind of flow—through the transformations. He noted, however, that one must differentiate between physically continuous growth processes and physically discontinuous metamorphic processes. A leaf, for example, passes through innumerable form changes as it grows, but between each leaf on a stem there is physical discontinuity (see fig. 10.2).

As an artist who also worked with clay, which is itself a fluid albeit highly viscous medium, Wilkes was already aware of the process of moving and shaping the form; it is this movement and activity out of which form arises. Form, in a sense, is born of movement and not merely determined by mass. In the realm of living organisms, Wilkes now saw form as arising and maintaining itself not through arbitrary movements but through precise, rhythmical processes.[13] In all living things, rhythms are present. The pulse of blood through arteries and veins, the alternating expansion and contraction of lungs, the peristaltic movement of an earthworm tunneling through the soil, the pulsating, unbrella-like body of a swimming jellyfish—each of these movements in nature gives expression to specific rhythms. Wilkes believed that somewhere hidden in this phenomenon of rhythmical movement was the secret to water's way of being. For him, the fact that all living things depend on water implied that regenerative processes are continually at work within flowing water, otherwise it would be unable to maintain its function as a life-sustaining element.

As Schwenk had observed, rhythmical motions are frequently evident in water phenomena: the rising and falling of tides, the repeated crashing of waves on a beach, the movement of ocean currents, and the earth's hydrologic cycle. Without careful control and a treatment to increase viscosity, as shown in the vortex train described earlier, orderly forms exist only fleetingly and then quickly disintegrate. Apparently, water can manifest its potential for creating orderly forms within itself only momentarily and then returns to the state the poet Novalis called "sensitive chaos," the phrase Schwenk chose for the title of his book.[14]

The Creation of Flowforms

In nature, water's tendency to create internal order out of disorder is much less apparent than in controlled demonstrations. Wilkes wondered if it might be possible to design a sequence of forms through which water could fulfill its potential to manifest an orderly metamorphic process. Could one create artistically an "organ of metamorphosis" for water? Such a sequence of forms might bring to physical expression the delicate potential for ordered movement that appears to be inherent in the nature of water.

The most obvious question was what these forms should look like. Here, again, Wilkes turned to nature for a clue. Freely flowing water rarely shows any kind of consistent order or symmetry; rather, chaos and asymmetry are the rule. In living organisms, however, water is contained within symmetrical forms where order and rhythm predominate. As the main constituent of sap, blood, lymph, and other bodily fluids, water circulates continuously in distinct rhythms. Although it is in constant movement, water can nevertheless become the "bearer of symmetry" when it is internalized in living organisms. What might happen if a freely flowing asymmetrical watercourse were similarly contained within a symmetrical form—that is, by mirroring its boundaries?

Water moving down a slope, as seen in a river or in rain running down a windshield, takes a meandering course, veering to one side and then to the other. Mimicking this pattern, Wilkes built a flat, sloping base on which he made an experimental channel with meandering walls that were mirrored on either side of a central axis. The meandering walls alternately curved outward and then drew in to form narrow apertures (fig. 10.3). The flow rate was determined by adjusting the slope and regulating the volume of incoming water.

As water flowed through the symmetrical channel, Wilkes observed a remarkable occurrence. At one place in the system, the dimensions of the aperture were such that there was a momentary hesitation as water flowed from one section into the next. Had the aperture been wider, water would have flowed through uninterrupted; if narrower, the upper section would have filled and overflowed. The unanticipated hesitation induced an alternating left and right deviation of flow into the lateral cavities of the channel. With additional experimentation, it was possible to achieve a similar vortical movement in each cavity. The overall movement became a figure eight, or lemniscate, with one side rotating clockwise, the other counterclockwise (fig. 10.4).

Left and right rotational motions were thus joined in one rhythmical movement, which Wilkes later termed a "vortical meander." This rhythmical motion, induced by the interrelationships of the channel's surfaces, was also evident as water streamed from the exit in a waterfall. The regular, rhythmic pulsation reminded Wilkes of his own pulse and strengthened his impression that, solely through resistance and not through a mechanism, water in this system had been brought into a

Fig. 10.3. Diagram (*lower left*), showing the influence of streaming water on a straight channel. The meander, mirrored, creates an expanding and contracting channel. Water rotates in the cavities (*middle section*); with special proportions (*lower section*), the flow begins to oscillate.

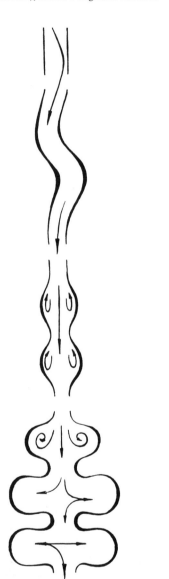

Fig. 10.4. Schematic representation (upper right), showing the development of water movement from a rotation to the lemniscatory pulse within the cavities of a Flowform.

Drawings © John Wilkes, used with permission.

condition of movement and rhythm similar to the circulation within living organisms.

DEVELOPMENTS IN FLOWFORM
RESEARCH AND DESIGN

Thus, through empirical studies and the grace of serendipity, the *Flowform Method*—the technique used to design channels that enable rhythmical movements to be generated in water streaming through them—was discovered in early 1970.[15] The design of the channel soon evolved into a series of independent vessels, each corresponding to a section of the original experimental conduit. The vessels were typically arranged on an incline to form a cascade (fig. 10.5).

Through subsequent experimentation, Wilkes found that the condition of symmetry could be relaxed without losing the oscillating, lemniscatory flow and, consequently, the movement became potentially much more dynamic. The proportions of the vessels, however, had to be precise for the Flowform to function. The determination of the parameters—dimension and shape of the inlet and outlet; the distance between them; the flow, the gradient, and the shape of each vessel—was made empirically by trial and error. Countless adjustments, removals and additions of materials, reshaping, restructuring, testing and retesting were necessary to arrive at a form that produced the characteristic lemniscatory flow.

Now was the time to return to Adams' initiative concerning an investigation of the possible relationship between the movement of water and path-curve surfaces. The Flowform Method afforded an opportunity, hitherto unavailable, to allow water to make contact with mathematical surfaces by means of rhythmical vortical movements. Wilkes demonstrated how variations in path-curve surfaces had resultant effects on water movement and thus how path curves could be studied and understood.[16]

To date, numerous Flowform designs of all kinds have been developed, cast in a variety of materials—mainly reconstituted stone—and integrated as aesthetic features in cities, gardens, offices, schools, and park landscapes.[17] Initially, designs consisted of a single symmetrical, or asymmetrical, form repeated in a series. By the mid-1970s, however, metamorphic sequences were developed that incorporated forms of different sizes and shapes. One such cascade, the "Akalla" model in Stockholm, designed in 1974, is set on a rocky slope of a children's recreation center, and contains Flowforms of three sizes, which are used in no fixed order but in a number of combinations. For the "Olympia"

Fig. 10.5. The "Malmö" Flowform at Sundet in the Norwegian mountains. Photograph © John Wilkes, used with permission.

cascade in London, a set of Flowforms was designed in 1977 to demonstrate a sequential development of the lemniscatory movement. For the Nederlandse Middenstands Bank headquarters (now ING) in Amsterdam, in addition to a series of large Flowforms, in the early 1980s, Wilkes, with the assistance of Nigel Wells, developed small-scale forms, which are used in a gently sloping ramp handrail over forty meters long; water circulating through the building helps regulate humidity, enhances aesthetics, and was intended to provide oxygenated water for the indoor plants.[18] A further innovation in Flowform design, which made its debut in Holland in 1981, is a circular sculpture three meters in diameter in which water rises through a central orifice and flows down into three paired cavities to generate three shifting leminscatory movements (fig. 10.6 and fig. 10.7).

A special convex-based "Rocker" Flowform has been created by designer Andrew Joiner for children (fig. 10.8). Water is placed in a central four-leaf clover depression and made to oscillate by a child, or two children, standing on the sculpture and rocking back and forth. This Flowform can be used therapeutically with autistic children, who must face each other, reach out to grasp the other for support, and coordinate their movements in order to produce the figure-eight forms in the water beneath. In this sense, Flowforms can work as a powerful visual, tactile, and auditory stimulus.

THE ECOLOGICAL VALUE OF FLOWFORMS

In addition to their aesthetic appeal, Flowforms have significant environmental applications.[19] In fact, the original research of Schwenk, Adams, and Wilkes was motivated by a concern for the quality of the earth's water, a globally threatened resource. Behind Wilkes' efforts is the wish to discover whether water's life-supporting capacities can be regenerated optimally through rhythmical movement, especially in relationship to either empirically or mathematically designed surfaces. He points to the fact that a river, if allowed to move freely, will purify and regenerate itself, in part, through biological processes. Can applications of the pulsating vortical meander induced by Flowforms significantly enhance such processes, particularly when they are under stress?

Preliminary investigations indicated that Flowform-treated water not only was penetrated by rhythmical movements in support of biological processes but also became highly oxygenated and thus showed promise for wastewater treatment. This potential became reality for a college community of some two hundred people in Järna, Sweden. Dissatisfied with its original biological water purification system, the community

Fig. 10.6. Diagram of water movement in the radial "Ashdown" Flowform. Drawing © John Wilkes, used with permission.

Fig. 10.7. The "Amsterdam" Flowform. Located at the International Landscape Exhibition 82, in Amsterdam, the Netherlands. The Flowform was designed in the United Kingdom and installed by Herbert Dreiseitl. Photograph by Herbert Dreiseitl, used with permission.

Fig. 10.8. The "Rocker" Flowform
Designed by Andrew Joiner, this
Flowform can be used by children or
adults.
Photograph © John Wilkes, used with
permission.

founder, Arne Klingborg, looked to Flowforms for a functional yet artistic solution. Renovation began in 1973, using several cascades designed to induce vigorous and varied rhythmical movements (fig. 10.9).

Since then, a number of Flowform cascades have been added to the Järna system in association with more ponds and filter beds, representing various wetland ecosystems. Although there are seasonal fluctuations in efficiency, coliform bacterial concentrations in the treated water have generally been below officially acceptable levels permissible for public swimming pools. As well as its cleaning function, the entire site serves as a bird sanctuary and community park to which thousands of visitors are welcomed annually. To accommodate the community's increasing population, an additional system has been added along with current improvement of the original system to enhance efficiency.

How do Flowforms affect water quality? Funds for intensified research are sorely lacking, but modest beginnings have been made.

Fig. 10.9. The "Akalla" Flowform. Located in Järna, Sweden, it is used for wastewater treatment. Photograph © John Wilkes, used with permission.

Researchers at Warmonderhof, a Dutch Biodynamic agricultural college, compared the life-supporting qualities of Flowform-treated water with those of water subjected to a simple step cascade. Polluted water was diverted through the parallel cascades, from which it streamed through separate pond and channel systems (fig. 10.10).

In these particular circumstances, both cascades demonstrated the capacity to aid the purification process. Four years of analyses, reported in 1986, found no consistent differences in chemical constitution between the two treatments. Plant growth in water from the two cascades, however, showed a marked distinction. The step-cascade water stimulated vegetative plant growth—leaf development—comparable to that of a shaded, calm, downstream, eutrophic section of a river. The movements induced by Flowforms supported relatively more generative, or floral and seed, development similar to that of well-illuminated, open rapids in an upstream, oligotrophic part of a river system.

In other words, the animated, rhythmical motions of water passing through Flowforms produced a more ecologically vital condition. Furthermore, the macrofaunal composition in the step-cascade pool was biased toward species that prefer a darker habitat and whose life cycle includes a winged stage, for example, species such as midges. The Flowform-associated pond tended to support macrofauna with a fully

Fig. 10.10. A purification system for comparative research. *Right* with three Flowform cascades; *far left* a step cascade. Located at Warmonderhof, a Dutch Biodynamic agricultural college. Photograph © John Wilkes, used with permission.

aquatic life cycle, such as crustaceans and water mites, typical of the upper water column and surface.

Besides their potential use in water purification, Flowforms hold promise in stored-water treatment and transport, irrigation, treatment of desalinated water, and pharmaceuticals. They may also be useful in aquaculture systems and as fish ladders for seasonally migrating species. In recent years, especially in Germany, there has been an emphasis on designs for water treatment in food processing activities, ranging from beer brewing and bread baking to air-conditioning for milk and meat-product curing cellars. In addition, applications are being designed for treatment of drinking water for cattle and for purification in lagoon and reed-bed systems, as well as a project for a new bakery in which water will be carefully prepared by running over long granite channels and then moved rhythmically through Flowforms.

THE SEVENFOLD FLOWFORM CASCADE

In an ambitious project, John Wilkes, together with colleagues Nigel Wells, Hansjörg Palm, and others, designed a Flowform sequence that artistically mirrors the rhythms of the earth's hydrologic cycle. With his artist's eye, Wilkes sees the hydrologic cycle in two gestures—contraction and expansion—a key polarity central to Goethe's world view. Clouds, rainfall, and the confluence of a river's tributaries are part of a contracting movement that brings water to the earth. Then the delta, the ocean into which it empties, and evaporation release water again into the atmosphere in a gesture of expansion.

This imaginative view of the hydrologic cycle inspired the design of a cascade consisting of seven vessels (fig. 10.11); although its idea was conceived in 1970, it was not until 1985 that it was possible to finance the construction of the first prototype. In the so-called Sevenfold Flowform Cascade, each vessel inlet is narrow, while the main body of the vessel widens, allowing freedom of movement, before closing in again to form the outlet. So, too, does the whole Sevenfold Flowform Cascade begin with three smaller forms, in which gravity acts strongly to create vigorous movements. The broader, more horizontal middle vessel is less dominated by gravity, and thus the water exhibits more freedom of movement outward toward the periphery in slow rhythms. The next forms progressively contract in size, and rhythms accelerate again.

Throughout this cascade, the gestures of the lemniscates change from one vessel to the next. From the entry vessel to the last in the series, the wings of the lemniscates shift their axes forward in the direction of the flow, while the crossing points gradually migrate to the rear (fig. 10.12). Thus, in the Sevenfold Flowform Cascade, Wilkes attempts to recreate artistically a wide spectrum of qualities and rhythms naturally inherent in water (fig. 10.13 and fig. 10.14).

The Sevenfold Flowform Cascade is being studied mathematically to identify its rhythmical processes and to understand their relationships. In efforts to quantify the rhythms, mathematician Nick Thomas in England, as well as a group of scientists in Trondheim, Norway, has used Fast-Fourier Transformations calculated from computer data collected by special probes that Thomas developed.[20] It is evident that each vessel induces not only a swinging rhythm as liquid flows from one side to the other, but also secondary and tertiary rhythms as well: water level repeatedly rises and falls in the vessels, and water exits each one in a rhythmical pulsation.

Just as the human organism embodies a rhythmical relationship between pulse and breath of 4 to 1, so too can Flowforms be developed to generate specific relationships between the various rhythms they produce. Rhythms within and between vessels can thus be attuned and harmonized to create a veritable symphony of movement.

As discussed above, such motions apparently enhance water's life-supporting capacity. What combinations of surface relationships and

Fig. 10.11. Original concept (*below, left*) for a sevenfold Flowform cascade.

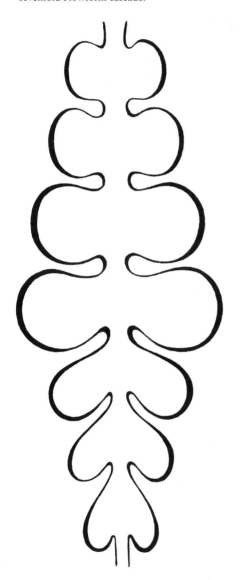

Fig. 10.12. Diagram (*above, right*) of the transformation of the lemniscate as water moves from an entry vessel through the Sevenfold Flowform Cascade I. Designers: John Wilkes and Nigel Wells. Drawings © John Wilkes, used with permission.

Fig. 10.13. The Sevenfold Flowform Cascade II Located at Chalice Well, Glastonbury, England. Designers: John Wilkes and Hansjöerg Palm.

Fig. 10.14. Diagram of the Sevenfold Flowform Cascade II Located at Chalice Well, Glastonbury, England. Designers: John Wilkes and Hansjöerg Palm.

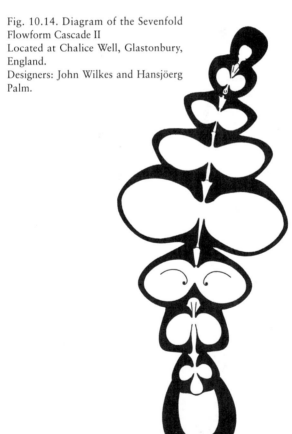

rhythm harmonics would best meet the requirements of wastewater treatment? irrigation? storage? drinking? Answers to these and other questions await further investigation. As with the discovery and initial development of Flowforms, the path of inquiry will be one that unites artistic skill and insight with scientific clarity and precision, much in the Goethean tradition.

NOTES

1. This essay is a revised version of an article originally published in *Orion Nature Quarterly* 7, 1 (winter 1988): 50–57. The authors and editors wish to thank the publisher for permission to draw on this earlier work.

2. Goethe, *Goethe: Scientific Studies*, ed. and trans Douglas Miller (New York: Suhrkamp, 1988). For a useful cross section of professional reactions to Goethean science, see F. Amrine, F. J. Zucker, and H. Wheeler, eds., *Goethe and the Sciences: A Reappraisal* (Dordrecht: D. Reidel, 1987).

3. Theodor Schwenk, *Sensitive Chaos: the Creation of Flowing Forms in Water and Air*, trans. O. Whicher and J. Wrigley (London: Rudolf Steiner Press, 1965), p. 80.

4. R. H. Brady, "Form and Cause in Goethe's Morphology," in F. Amrine, F. Zucker, and H. Wheeler, eds., *Goethe and the Sciences: A Reappraisal* (Dordrecht: D. Reidel, 1987), pp. 257–300; see also Brady's chapter 5 in this volume.

5. On this kind of active cognition, see H. Bortoft, *The Wholeness of Nature: Goethe's Science of Conscious Participation in Nature* (Hudson, N.Y.: Lindesfrane Press).

6. See, for example, R. Steiner, *Goethe's World View*, trans. W. Lindeman (Spring Valley, N.Y.: Mercury Press, 1985; originally published 1918); and R. Steiner, *Goethean Science*, trans. W. Lindeman (Spring Valley, N.Y.: Mercury Press, 1988; originally published as introductions to Goethe's natural-scientific works, edited by R. Steiner, 1883–1897).

7. Steiner, *Goethean Science*, p. 91.

8. Schwenk, *Sensitive Chaos* (see note 3); see also M. Riegner, "The Many Faces of Water." *Golden Blade* 41 (1989): 114–23.

9. One example is *Vorticella*; see Schwenk, *Sensitive Chaos*, pp. 20–21.

10. Schwenk, *Sensitive Chaos*, p. 11.

11. See L. Edwards, *The Vortex of Life: Nature's Patterns in Space and Time* (Edinburgh: Floris Books, 1993).

12. For an introduction to Adams' work, see O. Whicher, *Projective Geometry* (London: Rudolf Steiner Press, 1971); for an in-depth treatment of Adams' application of projective geometry to the study of organic form, see G. Adams and O. Whicher, *The Plant between Sun and Earth*, 2nd ed. (London: Rudolf Steiner Press, 1980).

13. J. Wilkes, "Flow Design Research Relating to Flowforms," *Golden Blade* 46 (1993): 72–84.

14. Schwenk, *Sensitive Chaos*, p. 9.

15. J. Wilkes, "The Flowform Method," *Transforming Art* 4, 2 (1994): 41–48.

16. This theme has been explored by mathematician Lawrence Edwards; see L. Edwards, *The Vortex of Life* (note 11); and L. Edwards, "The Universe as Organism in Space and Time," *Golden Blade* 46 (1993): 11–22.

17. Currently, examples of Flowforms are found in a dozen European countries. They are also represented in New Zealand, Australia, South Africa, Brazil, Taiwan, India, Canada, and the United States. The early designs were made by Wilkes in his workshop at Emerson College in Sussex, England, and later in collaboration with colleagues Nigel Wells, Andrew Joiner, Iain Trousdell, Mark Baxter, Hansjörg Palm, Nick Weidmann, and others. Associated work has been developed in Germany beginning in 1979 by Herbert Dreiseitl and later in 1987 in Denmark by Hanne Keis.

In the United States, individuals working with Flowforms include Christopher Mann of Michael Fields Agricultural Institute, East Troy, Wisconsin; Chris Hecht of Sandpoint, Indiana; and Jennifer Greene, of the Water Research Institute of Blue Hill, Maine, and authorized to distribute Flowforms designed in the United Kingdom. Activities have extended to a number of other countries with the intention to create a worldwide association to support Flowform research and development.

For a discussion of Flowforms as landscape features, see D. Valbracht, "Flowforms in Landscape Architecture" (master's thesis, Department of Landscape Architecture, Graduate School of Design, Harvard University, 1983).

18. See H. Maclean, "Banking on Nature's Power and Poetry," *Design Spirit* 2 (winter/spring 1990): 8–14.

19. See I. Trousdell, "Virbela Flowforms: Increasing Water's Capacity to Support Life," in *New Directions for Farming and Gardening in New Zealand* (Auckland: Random House, 1989).

20. N. Thomas, "Flowform Rhythms," *Science Forum* 4 (1983): 16–19.

III

The Future of
Goethean Science

11

Alan P. Cottrell

The Resurrection of Thinking and the Redemption of Faust

Goethe's New Scientific Attitude

In the first "study" scene of Goethe's *Faust*, the eminent theologian soon realizes the poodle he has allowed to follow him home is no ordinary beast.[1] A series of incantations quickly conjures forth the devil Mephistopheles, who describes his destructive vocation:

> I am the Spirit that Denies!
> And justly so: for all things, from the Void
> Called forth, deserve to be destroyed:
> 'T were better, then, were naught created.
> Thus, all which you as sin have rated,—
> Destruction,—aught with evil blent,—
> That is my proper element.[2]

In our times when humankind has achieved the dubious distinction of elevating the arts of destruction to the potential for total annihilation, these words speak more powerfully than ever. Goethe knew the perversity of denial's spirit intimately. Yet in his time the threat seemed perhaps rather less than the all-encompassing mood of obliteration that casts its paralysis today. A certain optimism prevailed, which reveals itself in Mephistopheles' sense of frustration as a would-be destroyer:

And truly 'tis not much, when all is done.
That which to Naught is in Resistance set,—
The Something of this clumsy world,—has yet,
With all that I have undertaken,
Not been by me disturbed or shaken:
From earthquake, tempest, wave, volcano's brand,
Back into quiet settle sea and land!
And that damned stuff, the bestial, human brood,—
What use, in having that to play with?
How many I have made away with!
And ever circulates a newer, fresher blood.
It makes me furious, such things beholding:
From Water, Earth, and Air unfolding,
A thousand germs break forth and grow,
In dry, and wet, and warm, and chilly;
And had I not the flame reserved, why, really,
There's nothing special of my own to show![3]

Mephistopheles lies, of course, in claiming fire as his own. In the end it will burn him as well.[4] Nevertheless, his frustration is real. The earth is healthy and reconstitutes itself after every catastrophe. In the elements air, water, and earth and the four qualities of which the Greeks considered them to be composed ("In dry, and wet, and warm, and chilly"), countless seeds spring to life: "A thousand germs break forth and grow." Here is the optimism of an earlier age: destruction spread right and left, yet always in the end overcome by the natural vitality of the earth itself. Nature provides the seeds of this renewal, and it provides them in abundance.

How can we look at the picture today? The earth's vitality deteriorates. Through unthinking acts of exploitation, the soil dies and the list of newly extinct species grows daily, while the specter of atomic incineration remains.

OBJECTIVE THINKING

This essay suggests that, in Goethe's new scientific attitude, beginnings have been made that, if clearly understood and put into practice, may illuminate the image of the "thousand germs" in quite a new way in keeping with the realities of our contemporary state of affairs. With this in mind, we shall now have a closer look at one central element in Goethe's endeavors: his *gegenständliches Denken,* or "objective thinking."

Goethe owes the term to Heinroth's *Lehrbuch der Anthropologie* (1822), in which the author applies it to Goethe's thought. Goethe's acknowledgment and elaboration of the term as a description of his method is developed in the essay "Significant Help from a Single, Ingenious Phrase" (1823).[5] After acknowledging the origin of the term, Goethe explains that he has been concerned to describe his way of viewing both *Nature* and also *himself*. In this connection he refers to the essay, "The Experiment as Mediator between Object and Subject" (1792, published 1823).[6] There then follows an important caveat on the dangers of one-sided introspection:

> I hereby confess that the great and so important-sounding admonition "Know thyself" has ever seemed suspicious to me—a cabal on the part of secretly conspiring priests wanting, by means of unattainable demands to confuse mankind, to seduce it away from activity directed toward the outer world into an inward-directed, false contemplativeness. Man knows himself only to the extent that he knows the world; he becomes aware of himself only within the world, and aware of the world only within himself. Every object, well contemplated, opens up a new organ within us.[7]

Goethe's skepticism is eminently healthy, for the one-sidedly introspective pursuit of self-knowledge can easily veer off into illusion and the hubris that prompts Faust to equate his spiritual stature with that of the Earth Spirit, until he is brought back to his senses by the spirit's stinging rejection: "Thou'rt like the Spirit which thou comprehendest,/Not me!"[8] Here, Goethe rejects only the overly introspective pursuit of self-knowledge, not the pursuit itself. When balanced by a healthy study of the world, it is appropriate, for the contemplation of every object unfolds new organs of awareness. As always with Goethe, it is a question of establishing and sustaining a healthy balance.

We may recall that Faust, too, sought knowledge of the world—deeper knowledge than the reductionistic methodologies of academic thought could yield:

> That I may detect the inmost force
> Which binds the world, and guides its course;
> Its germs, productive powers explore,
> And rummage in empty words no more![9]

The "germs" or "seeds" of which Faust speaks are not those scattered outwardly by nature. The word *Samen*, which Goethe very likely owes to Paracelsus, refers to the living spiritual essence of nature itself. Faust's knowledge of the world shall be alive—not divorced from the realm of value or from the moral domain. As Faust says, "I do not pretend I could be a teacher / To help or convert a fellow-creature."[10]

Faust's dilemma is that of modern individuals as well. We also seek to grasp the world not in terms of archaic consciousness but through that freedom that exercises mature self-determination. We also seek to know ". . . the inmost force / Which binds the world, and guides its course," but our reductionistic thinking prompts us to conceive of this inner essence not as living spirituality but as an increasingly finite set of physical particles, units of energy, and, in the end, varying "probabilities." Such thinking is enticing, for it is inwardly consistent and also manipulative. It is fundamentally "value-free." For this reason, it can result in the temptation to exercise power without regard for ethical considerations. And that, of course, is "magic." Faust's involvement with such forces leads him ever deeper into guilt and in the end to the nascent under-standing of what he has done. These weighty words of self-examination, he finally realizes, contain the very definition of what it is to be human:

> Not yet have I my liberty made good:
> If I could banish magic's fell creations,
> And totally unlearn the incantations,—
> Stood I, O Nature! Man alone in thee,
> Then were it worth one's while a man to be![11]

This declaration ought to be the cry of every responsible human being today, since our mechanical, reductionistic thinking has profound moral implications. Its self-styled "objectivity," which Goethe clearly recognized as an illusion, prides itself as value-free and amoral. But human beings are *not* amoral. And if their present-day thought is con-sistently amoral, its cultivation will engender amoral *habits* in thinking. Faust longs for a science that is inwardly alive and moral, that he may teach it to his pupils. Because he cannot find it, he falls into the practice of magic. How, then, may Faust—that is, modern Western humanity—be redeemed? Goethe offers us the first step in his "*gegenständliches Denken.*" We must grasp its meaning and then put it systematically to work and on a deeper level than in the past. A closer look at Goethe's thought suggests how this possibility may be understood.

HEIGHTENED CAPACITIES

Just as for Goethe the pursuit of self-knowledge encompasses both the outer and inner worlds, so too does the first step in this process, the harmonious interaction of observation and thinking. As this process is heightened, thinking weaves through the phenomena as an active beholding and, conversely, the essence of the phenomena comes alive in thinking. Thus Heinroth, says Goethe, observes properly

> that my faculty of thinking is objectively active, whereby he means to say that my thinking does not separate itself from its objects; that the elements of the objects, the concrete intuitions (*Anschauungen*) enter into that thinking and are most inwardly permeated by it in form; that my way of seeing (*Anschauen*) is itself a thinking, my thinking a way of seeing—a procedure said friend does not wish to deny his approbation.[12]

Goethe's thinking is not predicated upon an analysis of the structure of the intellect. Nor does it assume dogmatically that we can only *know* the world in terms of observations conveyed to the subject via the senses. It has no need, therefore, to postulate a realm of the "*Ding an sich*," a spiritual essence that is felt to exist but by definition can never be known. Goethe's thinking is not intellectually atomistic. It is *organic* and *participatory*. The doctrine of the unbridgeable dualism of subject and object dissolves as thought becomes *Anschauen* and *Anschauen* thought. Goethe also describes his epistemology as a "delicate empiricism." He writes: "There is a delicate empiricism, which identifies itself with the object in the most inward way and thereby becomes actual theory. This heightening (*Steigerung*) of spiritual capacities belongs, however, to a highly cultivated age."[13]

As thinking comes alive in nature, and nature comes alive in the activity of thinking, knowledge of the world and knowledge of the self unite at a higher level where the danger of "false contemplativeness" is overcome. After years of painstaking observation and thought in the sense of "delicate empiricism," the idea of plant metamorphosis, which is not a subjective cognitive construct tested against nature but an objective constituent element of nature, lights up within thinking:

> If I turn now to the *objective thinking* that I am granted, then I find that I was compelled to employ the very same procedure in natural history as well. What course of observation (*Anschauung*) and contemplation did I not pursue until the idea of the metamorphosis of plants dawned upon me!—as my *Italian Journey* confided to my friends.[14]

For Goethe, the *idea* of plant metamorphosis was not an abstraction but a perceived reality in constant flux. He followed the series of gradually metamorphosing forms both forward and backward through the entire sequence of the organs of the plant. The one fundamental form that he experienced proceeding through all these protean changes of shape he termed quite simply the "leaf" (*Blatt*):

> Namely, it occurred to me that within the organ of the plant which we are wont to term the leaf lies hidden the true Proteus, who is able to conceal and to reveal himself in all formations. Forwards and backwards the plant is always leaf, and leaf alone, so inseparably united with the future seed that one is unable to think one without the other.[15]

The final observation is crucial: the entire plant is indivisibly united with the seed. The seed "contains" the plant itself as living potential. Inasmuch as Goethe discovered this truth in the activity of cognition as he practiced it, thinking itself was a seed in which the entire content of the world lay as if enchanted and could be revealed in the deepened exercise of "*gegenständliches Denken*" as a path of self-knowledge. Little wonder, then, that few understood his intent. As R. H. Brady observes:

> The comprehension of such work demands the development of a new faculty, but Goethe's critics were all too willing to rely upon their established mental habits. What he claimed to have seen, they judged he merely theorized; what he called experience, they termed a speculative idea. When Goethe wrote that in his investigations "my observation is itself a thinking, and my thinking a way of observation," the implicit suggestion that an idea could be an experience as well was reason enough to suppose him wrong. That thinking could become an organ of perception seemed a contradiction in terms.[16]

PARTICIPATION

The assumption of an essential dichotomy between a consciously thinking subject and an observed nonconscious nature lies at the root of the inability of Goethe's critics to comprehend him and has antecedents that may be traced back through Western thought. This dualistic mode of thinking militates against taking the notion of *participatory* thinking seriously. So much so, indeed, that it has become a mental habit. Owen Barfield suggests that participation is still a fact, although we are unaware of it and even deny it. He sees this denial formulated in René Descartes' division of the universe into "extended substance" and "thinking substance" (matter and mind). Barfield writes: "And it is on that denial of participation that the whole methodology of natural science is based."[17] From this premise we extrapolate and conclude that there never was any such thing as participation. "The fact remains," however, "that the denial is an illusion."[18] Our current scientific thinking is largely abstract in that it concentrates on those ways in which various diverse entities appear identical. The category "two-legged," for instance, is such an abstraction, as it can contain human beings, pelicans, and ladders. Barfield continues:

> The opposite of abstract thought is imagination, which deals not with identities, but with resemblances; not with side-by-sideness, but with *interpenetration*; and if we want to see the whole system of abstract thought, in which we're so deeply immersed, from outside of itself, so to speak, we must begin by seeing it in the light of imagination.[19]

It is just this imaginative faculty of cognition, imaginative in the literal sense of the word, this "viewing" (*Anschauen*) as "thinking" and vice versa, that rests at the core of Goethe's undertaking. He evolves it gradually by trial and error, a "delicate empiricism" which is the opposite of vague reverie. It is what one might term an "exact imagination." It is a painstaking and arduous path of systematic schooling which leads from the abstract "onlooker consciousness" of the dualistic kind to the "participatory consciousness" of Goethe's "*gegenständliches Denken.*"

On this path of inner schooling it is the consciously willed, focused *activity* that counts. Once it is discovered and applied to nature, one finds that what seemed an impossibly complex conundrum is not so at all. This helps to explain the delight expressed in Goethe's letter to Johann von Herder from Naples on 17 May 1787: "Furthermore, I must confide to you that I am quite close to the mystery of the generation and organization of the plant, and that it is the simplest thing imaginable."[20] Goethe continues, likening the discovery to a model and a key:

> The archetypal plant will be the most marvelous creation in the world, which nature itself shall envy me. With this model and the key to it one can then invent further plants *ad infinitum*—plants that must be logical (*konsequent*); i.e., even if they do not exist, they could exist, and are not some kind of painter's or poet's shadow or illusion, but rather something with an inner truth and necessity. The same law will be applicable to everything living.[21]

Symbols, of course, are what they are by virtue of their multiple referents. It may be permissible, in any case, to suggest that in this instance the "model" may possibly refer to the constituent laws that determine the plant's being (e.g., "polarity," "heightening" (*Steigerung*), and "spiral tendency"), while the "key" that must be applied actively to "unlock" the "model" is the changing awareness of the thinker. We recall Goethe's suggestion that contemplation of the object alters the faculty of cognition: "Every new object, well contemplated, opens up a new organ within us." The verb *aufschliessen* refers, among other things, to the activity of "unlocking" made possible by the use of a *key*. The intentionality of the participatory mode of "thinking" as "viewing" (*Anschauen*) unites with the flowing life of the plant forms and unlocks their mysteries, as in contemplating them Goethe allows them to awaken ever new organs of perception in the organism of thought itself. We recall Brady's observation that to Goethe's critics the notion "that thinking could become an organ of perception seemed a contradiction in terms." Brady continues:

> The "new faculty" . . . cannot be developed without entering into the unusual state of awareness through which we become conscious of our own intentional activity. It is necessary to turn the attention from our *thoughts* to an awareness of ourselves *thinking*. Only then do we discover that while a *thought* may indeed be devoid of perceptual content, things are quite otherwise with the activity of *thinking* (or intending), which activity provides an inner realm of experience. . . . When Goethe attempted to make the forms move, he entered into this unusual standpoint.[22]

Once this standpoint is reached, the dichotomy of self and world is bridged in the intentional activity of thinking, and a self-knowledge is attained that leaves the danger of "false contemplativeness" behind. One is reminded of Heinrich Henel, who counters the often-expressed view that in Palermo Goethe sought a specific physical plant as a pure expression of the "archetypal plant": "What Goethe sought was the confirmation of a thought, a representation, an idea. It may be that he found this confirmation in a single plant in Padua or in Sogesta and then solidified it through further observations, especially of proliferated flowers."[23]

New Organs of Cognition

A significant light is shed on this way of thinking by an exchange of thoughts in Goethe's treatise on art entitled "The Collector and His Own":

> Guest: I have noted, Sir, that philosophers have a way of sallying forth into battle behind strange words, as behind an aegis.

> I: This time I can assure you that I have not spoken as a phi-
> losopher; they were entirely matters of experience.
> Guest: You call that experience, of which one can comprehend nothing!
> I: Every experience has its organ.
> Guest: A special organ, you mean?
> I: Not a special one, but it must have a certain quality.
> Guest: And that would be?
> I: It must be able to produce.
> Guest: Produce what?
> I: The experience! There is no experience that is not produced,
> called forth, created.[24]

We recall that every object calls forth, when contemplated, a new inner organ. We now learn that such an inner organ itself *produces* the world of experience. The organ of perception is at the same time an organ of creation. In this context, Goethe applies the thought to the the artist, though it is also applicable to the scientist. Even at the rudimentary level of the organ of sight—the eye—Goethe sees these seemingly contradictory attributes at work. While, on one hand, the eye *perceives* colors, on the other hand, it *produces* the complementary colors as after-images of those perceived. For Goethe, the eye is an organ that is eminently *active* in the *systole* and *diastole* of transmitting percepts from the outer world to the eye of the mind, while at the same time creating new ones inwardly in response, adding them to those received from without:

> When the eye perceives the color, it immediately becomes active, and it is in keeping with its nature to call forth on the spot, by a process as unconscious as it is necessary, another color which, together with that given, contains the color circle in its entirety. A single color calls forth within the eye by means of a specific sensation the striving for universality.[25]

This creative ability is always present in the eye, and the organ responds to a world that it experiences as related to its own inner nature:

> The colors that we perceive on the surfaces of bodies are not something utterly alien to the eye through which it receives, as it were, the stamp of this sensation. No, this organ is ever disposed to call forth colors of itself, and enjoys a pleasant sensation whenever something in keeping with its own nature is brought to it from without; when its deter-minability is significantly determined in a certain direction.[26]

It should by now be clear that the activity of the eye, for Goethe, is vividly analogous to that of the mind itself. And indeed we find that he consciously compares the two and tells us that his descriptions in the *Farbenlehre* will remain incomprehensible unless one activates both "the eyes of the body and of the spirit":

> Here we do not set forth arbitrary signs, letters, and whatever else you please in place of the phenomena; here we do not deliver phrases that can be repeated a hundred times without thinking anything thereby nor giving anyone else pause to think. Rather, it is a matter of phenomena that one must have present before the eyes of the body and of the spirit in order to be able to evolve clearly their origin and development for oneself and others.[27]

The key phrase is "without thinking anything thereby." The eye of the body is stimulated by light and color and responds actively by its very nature. The eye of the spirit or mind is stimulated by observations and thoughts, and responds through the intentional activity of *thinking*. The activity that occurs in *perception* on a rudimentary level of consciousness is raised by the mind to the fully conscious clarity of thinking. And from there it passes over, as Brady notes, to the even more intensely conscious activity of the observation of thinking itself.

At this level, the "organ" of thinking not only perceives but *produces* the content of experience as was suggested in "The Collector and his Own." And when it does so consistently as a path of meditative activity, knowledge of the world rises through a true resurrection of thinking and merges with knowledge of the self. The facile distinction between "objective" and "subjective" knowledge is thus overcome through the new participatory mode of cognition, which is Goethe's legacy to modern science, and which answers in a responsible and healthy way the age-old call: "Know thyself." In such thinking, subject and object merge in one fully awake activity, and one experiences every attendant perception and deed in the light of freedom and responsibility.

The contemporary problem of science and "values" is shifted from the realm of abstract speculation to that of inner experience. This new cognitional mode may be described as the *key* to the future of science, to the degree that science wills to embrace *conscience*. It is the key that can unlock this future, just as focused intentionality of thinking is the key that for Goethe "unlocked" the "archetypal plant."

The Poet as Thinker

Goethe's scientific and poetic endeavors spring from a common root, and an understanding of one illuminates the the other. While it lies beyond the scope of this essay to pursue the subject of Goethe's poetry systematically, a few illustrations will characterize what is meant. The intentionality actively at work in Goethe's poetic imagination is revealed in keeping with our discussion in such a youthful outpouring of life as the poem "May Festival" (1771), in which we find the stanza:

> Blossoms press forth
> From every branch
> And a thousand voices
> From out of the bush.[28]

One does not in any external sense "see" blossoms pressing forth out of the branches, for they do so over an extended period of time. But the young Goethe telescopes that process and presents it as though in "slow motion" through his poetic imagination. So alive is that imagination that in this early lyric, penned long before he "unlocked" the secrets of the "archetypal plant," we find him already naively drawing on its inner life with the "eyes of the spirit" and pouring that life into his artistic creation.

Another remarkable lyric passage of this sort is found in "Upon the Lake" (1775), in which the oarsman describes the distant mountains as if they were coming forward to meet him: "And mountains, cloudy heavenward, / Meet us on our course."[29] In the earlier version, the lines read: "And mountains, touched by clouds / Come forth to meet our course." The verb used in the first version—*entgegnen* (come forth)— expresses even more vividly than the second version's *begegnen* (meet) the gradual looming motion that seems to animate the mountains.

And who, having worked for years with Goethe's thought as a whole, can fail to hear in the "*-gegnen*" contained in both words a delicate echo of *gegenständlich*, which Goethe found so happily applied to his thinking? The German *Gegen-stand* aptly characterizes an object in its tendency to "stand forth" toward the observer. Participatory consciousness comes forth to meet it and in contemplation enters into its inner essence, so that it evokes a new "organ" in the beholder. This entire attitude is prefigured here, again naively, and as if rising forth from the pregnant matrix of the poetic imagination.

That creative matrix, as source of both scientific and artistic intentionality, is later itself described by Goethe. It is given in the mysterious realm of the "Mothers" to which Faust must "descend" (or "rise") to fetch forth the shades of Helen and Paris for the amusement of the emperor at court. It is a realm beyond the world of sensory experience, a realm of constant transformation: "Formation, Transformation, / The Eternal Mind's eternal recreation."[30] Interestingly, Faust will find his

way to it and unlock its mysteries with a small key received from
Mephisto—a key that gleams, flashes, and grows in Faust's hand.[31]
Mephisto knows the realm of the Mothers and can tender Faust the
possibility of entering it with the "key" of thinking. In Faust's hand, the
key begins to grow. Faust's thinking is alive, but Mephisto can think only
abstractly and can therefore only point the way but not *participate* in the
activity.[32]

When he reappears on the stage, Faust steps forth clad as a priest
and intones solemn words evoking the eternal realm of the Mothers with
its images of life:

> And ye allot it, with all-potent might,
> To Day's pavillions and the vaults of Night.
> Life seizes some, along his gracious course:
> Others arrest the bold Magician's force;
> And he, bestowing as his faith inspires,
> Displays the Marvellous, that each desires.[33]

Wilhelm Emrich points out convincingly that the image of the day is
here coordinated with life, and the image of night with poetry. He notes
that a manuscript variant to *Magier* (magician) is *Dichter* (poet), in view
of which Goethe's underlying meaning becomes clear.[34] In this passage
from Faust, the mature Goethe gives us a picture of the inner realm of
meditative thought itself, which encompasses the source of deepened
"*gegenständliches Denken.*" As a young man, he drew from it instinc-
tively in his poetry. As he matured, he did so ever more consciously, in
both his art and scientific work.

THE PREGNANT POINT

Mephisto describes the realm of the Mothers as an eternally empty one in
which Faust will see *nothing*. And Faust replies in the well-known words:
"In this, thy Nothing, may I find my *ALL*!"[35] Ordinary intellect cannot
pass through this needle's eye, the point of absolute nothingness. Participatory thinking, however, can and, in doing so, reemerges in the spiritual
"All." This is the crucial "point," the "zero point" of Goethe's
epistemological breakthrough. It is a "vanishing point" for the calculating
intellect, which grasps things only in their "side-by-sideness" with the logic
of the physical world. It is a "growing point" for the intentional activity of
participatory thinking, which grasps things in their "interpenetration" with
the imaginative faculty of the "eyes of the mind." At this point, intellectual
thinking must *die*. And at this point, if we will it, thinking may resurrect.

Toward the end of the essay, "Significant Help . . . ," after having pointed to the significance of "*gegenständliches Denken*" for his work in botany, osteology, and geology, Goethe makes an observation that is easily overlooked. In Italy, he had exclaimed that, with the "model " of the "archetypal plant" and the "key" to it, he could invent (*erfinden*) all possible existent and nonexistent plants. Furthermore, he saw the entire plant, in a sense, contained ideally, as potential, within the germ or seed. This seed, in fact, he termed the "main point": "The main point, where the germ dwells, I have quite clearly and indubitably found. I see everything else in its entirety already as well: only a few points must still become more definite. The archetypal plant will be the most marvellous creation in the world."[36] That was in 1787. And now, thirty-six years later (1823), he explains:

> Excited by just these contemplations, I continued examining myself and discovered that my whole method rests upon deduction. I do not rest until I have found a pregnant point, from which much can be deduced, or rather, that freely brings forth much out of itself and bears it toward me, since in working and perceiving I proceed carefully and faithfully.[37]

Here Goethe writes out of the distilled encompassing vision of a lifetime of experience. The verb *erfinden* (invent) used in Italy has yielded to *ableiten* (deduce), which encompasses Goethe's cognitive mode as applied in all areas of science. In the physical sciences, the insights are derived from the archetypal phenomenon, which contains the simplest ultimate nexus of factors that must be present for a physical event to take place. The event can be derived from the essential conditions that constitute the archetypal phenomenon, but it can not be so derived if any one of those factors is removed. The archetypal phenomenon is thus a "pregnant point."

In the plant world, the archtetypal plant is the pregnant point, and the "main point" (*Hauptpunkt*) in the organism of the plant is, as we have seen, the "germ" (*Keim*). In the animal world, the type (*Typus*) is the pregnant point. Goethe says one may "derive" (*ableiten*) much from such a point. He then turns the thought around, describing the event, as it were, from the "point of view" of the pregnant point itself, which "freely brings forth much out of itself and bears it toward me."

That is what it means for a point to be pregnant in Goethe's sense. It is not merely a noncommital figure of speech but, rather, an exact description of what he wishes to say: the "point" of cognition is spiritually alive. It brings forth much "from out of itself," just as the blossoms "bring themselves forth" from the branch in May and the archetypal plant brings forth the splendor of all the plant kingdom, a veritable "world-garden" (*Weltgarten*) from the mother-ground of spiritual life. Indeed, having discovered the archetypal plant in Palermo, Goethe exclaims: "A world-garden had opened up before me."[38] What the pregnant point thus brings forth, says Goethe, is something that it "bears toward me" (*mir entgegenträgt*).

Again that wonderful word *gegen—Gegenstand, entgegnen, begegnen,* and now *entgegenträgt*. As we pursue the sentence further, we read that there is a reason why the pregnant point can release its life: ". . . since in working and perceiving I proceed carefully and faithfully." That, of course, is what the *eye* does, as noted above. It is a gesture of alternating inbreathing and outbreathing. First it receives color impressions from the world (a "perceiving" [*Empfangen*]), and then through its innate life it produces the complementary colors as well (a "working" [*Bemühen*]). This picture of the "eye of the body" now reemerges in the essay "Significant Help . . ." as a description of the activity of the "eye of the mind" in *all* spheres of scientific work.

And how does Goethe go about this work? Carefully (literally, "seeing forth" or "looking ahead" [*vorsichtig*]) and faithfully (*treu*)— faithful to his cautious mode of study and above all faithful to the phenomena themselves. It should also not escape our notice that this whole statement contains an unobtrusive shift of grammatical tense. It begins in the past ("I continued," "discovered") as he describes the search that led to the discovery of the principle of derivation. He then moves to the present ("I do not rest until I have found a pregnant point.") as he leads the reader into what for him is a never-ending process.

The outwardly invisible point that for Mephisto is a "Nothing" and for Faust holds the "All" is just this pregnant point of intentionality in the inmost sanctuary of contemplative thought. It is a point pregnant with life, a dry "seed" that contains as potential that which through its nourishment and cultivation can emerge, as human deed, into the world of the actual. Goethe sees in it the "source" and "ground" of all thinking. In the *Maxims and Reflections*:

> When the youth begins to understand that a visible point must be preceded by an invisible one; that the shortest distance between two points has already been thought as a line before it is drawn on paper with the pencil, then he feels a certain pride, a certain pleasure. And rightfully so, for the source of all thinking has opened up before him, idea and act; "*potentia et actu*" has become clear to him; the philosopher reveals nothing new to him; from his own side the fundament of all thinking had dawned upon the geometer.[39]

When the admonition "Know thyself" is grasped in this context and at this level, it is freed of all danger of asceticism and "false contemplativeness." It reveals its proper role as "good advice" for every active and diligent human being. Thus we read in the following maxim:

> If we then take the significant maxim "Know thyself," we are not obliged to interpret it ascetically. In no way is the *heautognosis* of our modern hypochondrists, humorists and *heauton timoroumenoi* implied. Rather, it means simply: Give a certain regard to yourself; take note of yourself so that you become aware how you come to stand in relation to your peers and to the world. This requires no psychological torments: every diligent person knows and has experienced what this is supposed to mean. It is good advice that is of the greatest practical good.[40]

GOETHE'S LEGACY

We now return to the importance of these matters for today's situation. Our contemporary science is deeply imbued with mechanistic thinking in the mode of causality. This mode is altogether appropriate within the realm of physical phenomena such as mechanics and physical chemistry. In the sphere of biology, however, one already reaches a borderline where, for many contemporary scientists, the exclusive application of the concept of physical causality becomes highly questionable. In the plant kingdom, physical matter is enhanced by the phenomenon *of life*. In the animal kingdom, these two levels are further enhanced by the phenomena of *sentient consciousness*. In the human being, these three levels are complemented by the emergence of the individuality as conscious *self*.

When concepts of causality and randomness are applied exclusively to these further realms, phenomena of a higher qualitative order are reduced to physical terms, and we therefore speak of "reductionistic" thinking. In the mindless application of such thinking, we may find the cause of an entire spectrum of problems in nature and society today. Reductionistic thinking does not grasp the delicate interplay of life forces in the biosphere, and we have the proliferating deterioration of interpenetrating life-supporting systems known as the "ecological problem."

In addition, reductionistic thinking fails to rise methodologically to the challenge of the role of intentionality, with the result that the activity of the mind is seen to be an epiphenomenon of physiology. Finally, reductionistic thinking cannot find a conscious self able to act from moral intuition and therefore substitutes a shadow-image of that self, an entity propelled by hereditary and environmental determinism. It is hardly surprising that such thinking seeks answers to the social question primarily in the sphere of technology.

In contrast to these usages of reductionistic thinking, Goethean thinking embraces the qualitatively ascending levels of existence by means of an epistemology that is truly critical and at pains both to respond to and to handle the phenomena in keeping with the quality of their articulation at each level. Such thinking, constantly practicing self-evaluation as it proceeds, gradually grows to encompass the realities of life, of consciousness, and of values, the sphere of the moral. As such, human thinking in this new modality is a legacy to our time. Goethe's seven-stanza "Legacy" (*Vermächtnis*), a poem written in Goethe's eightieth year and placed at the end of his novel, *Wilhelm Meister's Journeymanship*, is a poetic distillation of his mature wisdom and illuminates the resurrection of thinking as we have discussed it:

Legacy
No being can decay to nothing!
The eternal is active in all things,
Take sustenance joyously from Being!
Being is eternal; for laws
Conserve the living treasures,
From which the All has adorned itself.

The true was found already long ago
Bound community of noble spirits together,
That which is true of old — take hold of it!
Thank for this, son of earth, the Wise One,
Who showed it how to orbit the sun
And to its siblings showed the path.

Now immediately turn inward,
The center you will find therein,
Something no noble one would doubt.
There you will not miss any rules:
For the independent conscience
Is sun to your day of morals.

Then you must trust the senses
They do not allow you to view anything false,
If your understanding keeps you awake.
With fresh glance note gladly,
And wander surely and lithely
Through fields of a richly-endowed world.

Enjoy moderately plenty and blessing,
Let reason be present everywhere,
Where life takes joy in life.
Then the past continues on,
The future is alive betimes,
The moment is eternity.

And if you finally have succeeded,
And if you are permeated by the feeling:
Only that which is fruitful is true,
You test the universal reigning,
It will proceed after its own fashion,
Ally yourself with the smallest group.

And as from ages hence in quiet
A labor of love according to his own will
Was created by philosopher and poet,
So will you gain the most beautiful favor:
For to anticipate the feelings of noble souls
Is the most desirable occupation.[41]

The entire poem is an admonition in the sense of "Know thyself." It opens with the thought of Permanency in Change (*Dauer im Wechsel*), the spiritual womb of Being, of eternity, of lawfulness within flux. The second stanza celebrates the thinkers who described the movement of the planets in relation to the earth. Lawfulness is here seen to be concretely embodied in nature. In the third stanza, the poet tells us that the center of the universe is to be sought *within*. And the image of the sun, which appears outwardly in stanza two as the pivotal point of the universe, is now reintroduced as the image for the human conscience, the center of the moral universe. Through the metaphor of the sun, the phenomena of nature and the realm of values are united as, in fact, we have found them to be for the epistemological mode underlying Goethe's view of scientific thought.

Just as we may find certainty in the fulcrum of conscience, so stanza four reminds us that we may also trust the experience of our senses. The cultivation of sensory observation to a high degree of accuracy is a central concern of such a study as the *Theory of Color* and is expressed in various ways throughout Goethe's work. It is summed up in the saying: "The senses do not deceive; it is judgement that deceives."[42]

Verstand (understanding, stanza 4) keeps the mind awake. *Vernunft* (reason), in Goethe's sense, is the faculty that grasps growth, *das Werdende* (that which is becoming): "Let reason be present everywhere, / Where life takes joy in life." When this living thinking is experienced, the boundaries between past, present, and future are transcended and the participating mind penetrates through the zero-point of time and space into the pregnant point of the Mother-ground of existence, a moment that as life-filled eternity is a seed of future worlds: "Then the past continues on, / The future is alive betimes, / The moment is eternity."

When this experience is attained, the soul is permeated by the feeling: "Only that which is fruitful is true." Goethe's ultimate test of truth—the truth of sense-experience and of thinking—is that it shall be "fruitful" and further life and health. The extension of this attitude from the natural to the societal sphere is exemplified by the vision of the *Wanderjahre*, to which Goethe appends this poem. Wilhelm has embraced the vocation of medicine and thereby himself embodies this theme of health-bestowing activity. Only a few will attain to a living realization of the inner experience of spiritual truth and will bear the burden of isolation: "Ally yourself with the smallest group."

Yet, the burden of creating freely a work born in the stillness of meditative thought is a burden born lightly. It brings with it the most beautiful of favors: "For to anticipate the feelings of noble souls / Is the most desirable occupation." Noble souls are on the way, as though drawing closer from out of the future. To evolve through inner work the new ideas that such *"edle Seelen"* will need to work with is to plant good seeds. To leave such a legacy is about all anyone can hope to accomplish and is thus the most desirable calling (*Beruf*).

"Gegenständliches Denken"—meditative practice in Goethe's sense—is centered inwardly and is illumined by the sun of conscience. As the living source of scientific and moral intuitions, it is a *cognitive modality* as a seed for the future.[43] Furthermore, *each individual moral intuition* is itself a "seed of thought" for the future. These many thoughts are the "thousand seeds" that must be planted by us individually today, if Mephisto is to be countered in keeping with the realities of the twentieth and twenty-first centuries. In Goethe's time, Mephisto felt impeded by the "thousand seeds" provided in the course of things *outwardly*, by nature herself. Today the image takes on a new and sobering meaning. It is an image for events that may be brought about *inwardly*, in the domain of cognition, where Mephisto has presently chosen to launch his most pernicious attack—the assault on the spiritual nature of humanity.

The image of the seed, reevaluated in the light of Goethe's epistemological stance as a "resurrection of thinking," casts light on the dilemma of Faust; for Faust is Goethe's representative of modern consciousness. The aged Faust exclaims:

> If I could banish Magic's fell creations,
> And totally unlearn the incantations,
> Stood I, O Nature! Man alone in thee,
> Then were it worth one's while a man to be![44]

Magic, the illegitimate use of power, is resisted and overcome only through the moral development of one's faculties in the sunlight of conscience. And with respect to science, this is not possible without the resurrection of thinking. To bring about the conditions that may lead to this resurrection has therefore now become the first task of the scientist in our time.

Goethe holds the view that modern human beings must systematically work toward increasing freedom and self-determination. They cannot redeem themselves, but they can create the conditions that enable the higher worlds, through Grace, to do so. In the words of the angels: "Whoe'er aspires unweariedly / Is not beyond redeeming."[45] It is the calling of each free spirit to evolve those intuitions that, as seeds, embody the potential for the redemption of Faust in the present time. Such a vocation is a heavy burden, yet uplifting to the bearer and perhaps the most desirable vocation.

Notes

1. This essay was written shortly before Cottrell's death in 1984. Though it has taken over a decade for its actualization, the idea for the present volume was originally inspired by Cottrell, and he wrote this essay especially for inclusion. We are pleased that it is finally being published—EDS.

2. J. W. von Goethe, *Faust*, trans. B. Taylor (New York: Modern Library, 1912) (hereafter Taylor), p. 46. The original can be found in J. W. von Goethe, *Faust, Goethes Werke: Hamburger Ausgabe*, vol. III (Hamburg: Christian Wegner, 1948–1960), ll.1338–44. All further references to the German text of *Faust* will be to the line numbers in the *Hamburger Ausgabe* (hereafter *HA*).

3. Taylor, p. 47; *HA*, III, ll.1362–78.

4. My head, heart, liver, by the flames are rent! / An over-devilish element!— / Sharper than Hell's red conflagration! (Taylor, p. 247).

5. *HA*, XIII:37–41.

6. *HA*, XIII:10–20.

7. *HA*, XIII:38. All translations, except those from *Faust*, are by Frederick Amrine and used with his permission.

8. Taylor, p. 20. *HA*, III, ll.512–13.

9. Taylor, p. 15; *HA*, III, ll.382–85.

10. Taylor, p. 15; *HA*, III, ll.372–73.

11. Taylor, p. 235; *HA*, III, ll.11403–7.

12. *HA*, XIII:37.

13. Goethe, *Maximen und Reflexionen*, no. 509, *HA*, XII:435.

14. Goethe, "Bedeutende Fördernis", *HA*, XIII:39.

15. Goethe, *Italienische Reise*, *HA*, XI:375.

16. R. H. Brady, "Goethe's Natural Science. Some Non-Cartesian Meditations," in *Toward a Man-Centered Medical Science*, edited by K. Schaefer, H. Hensel, and R. H. Brady (Mt. Kisco, N.Y.: Futura, 1977), pp. 159–60; also see Brady's chapter 5 in this volume.

17. O. Barfield, "Participation and Isolation: A Fresh Light on Present Discontents," in *The Rediscovery of Meaning and Other Essays* (Middletown, Conn.: Wesleyan University Press, 1977), p. 205.

18. Ibid., p. 209.

19. Ibid.

20. *Italienische Reise*, *HA*, XI:323.

21. Ibid., p. 324.

22. Brady, "Goethe's Natural Science," p. 160.

23. H. Henel, "Typus und Urphänomen in Goethes Naturlehre," in *Goethezeit: Gesammelte Aufsätze* (Frankfurt: Insel, 1979), p. 368, note 29; translated as "Type and Proto-Phenomenon in Goethe's Science," *Proceedings of the Modern Language Association* 71 (1956): 651–68.

24. Goethe, "Der Sammler und die Seinigen," *HA*, XII:85.

25. Goethe, *Zur Farbenlehre*, *HA* XIII:501.

26. Ibid., p. 494.

27. Ibid.

28. Goethe, "*Maifest*," *HA*, I:30–31, ll.5–8.

29. 2nd version, *HA*, I:102, ll.7–8.

30. Taylor, p. 55; *HA*, III, ll.6287–88.

31. Taylor, p. 54: "It glows, it shines,—increases in my hand!"

32. In contrast to superficial readings of the image of the key as phallic symbol, the connection of the image with Goethe's botanical thought was first pointed out in 1961 by Gottfried Diener in his *Fausts Weg zu Helena, Urphänomen und Archetypus* (Stuttgart: Klett, 1961), pp. 98–99.

33. Taylor, p. 60; *HA*, III, ll.6433–38.

34. W. Emrich, *Die Symbolik von Faust II: Sinn und Vorformen*, 4th ed. (Wiesbaden: Akademische Verlagsgesellschaft Athenaion, 1978), pp. 217–19.

35. Taylor, p. 53, *HA*, III, l.28.

36. Goethe, *Italienische Reise*, *HA*, XI:323–24.

37. *HA*, XIII:40.

38. Ibid., p. 267.

39. Goethe, *Maximen und Reflexionen*, no. 355, *HA*, XII:413.

40. Ibid., no. 356, p. 413.

41. *HA*, I:369–70.

42. Goethe, *Maximen und Reflexionen*, no. 295, *HA*, XII:406.

43. For this interpretation of "moral intuition," I am indebted to Rudolf Steiner, *The Philosophy of Freedom* (London: Rudolf Steiner Press, 1964).

44. Taylor, p. 235; *HA*, III, ll.11404–07.

45. Taylor, p. 252.

12

Henri Bortoft

Counterfeit and Authentic Wholes

Finding a Means for Dwelling in Nature

What is wholeness?[1] To answer this question, it is helpful to present a specific setting. Imagine someone who did not yet recognize it asking, "What is roundness?" We might try to answer by giving a number of instances, such as "the moon is round," "the plate is round," "the coin is round," and so on. Of course, "round" is none of these things, but by adducing a number of such instances we might hope to provoke in the person the recognition of roundness. This happens when the person's perception of the specific instances is reorganized, so that they now become like mirrors in which roundness is seen reflected. In spite of what many people might think, this process does not involve empirical generalization, that is, abstracting what is common from a number of cases. The belief that concepts are derived directly from sensory experiences is like believing that conjurors really do produce rabbits out of hats. Just as the conjuror puts the rabbit into the hat beforehand, so the attempt to deduce the concept by abstraction in the empiricist manner presupposes the very concept it pretends to produce.

My aim in this essay is to understand wholeness. I adduce a number of examples of wholeness, with the aim of learning more about wholeness itself by seeing its reflection in these particular cases. I distinguish authentic wholeness from counterfeit forms in terms of the relationship between whole and part. The result leads to an understanding of how the

277

whole can be encountered through the parts. Finally, I argue that the way of science developed by Goethe exemplifies the principle of authentic wholeness. Goethe's mode of understanding sees the part in the light of the whole, fostering a way of science that dwells in nature.

HOLOGRAMS AND THE
UNIVERSE OF LIGHT AND MATTER

The advent of the laser has made possible the development of a radically different kind of photography. "Hologram" is the name given to the special kind of photographic plate produced with the highly coherent light of a laser—that is, light that holds together and does not disperse, similar to a pure tone compared to noise. Whereas the ordinary photographic plate records and reproduces a flat image of an illuminated object, the hologram does not record an image of the object photographed but provides an optical reconstruction of the original object. When the hologram plate itself is illuminated with the coherent light from the laser with which it was produced, the optical effect is exactly as if the original object were being observed. What is seen is to all optical appearances the object itself in full three-dimensional form, being displaced in apparent position when seen from different perspectives (the parallax effect) in the same way as the original object.

A hologram has several remarkable properties, in addition to those related to the three-dimensional nature of the optical reconstruction that it permits. The particular property that is of direct concern in understanding wholeness is the pervasiveness of the whole optical object throughout the plate.[2] If the hologram plate is broken into fragments and one fragment is illuminated, we find that the same three-dimensional optical reconstruction of the original object is produced. There is nothing missing; the only difference is that the reconstruction is less well defined. The entire original object can be optically reconstructed from any fragment of the original hologram, but as the fragments get smaller the resolution deteriorates until the reconstruction becomes so blotchy and ill-defined as to become unrecognizable. This property of the hologram is in striking contrast to the ordinary image-recording photographic plate. If this type of plate is broken and a fragment illuminated, the image reproduced will be that recorded on the particular fragment and no more. With orthodox photography the image fragments with the plate; with holography the image is undivided with the fragments.

What can be seen straightaway about wholeness in this example of the hologram is the way in which the whole is present in its parts. The entire picture is wholly present in each part of the plate, so that it would not be true in this case to say that the whole is made up of parts. This point will be explored in detail shortly, but the advantage of beginning with the hologram is that it is such an immediately concrete instance of wholeness.

A second example of wholeness involves the ordinary experience of looking up at the sky at night and seeing the vast number of stars. We see this nighttime world by means of the light "carrying" the stars to us, which means that this vast expanse of sky must all be present in the light that passes through the small hole of the pupil into the eye. Furthermore, other observers in different locations can see the same expanse of night sky. Hence, we can say that the stars seen in the heavens are all present in the light that is at any eye-point. The totality is contained in each small region of space, and when we use optical instruments like a telescope, we simply reclaim more of that light.[3] If we set off in imagination to find what it would be like to be light, we come to a condition in which here is everywhere and everywhere is here. The nighttime sky is a "space" that is one whole, with the quality of a point and yet including all within itself.

Matter also turns out to behave in an unexpectedly holistic way at both the macroscopic and the microscopic level. We tend to think of the large-scale universe of matter as being made up of separate and independent masses interacting with one another through the force of gravity. The viewpoint that emerges from modern physics is very different from this traditional conception. It is now believed that mass is not an intrinsic property of a body, but in fact a reflection of the whole of the rest of the universe in that body. Einstein imagined, following Ernst Mach, that a single particle of matter would have no mass if it were not for all the rest of the matter in the universe.[4] Instead of trying to understand the universe by extrapolating from the local environment here and now to the universe as a whole, it may be useful to reverse the relationship and understand the local environment as being the result of the rest of the universe.[5]

Similarly, at the microscopic level, we tend to think of the world as being made up of separate, independent subatomic particles interacting with one another through fields of force. But the view that emerges from physics today is very different. "Particle physicists," as they are called, have found that subatomic particles cannot be considered to be made up of ultimate, simple building blocks that are separate and outside of each other. Increasingly, it becomes clear that analysis in this traditional way is inappropriate at the microscopic level. Thus, in the "bootstrap" philosophy of Geoffrey Chew, the properties of any one particle are determined by all the other particles, so that every particle is a reflection of all the others. This structure whereby a particle contains all other particles, and is also contained in each of them, is expressed succinctly by the phrase, "every particle consists of all other particles."[6]

Just as there are no independently separate masses on the large scale, there are also no independent elementary particles on the small scale. At both levels, the whole is reflected in the parts, which in turn contribute to the whole. The whole, therefore, cannot simply be the sum of the parts—that is, the totality—because there are no parts that are independent of the whole. For the same reason, we cannot perceive the whole by "standing back to get an overview." On the contrary, because the whole is in some way reflected in the parts, it is to be encountered by going further into the parts instead of standing back from them.

THE HERMENEUTIC CIRCLE

A third instance of wholeness is externally somewhat different from the previous two. It is concerned with what happens when we read a written text. If reading is to be meaningful, it is not just a matter of repeating the words verbally as they come up in sequence on the page. Successful reading is not just a matter of saying the words. It is an act of interpretation, but not interpretation in the subjective sense. True interpretation is actively receptive, not assertive in the sense of dominating what is read. True interpretation does not force the text into the mould of the reader's personality, or into the requirements of his or her previous knowledge. It conveys the meaning of the text—"conveys" in the sense of "passes through" or "goes between." This is why readers sometimes can convey to others more of the meaning of a text than they understand themselves.

Authentic interpretation, and hence successful reading, imparts real meaning, but the question becomes, what or where is this meaning? We often say, "I see," when we wish to indicate that we have grasped something. If we try to look at what we imagine is in our grasp, however, we find ourselves empty-handed. It does not take much experimentation here to realize that meaning cannot be grasped like an object.

The meaning of a text, therefore, must have something to do with the whole text. What we come to here is the fundamental distinction between whole and totality. The meaning is the whole of the text, but this whole is not the same as the totality of the text. That there is a difference between the whole and the totality is clearly demonstrated by the evident fact that we do not need the totality of the text in order to understand its meaning. We do not have the totality of the text when we read it, but only one bit after another. But we do not have to store up what is read until it is all collected together, whereupon we suddenly see the meaning all at one instant. On the contrary, the meaning of the text is discerned and disclosed with progressive immanence throughout the reading of the text.

We can begin to see how remarkably similar the meaning structure of a text is to the optical form of the hologram. The totality of the text can be compared to the pattern of marks on the hologram plate. But the meaning of the text must be compared to the whole picture that can be reconstructed from the hologram plate. This is the sense in which the meaning of the text is the whole. The whole is not the totality, but the whole emerges most fully and completely through the totality. Thus, we can say that meaning is hologrammatical. The whole is present throughout all of the text, so that it is present in any region of the text. It is the presence of the whole in any region of the text that constitutes the meaning of that region of the text. Indeed, we can sometimes find that it is just the understanding of a single passage that suddenly illuminates for us the whole meaning of the text.

What we come to here is the idea of the hermeneutical circle, which was first recognized by Frederich Ast in the eighteenth century and subsequently developed by Friedrich Schleiermacher in his program for general hermeneutics as the art of understanding.[7] At the level of discourse, this circle says that to read an author we have to understand him or her first, and yet we have to read the author first to understand him or her. It appears we have to understand the whole meaning of the text "in advance" to read the parts which are our pathway towards the meaning of the text as a whole. Clearly, this is a contradiction to logic and the form or reasoning that is based thereon. Yet, it is the *experience* we go through to understand the meaning of the text, as it is also the experience we go through in writing a text. The same paradox for logic can be found at the level of the single sentence. The meaning of a sentence has the unity of a whole. We reach the meaning of the sentence through reading the words, yet the meaning of the words in that sentence is determined by the meaning of the sentence as a whole.

The reciprocal relationship of part and whole that is revealed here shows us clearly that the act of understanding is not a logical act of reasoning because such an act depends on the choice of either/or. The paradox arises from the tacit assumption of linearity—implicit in the logic of reason—which supposes that we must go either from part to whole or from whole to part. Logic is analytical, whereas meaning is evidently holistic, and hence understanding cannot be reduced to logic. We understand meaning in the moment of coalescence when the whole is reflected in the parts so that together they disclose the whole. It is because meaning is encountered in this "circle" of the reciprocal relationship of the whole and the parts that we call it the hermeneutical circle.

THE WHOLE AND THE PARTS

The hologram helps us to see that the essence of the whole is that it is whole. If we had begun our discussion of the whole with the statement that the whole is whole, it would have seemed vacuous or trivially pedantic. But the optical instance of the hologram enables us to see that, far from being a trivial tautology, this statement expresses the primacy of the whole. No matter how often we break the hologram plate, the picture is undivided. It remains whole even while becoming many.

This essential irreducibility of the whole is so strong that it seems inconceivable that there is any way in which the whole could have parts. This is very much opposite to the view we usually have of the relation between parts and whole. We are accustomed to thinking of going from parts to whole in some sort of summative manner. We think of developing the whole, even of making the whole, on the practical basis of putting parts together and making them fit. In this conventional way of working, we see the whole as developing by "integration of parts." This way of thinking, however, places the whole secondary to the parts, though usually we do not notice this error. Such a way of seeing places the whole in secondary relationship because it necessarily implies that the whole comes after the parts. It implies a linear sequence: first the parts, then the whole. The implication is that the whole always comes later than its parts.

Faced with the primacy of the whole, as seen in the hologram, we may want to reverse the direction of this way of thinking of the whole. This we would do if we thought of the parts as being determined by the whole, defined by it, and so subservient to the whole. But this approach is not the true primacy of the whole, either. It puts the whole in the position of a false transcendental that would come earlier than the parts, and so would leave them no place. This approach effectively considers the whole as if it were a part, but a "superpart" that controls and dominates the other, lesser parts. It is not the true whole, and neither can the parts be true parts when they are dominated by this counterfeit whole. Instead, there is only the side-by-sideness of would-be parts and the counterfeit whole. This is a false dualism.

Inasmuch as the whole is whole it is neither earlier nor later. To say that the whole is not later than the parts is not to say that we do not put parts together. Of course we do—consider the action of writing, for example. But the fact that we often put parts together does not mean that in so doing we put the whole together. Similarly, to say that the whole is not earlier than the parts is not to deny the primacy of the whole. But, at the same time, to assert the primacy of the whole is not to maintain that it is dominant, in the sense of having an external superiority over the parts.

We can see the limitation of these two extreme approaches to the whole if we look at the act of writing. We put marks for words together on a page by the movement of the pen to try to say something. What is said is not the resultant sum of the marks, nor of the words that they indicate. What is said is not produced automatically by the words adding together as they come. But equally, we do not have what is said fixed and finished in front of us before it is written. We do not simply copy what is already said. We all know the familiar experience of having the sense that we understand something and then finding that it has slipped away when we try to say it. We seem to understand already before saying, but in the moment of expression we are empty. What appears is not ready-made outside the expression. But neither is expression an invention from a vacuum.

The art of saying is in finding the "right parts." The success or failure of saying, and hence of writing, turns upon the ability to recognize what is a part and what is not. But a part is a part only inasmuch as it serves to let the whole come forth, which is to let meaning emerge. A part is only a part according to the emergence of the whole that it serves; otherwise it is mere noise. At the same time, the whole does not dominate, for the whole cannot emerge without the parts. The hazard of emergence is such that the whole depends on the parts to be able to come forth, and the parts depend on the coming forth of the whole to be significant instead of superficial. The recognition of a part is possible only through the "coming to presence" of the whole. This fact is particularly evident in authentic writing and reading, where something is either to come to expression or to come to be understood.

We cannot separate part and whole into disjointed positions, for they are not two as in common arithmetic. The arithmetic of the whole is not numerical.[8] We do not have part *and* whole, though the number category of ordinary language will always make it seem so.[9] If we do separate part and whole into two, we appear to have an alternative of moving in a single direction, either from part to whole or from whole to part. If we start from this position, we must at least insist on moving in both directions at once, so that we have neither the resultant whole as a sum nor the transcendental whole as a dominant authority, but the emergent whole that comes forth into its parts. The character of this emergence is the "unfolding of enfolding," so that the parts are the place of the whole where it bodies forth into presence.[10] The whole imparts itself; it is accomplished through the parts it fulfills.

We can perhaps do something more to bring out the relationship between whole and part by considering the hologram again. If we break the hologram plate into fractions, we do not break the whole. The whole is present in each fraction, but its presence diminishes as the fractioning proceeds. Starting from the other end, with many fractions, we could put the fractions together to build up the totality. As we did so, the whole would emerge; it would come forth more fully as we approached the totality. But we would not be building up the whole. The whole is already present, present in the fractions, coming fully into presence in the totality. The superficial ordering of the fractional parts may be a linear series—this next to that, and so on. But the ordering of the parts with respect to the emergent whole, the essential ordering, is nested and not linear. Thus, the emergence of the whole is orthogonal to the accumulation of parts because it is the coming into presence of the whole that is whole, the whole that is immanent.

This process tells us something fundamental about the whole in a way that shows us the significance of the parts. If the whole presences within its parts, then a part is a place for the presencing of the whole.[11] If a part is to be an arena in which the whole can be present, if cannot be "any old thing." Rather, a part is special and not accidental, since it must be such as to let the whole come into presence. This speciality of the part is particularly important because it shows us the way to the whole. It clearly indicates that the way to the whole is into and through the parts. It is not to be encountered by stepping back to take an overview, for it is not over and above the parts, as if it were some superior, all-encompassing entity. The whole is to be encountered by stepping right into its parts. This is how we enter into the nesting of the whole, and thus move into the whole as we pass through the parts.

This dual movement, into the whole through the parts, is demonstrated clearly in the experience of speaking and reading, listening, and writing. We can see that in each case there is a dual movement: we move through the parts to enter into the whole that presences within the parts. When we understand, both movements come together. When we do not understand, we merely pass along the parts. Consider, for example, the interpretation of a difficult text, say, Immanuel Kant's *Critique of Pure Reason*. At first encounter, we just pass along the parts, reading the sentences without understanding. To come to understand the text, we have to enter into it, and we do this in the first place by experiencing the meaning of the sentences. We enter into the text as the medium of meaning through the sentences themselves, putting ourselves into the text in a way that makes us available to meaning. We do not stand back to get an overview of all the sentences, in the hope that this will give us the meaning of the text. We do not refer to some other, external text that will give us the meaning. There is no superior text that can be an authority in interpretation because there is no access to the meaning of Kant's book other than through itself. Even for Kant, there was no pure "meaning in itself," present as an object in his consciousness, which he then represented in language. The original text is already in interpretation, and every text written about Kant's book is itself an expression of the meaning that that book was written to make evident. The hermeneutic approach must recognize, as Martin Heidegger said, that ". . . what is essential in all philosophical discourse is not found in the specific propositions of which it is composed but in that which, although unstated as such, is made evident through these propositions."[12] Authentic interpretation recognizes the way in which the whole, which is the meaning of the text, comes to presence in the parts, which are the sentences.

ENCOUNTERING THE WHOLE:
THE ACTIVE ABSENCE

Everything we encounter in the world can be said to be either one thing or another, either this or that, either before or after, and so on. Wherever we look, there are different things to be distinguished from one another: this book here, that pen there, the table underneath, and so on. Each thing is outside the other, and all things are separate from one another. But in recognizing the things about us in this way, we, too, are separate from and outside each of the things we see. We find ourselves laid out side by side, together with and separate from, the things we recognize. This is the familiar spectator awareness. In the moment of recognizing a thing we stand outside that thing, and in the moment of standing outside that thing we turn into an "I" that knows that thing, for there cannot be an "outside" without the distinction of something being outside some other thing. Thus, the "I" of "I know" arises in the knowing of something in the moment of recognition of the thing known. By virtue of its origin, the "I" that knows is outside what it knows.

We cannot know the whole in the way in which we know these things because we cannot recognize the whole as a thing. If the whole were available to be recognized in the same way as we recognize the things that surrounds us, then the whole would be counted among those things as one of them. We could point and say, "here is this" and "there is that," and "that's the whole over there." If we had the power of such recognition, we would know the whole in the same way that we know its parts, for the whole itself would simply be numbered among its parts. The whole would be outside its parts in the same way that each part is outside all the other parts. But the whole comes into presence *within* its parts, and we cannot encounter the whole in the same way that we encounter the parts. We should not think of the whole as if it were a thing.

Awareness is occupied with things. The whole is absent to awareness because it is not a thing among things. To awareness, the whole is no-thing, and since awareness is awareness of *something*, no-thing is nothing. The whole that is no-thing is taken as mere nothing, in which case it vanishes. When this loss happens, we are left with a world of things, and the apparent task of putting them together to make a whole. Such an effort disregards the authentic whole.

The other choice is to take the whole to be no-thing but not nothing. This possibility is difficult for awareness, which cannot distinguish the two. Yet, we have an illustration immediately on hand with the experience of reading. We do not take the meaning of a sentence to be a word. The meaning of a sentence is no-word. But evidently this is not the same as nothing, for if it were we could never read! The whole presences within parts, but from the standpoint of awareness that grasps the external parts, the whole is an absence. This absence, however, is not the same as nothing. Rather, it is an *active* absence inasmuch as we do not try to be aware of the whole, as if we could grasp it like a part, but instead let ourselves be open to be moved by the whole.

A particularly graphic illustration of the development of sensitivity to the whole as an active absence is to be found in the experience of writing, where we saw earlier that we do not have the meaning before us like an object. Another illustration of the active absence is provided by the enacting of a play. Actors do not stand away from their parts as if they were objects to be captured by awareness. They enter into their parts in such a way that they enter into the play. If the play is constructed well, the whole play comes into presence within the parts so that the actors encounter the play through their parts. But they do not encounter the play as an object of knowledge over which they can stand like the lines they learn. They encounter the play in the parts as an active absence that can begin to move them. When this happens the actors start to be acted by the play, instead of trying to act the play. The origin of the acting becomes the play itself, instead of the actor's subjective "I." The actors no longer impose themselves on the play as if it were an object to be mastered, but they listen to the play and allow themselves to be moved by it. In this way they enter into the parts in such a way that the play speaks through them. This is how, their awareness occupied with the lines to be spoken, they encounter the whole that is the play—not as an object but as an active absence.

Developmental psychology now offers considerable support for this notion that the whole is "nothing" to our ordinary awareness, as well as for the notion that we can develop a sensitivity to the whole as an "active absence." Psychologists have discovered that there are two major modes of organization for a human being: the action mode and the receptive mode.[13] In the early infant state, we are in the receptive mode, but this is gradually dominated by the development of the action mode of organization that is formed in us by our interaction with the physical environment. Through the manipulation of physical bodies, and especially solid bodies, we develop the ability to focus the attention and perceive boundaries—that is, to discriminate, analyze, and divide the world up into objects. The internalization of this experience of manipulating physical bodies gives us the object-based logic that Henri Bergson called "the logic of solids."[14] This process has been described in detail by psychologists from Hermann Ludwig von Helmholtz down to Jean Piaget. The result is an analytical mode of consciousness attuned to our experience with solid bodies. This kind of consciousness is institutionalized by the structure of our language, which favors the active mode of organization. As a result, we are well prepared to perceive selectively only some of the possible features of experience.

The alternative mode of organization, the receptive mode, is one that allows events to happen—for example, the play above. Instead of being verbal, analytical, sequential, and logical, this mode of consciousness is nonverbal, holistic, nonlinear, and intuitive. It emphasizes the sensory and perceptual instead of the rational categories of the action mode. It is based on taking in, rather than manipulating, the environment.

For reasons of biological survival, the analytic mode has become dominant in human experience. This mode of consciousness corresponds to the object world, and since we are not aware of our own mode of consciousness directly, we inevitably identify this world as the only reality. It is because of this mode of consciousness that the whole is "nothing" to our awareness, and also that when we encounter it we do so an as "active absence." If we were reeducated in the receptive mode of consciousness, our encounter with wholeness would be considerably different, and we would see many new things about our world.

WHOLENESS IN SCIENCE

There are many hermeneutic illustrations of the active absence—speaking, reading, playing a game, and so on—that are similar to the actors playing their parts in the play. These examples can each demonstrate the reversal that comes in turning from awareness of an object into the encounter with the whole. This turning around, from grasping to being receptive, from awareness of an object to letting an absence be active, is a reversal that is the practical consequence of choosing the path that assents to the whole as no-thing and not mere nothing.

It is because of this reversal that the authentic whole must be invisible to the scientific approach, as currently conceived. The paradigm for modern scientific method is Kant's "appointed judge who compels the witnesses to answer questions which he himself has formulated."[15] Science believes itself to be objective, but is in essence subjective because the witness is compelled to answer questions that *the scientist themselves have formulated*. They never notice the circularity in this because they believe they hear the voice of "nature" speaking, not realizing that it is the transposed echo of their own voices. Modern positivist science can only approach the whole as an object of interrogation. So it is that science today, by virtue of the method that is its hallmark, is left with a fragmented world of things which it must then try to reassemble.

The introduction of a quantitative, mathematical method in science led to the distinction between primary and secondary qualities.[16] The so-called primary qualities—like number, magnitude, position, and so on—can be expressed mathematically. But such secondary qualities as color, taste, and sound cannot be expressed mathematically in any direct way. This distinction has been made into the basis for a dualism in which only the primary qualities are considered to be real. Any secondary quality is supposed to be the result of the effect on the senses of the primary qualities, being no more than a subjective experience and not itself a part of "objective" nature.

The result of this dualistic approach is that the features of nature which we encounter most immediately in our experience are judged to be unreal—just illusions of the senses. In contrast, what is real is not evident to the senses and has to be attained through the use of intellectual reasoning. Thus, one group of qualities is imagined to be behind or beneath the other group, hidden by the appearances, so that a secondary quality is understood when it is seen how it could have arisen from the primary qualities. The reality of nature is not identical to the appearances that our senses give, and a major aim of positivist science is to *replace the phenomenon with a mathematical model*, which can incorporate only the primary qualities. This quantitative result is then supposed to be more real than the phenomenon observed by the senses, and the task of science becomes a kind of "metaphysical archaeology" which strives to reveal an underlying mathematical reality.

The way this approach is done in practice can be illustrated by Sir Isaac Newton's treatment of the colors produced by a prism. His method was to correlate all observations of secondary qualities with measurements of primary qualities, so as to eliminate secondary qualities from the scientific description of the world.[17] Newton eliminated color by correlating it with the "degree of refrangibility" (what we could now call the "angle of refraction") of the different colors when the sun's light passes through a prism. Furthermore, refraction can be represented numerically, thus, the ultimate aim of substituting a series of numbers for the sensory experience of different colors is achieved (later the wavelength of light would replace refrangibility). Hence, something that can be measured replaced the phenomenon of color, and in this way color as color was eliminated from the scientific account of the world.

GOETHE'S WAY OF SCIENCE

Newton's approach to light and color illustrates the extraordinary degree to which modern science stands outside the phenomenon, the ideal of understanding being reached when the scientist is as far removed as possible from the experience.[18] The physics of color could now be understood just as well by a person who is color-blind. There is little wonder that the successful development of physics has led to an ever-increasing alienation of the universe of physics from the world of our everyday experience.[19]

Goethe's approach to color was very different from Newton's analytic approach. Goethe attempted to develop a physics of color which was based on everyday experience. He worked to achieve an authentic wholeness by *dwelling in the phenomenon* instead of replacing it with a mathematical representation.

Goethe's objection to Newton's procedure was that he had taken a complicated phenomenon as his basis, and tried to explain what was simple by means of something more complex.[20] To Goethe, Newton's procedure was upside down. Newton had arranged for the light from a tiny hole in a window shutter to pass through a glass prism onto the opposite wall. The spectrum of colors formed in this way was a well-known phenomenon at the time, but Newton's contribution was to explain it in a new way. He believed that the colors were already present in the light of the sun coming through the hole, and the effect of the prism was to separate them. It would be quite wrong to say, as is said so often in physics textbooks, that *the experiment showed* Newton this, or that he was *led to believe* this by the experiment. Rather, it was Newton's way of seeing that constituted the experiment's being seen in this way. He saw the idea (that white light is a mixture of colors which are sorted out by the prism) "reflected" in the experiment, as if it were a mirror to his thinking; he did not derive it from the experiment in the way that is often believed.

In contrast to Newton, Goethe set out to find the simplest possible color phenomenon and make this his basis for understanding color in more complex situations. He believed Newton erred in thinking colorless light was compounded of colored lights because colored light is darker than colorless light, and this would mean that several darker lights were added together to make a brighter light. Goethe looked first at the colors that are formed when the prism is used in light in the natural environment, instead of the restricted and artificial environment that he felt Newton had selected as the experimental basis for his approach. By doing this, Goethe recognized that the phenomenon of prismatic colors depended on a boundary between light and dark regions. Far from the colors somehow being already *contained* in light, for Goethe, they *came into being* out of a relationship between light and darkness.

To Goethe, the prism was a complicating factor, and so to understand the arising of colors, he looked for the more simple cases, which meant looking for situations where there are no secondary factors, only light and darkness. Such a case is what Goethe first called *das reine Phänomen* (the pure phenomenon), and for which he later used the term "*Urphänomen*" (primal or archetypal phenomenon).[21] He found the primal phenomenon of color in the color phenomena that are associated with opaque or semitransparent media. When light is seen through such a medium, it darkens first to yellow, and then to orange and red as the medium thickens. Alternatively, when darkness is seen through an illuminated medium, it lightens to violet and then blue. Such a phenomenon is particularly evident with atmospheric colors, such as the colors of the sun and the sky, and the way that these change with atmospheric conditions. Thus, it was in the natural environment that Goethe first recognized the primal phenomenon of color to be the lightening of dark to give violet and blue and the darkening of light to give yellow and red. He expressed this process poetically as "the deeds and sufferings of light."[22]

Once Goethe had found this primal phenomenon, he was in a position to see how the colors change from one to another as conditions change. He could see how these shifts were at the root of more complex phenomena such as the prismatic colors. One result is that a dynamic wholeness is perceived in the prismatic colors—a wholeness totally lacking in Newton's account. In other words, Goethe's presentation describes the origin of colors whereas Newton's does not. The colors of the spectrum are simply not intelligible in Newton's account because there is no inherent reason why there should be red, or blue, or green, as there is no reason why they should appear in the order that they do in the spectrum. But with Goethe's account, one can understand both the quality of the colors and the relationship between them, so that we can perceive the wholeness of the phenomenon without going beyond what can be experienced.

Goethe's method was to extend and deepen his experience of the phenomenon until he reached that element of the phenomenon that is not given externally to sense experience. This is the connection, or relationship in the phenomenon which he called the "law" (*Gesetz*), and which he found by going more deeply into the phenomenon instead of standing back from it or trying to go beyond it intellectually to something that could not be experienced.[23] In other words, Goethe believed that the organization or unity of the phenomenon is real and can be *experienced*, but that it is not evident to sensory experience. It is perceived by an intuitive experience—what Goethe called "*Anschauung,*" which "may be held to signify the *intuitive knowledge gained through contemplation of the visible aspect.*"[24]

In following Goethe's approach to scientific knowledge, one finds that the wholeness of the phenomenon is intensive. The experience is one of entering into a dimension that is in the phenomenon, not behind or beyond it, but which is not visible at first. It is perceived through the mind, when the mind functions as an organ of perception instead of the medium of logical thought. Whereas mathematical science begins by transforming the contents of sensory perception into quantitative values and establishing a relationship between them, Goethe looked for a relationship between the perceptible elements that left the contents of perception unchanged. He tried to see these elements themselves holistically instead of replacing them by a relationship analytically. As Ernst Cassirer said, "the mathematical formula strives to make the phenomena calculable, that of Goethe to make them visible."[25]

It seems clear from his way of working that Goethe could be described correctly as a *phenomenologist* of nature, since his approach to knowledge was to let the phenomenon become fully visible without imposing subjective mental constructs. He was especially scathing towards the kind of theory that attempted to explain the phenomenon by some kind of hidden mechanism. He saw this style of analysis as an attempt to introduce fanciful sensory-like elements behind the appearances, to which the human mind then had to be denied direct access. He thought René Descartes' attempt to imagine such mechanical models behind the appearances as debasing to the mind, and no doubt he would have felt the same way about Einstein's scientific investigator.[26] Goethe did not examine the phenomenon intellectually but, rather, tried to visualize the phenomenon in his mind in a sensory way—the process he called "exact sensorial fantasy" (*exakte sinnliche Phantasie*).[27] Goethe's thinking is concrete, not abstract, and can be described as one of dwelling in the phenomenon.[28]

THE URPHENOMENON

The notion of the *Urphänomen* is an invaluable illustration of the concrete nature of Goethe's way of thinking that dwells in the phenomenon.

The primal phenomenon is not to be thought of as a generalization from observations, produced by abstracting from different instances something that is common to them. If this result were the case, one would arrive at an abstracted unity with the dead quality of a lowest common factor. For Goethe, the primal phenomenon was a concrete instance—what he called "an instance worth a thousand, bearing all within itself."[29] In a moment of intuitive perception, the universal is seen within the particular, so that the particular instance is seen as a living instance of the universal. What is merely particular in one perspective is simultaneously universal in another way of seeing. In other words, the particular becomes symbolic of the universal.[30]

In terms of the category of wholeness, the primal phenomenon is an example of the whole that is present in the part. Goethe himself said as much when he called it "an instance worth a thousand," and described it as "bearing all within itself." It is the authentic whole that is reached by going into the parts, whereas a generalization is the counterfeit whole that is obtained by standing back from the parts to get an overview. Looking for the *Urphänomen* is an example of looking for the right part—that is, the part that contains the whole. This way of seeing illustrates the simultaneous, reciprocal relationship between part and whole, whereby the whole cannot appear until the part is recognized, but the part cannot be recognized as such without the whole.

For example, Goethe was able to "read" how colors arise in the way that the colors of the sun and the sky change with the atmospheric conditions throughout the day. Because there were no secondary, complicating factors, this was for him an instance of the primal phenomenon of the arising of colors. This phenomenon was perceived as a part that contained the whole, and it was, in fact, through the observation of this particular phenomenon that Goethe first learned to see intuitively the law of the origin of color. Yet, the way that the colors of the sun and sky change together does not stand out as a phenomenon until it is seen as an instance of how colors arise. The search for the primal phenomenon is like creative writing, where the need is to find the right expression to let the meaning come forth. By analogy, we can say that Goethe's way of science is "hermeneutical." Once the primal phenomenon has been discovered in a single case, it can be recognized elsewhere in nature and in artificial situations where superficially it may appear to be very different. These varying instances can be compared to the fragments of a hologram.

Newton, in contrast, tried to divide light into parts: the colors of the spectrum from red to blue. But these are not true parts because each does not contain the whole, and hence they do not serve to let the whole come forth. Colorless light, or white light, is imagined to be a summative totality of these colors; whole and parts are treated as separate and outside of each other. Newton tried to go analytically from whole to parts (white light separated into colors), and from parts to whole (colors combined to make white light). In contrast, Goethe encountered the wholeness of the phenomenon through the intuitive mode of consciousness, which is receptive to the phenomenon instead of dividing it according to external categories.[31]

CONCLUSION

The experience of authentic wholeness requires a new style of learning largely ignored in our schools and universities today. Typically, modern education is grounded in the intellectual faculty, whose analytical capacity alone is developed, mostly through verbal reasoning. One notes, for example, that science students are often not interested in observing phenomena of nature; if asked to do so, they become easily bored. Their observations often bear little resemblance to the phenomenon itself.[32] These students are much happier with textbook descriptions and explanations, a fact readily understandable once one recognizes that most educational experience unfolds in terms of one mode of consciousness—the verbal, rational mode.

The experience of authentic wholeness is impossible in this mode of consciousness, and a complementary style of understanding could usefully be developed. This can be done, first by learning to work with mental images in a way emulating Goethe—that is, forming images from sensory experiences. In turn, this process requires careful observation of the phenomenon. Authentic wholeness means that the whole is in the part, hence careful attention must be given to the parts instead of to general principles. In contrast, an intellectual approach to scientific education begins by seeing the phenomenon as an instance of general principles.

Working with mental images activates a different mode of consciousness that is holistic and intuitive. One area where this style of learning is now used practically is in transpersonal education.[33] Experiments with guided fantasy indicate that a frequent result is the extension of feelings, whereby the student experiences a deeper, more direct contact with the phenomenon imagined.[34] In this way, a more comprehensive and complete encounter with the phenomenon results, and aspects of the phenomenon otherwise unnoticed often come to light. In addition, students feel themselves to be more in harmony with the phenomenon, as if they themselves were participating in it. This leads to an attitude toward nature more grounded in concern, respect, and responsibility.[35]

Goethe's way of science is not the only direction for a way of learning grounded in authentic wholeness. In most general terms, such a style of education and science is phenomenological, letting things become manifest as they show themselves without forcing our own categories on them. This kind of learning and science goes beyond the surface of the phenomenon, but not behind it to contrive some causal mechanism described by a model borrowed from somewhere else. A contemporary illustration of such an approach is the work of biologist Wolfgang Schad in his zoological study *Man and Mammals*.[36] Schad shows how all mammals can be understood in terms of the way in which the whole is present in the parts. In addition, he demonstrates how each mammal can be understood in terms of its own overall organization.

Schad begins with the direct observation of the immediate phenomena, working to rediscover the uniqueness of individual animals. According to Schad's approach, every detail of an animal is a reflection of its basic organization. Thus, he does not begin by replacing the phenomenon with a stereotype, but rather searches for the animal's unique qualities. This approach does not lead to fragmentation and multiplicity. Instead, it leads to the perception of diversity within unity, whereby the unique quality of each mammal is seen holistically within the context of other mammals. With a wealth of drawings and photographs, Schad demonstrates how going into the part to encounter the whole leads to the perception of multiplicity within a holistic perspective. He shows that multiplicity in unity means seeing uniqueness without fragmentation.

The counterfeit approach to wholeness—that is, going away from the part to get an overview—leads only to the abstraction of the general case, which has the quality of uniformity rather than uniqueness. Schad indicates how a biology grounded in authentic wholeness can recognize the inner organic order in an animal in such a way that its individual features can be explained by the basic organization of the animal itself. In short, the mammal "explains" itself. For example, the formation of the hedgehog's horny quills is explained in terms of the basic organization of the hedgehog itself. Other questions for which Schad provides answers are why cattle have horns, and deer, antlers; why leopards are spotted, and zebras, striped; why otters, beavers, seals, and hippopotamuses live in water; why giraffes' necks are long; why rhinoceroses are horned. Schad convincingly demonstrates that features such as these can be explained through careful observation of an animal's organization in relation to the organization of other mammals.

Like Goethe's, Schad's way of science is phenomenological and hermeneutical. It is phenomenological because the animal is capable of disclosing itself in terms of itself. Phenomenology, said Heidegger, is the effort "to let that which shows itself be seen from itself in the very way in which it shows itself from itself."[37] Phenomenology brings to light what is there but at first may be hidden. Schad discovers in the animal the qualities that make that animal what it is rather than some other creature. In addition, Schad's work is hermeneutical, since when the point is reached where the animal discloses itself, the animal becomes its own language. In this moment, the animal *is* language. As an authentic discovery, this moment can only be experienced directly; it cannot be "translated" adequately into the verbal language of secondhand description. In this sense, Schad's way of seeing echoes the universal sense of Hans-Georg Gadamer's hermeneutics, in which "being that can be understood is language."[38]

As Schad's work suggests, Goethe's way of science did not end with him. His style of learning and understanding belongs not to the past but to the future. It is widely acknowledged today that, through the growth of the science of matter, the Western mind has become more and more removed from contact with nature. Contemporary problems, many arising from the modern scientific method, confront people with the fact that they have become divorced from a realistic appreciation of their place in the larger world. At the same time, there is a growing demand for a renewal of contact with nature. It is not enough to dwell in nature sentimentally and aesthetically, grafting such awareness to a scientific infrastructure that largely denies nature. The need is a *new* science of nature, different from the science of matter, and based on other human faculties besides the analytic mind. A basis for this science is the discovery of authentic wholeness.[39]

NOTES

1. This essay was originally published in David Seamon and Robert Mugerauer, eds., *Dwelling, Place and Environment* (Dordrecht: Martinus Nijhoff, 1985; New York: Columbia University Press, 1989), pp. 281–302. The editors and author thank Kluwer Academic Publishers and Martinus Nijhoff Publishers for allowing the article to be reprinted here. ©1985 by Martinus Nijhoff Publishers, Dordrecht, the Netherlands.

2. T. Leith and H. Upatnieks, "Photography by Laser," *Scientific American* 212 (1965): 24–35.

3. David Bohm, *Wholeness and the Implicate Order* (London: Routledge and Kegan Paul, 1980), p. 149.

4. C. W. Kilmister, *The Environment in Modern Physics* (London: English University Press, 1965), p. 36.

5. Jayant Narlikar, *The Structure of the Universe* (Oxford: Oxford University Press, 1977), p. 250.

6. Fritjof Capra, *The Tao of Physics* (London: Wildhouse, 1975), p. 313.

7. Richard E. Palmer, *Hermeneutics* (Evanston, Ill.: Northwestern University Press, 1969), chap. 7.

8. P. H. Bortoft, "A Non-reductionist Perspective for the Quantum Theory" (master's thesis, Department of Theoretical Physics, Birkbeck College, 1982), chap. 5.

9. The difficulty with talking about part *and* whole is that a distinction is made that is extensive, and this leads to dualism. The difficulty disappears with the recognition that there can be an *intensive* distinction; see Bortoft, "Non-reductionist Perspective."

10. See the notion of unfolding (*explicatio*) and enfolding (*complicatio*) in the work of Nicholas of Cusa, discussed in Karl Jaspers, *The Great Philosophers*, vol. 2 (London: Rupert Hart-Davis, 1966), p. 129; also, see Bohm, *Wholeness and the Implicate Order*, chap. 7.

11. The terminology of presence and presencing is adopted from Martin Heidegger as an attempt to escape dualism. See G. J. Seidel, *Martin Heidegger and the Pre-Socratics* (Lincoln: University of Nebraska Press, 1964), chap. 3.

12. Martin Heidegger, *Kant and the Problem of Metaphysics* (Bloomington: Indiana University Press, 1962), p. 206.

13. Arthur J. Deikman, "Bimodal Consciousness," in *The Nature of Human Consciousness*, edited by Robert E. Ornstein (San Francisco: W. H. Freeman, 1973).

14. Henri Bergson, *Creative Evolution* (London: Macmillan, 1911), p. ix; also see Milič Čapek, *Bergson and Modern Physics* (Holland: Reidel, 1971), pp. 56, 69, 72–74.

15. Immanuel Kant, *Critique of Pure Reason*, trans. Norman Kemp Smith (London: Macmillan, 1964), p. 20.

16. E. A. Burtt, *The Metaphysical Foundations of Modern Science* (London: Routledge and Kegan Paul, 1980), p. 83.

17. Michael Roberts and E. R. Thomas, *Newton and the Origin of Colours* (London: Bell, 1934), pp. 60, 110.

18. Idries Shah, *The Sufis* (New York: Doubleday, 1964), p. xvi.

19. Aron Gurwitsch, *Phenomenology and the Theory of Science* (Evanston, Ill.: Northwestern University Press, 1974), chap. 2. See also Aron Gurwitsch, "Galilean Physics in the Light of Husserl's Phenomenology," in *Phenomenology and Sociology*, edited by Thomas Luckmann (Harmondsworth: Penguin Books, 1978).

20. Ernst Lehrs, *Man or Matter*, 3rd rev. & enl. (London: Rudolf Steiner Press, 1985), p. 314.

21. H. B. Nisbet, *Goethe and the Scientific Tradition* (University of London: Institute of Germanic Studies, 1972), p. 39.

22. Lehrs, *Man or Matter*, p. 314.

23. Nisbet, *Goethe and the Scientific Tradition*, p. 36, n.140.

24. Agnes Arber, *The Natural Philosophy of Plant Form* (Cambridge: Cambridge University Press, 1950), p. 209, italics in the original.

25. Quoted in A. G. F. Gode von Aesch, *Natural Science in German Romanticism* (New York: Columbia University German Studies, 1941), p. 74.

26. Nisbet, *Goethe and the Scientific Tradition*, p. 54; Albert Einstein and Leopold Infeld, *The Evolution of Physics* (Cambridge: Cambridge University Press, 1947), p. 33.

27. Lehrs, *Man or Matter*, p. 109.

28. The difference between these two kinds of scientific thinking illustrates, and is illustrated by, the distinction Martin Heidegger makes between "belonging *together*" and "*Belonging* together" in Martin Heidegger, *Identity and Difference* (New York: Harper and Row, 1969), p. 29. In the first case, belonging is determined by together, so that "to belong" means to have a place in the order of a "together"—that is, in the unity of a framework. But in the case of belonging together, the "together" is determined by the *belonging*, so that there is "the possibility of no longer representing belonging in terms of the unity of the together, but rather experiencing this together in terms of belonging" (ibid.). Thus, we could say that Goethe experienced the *belonging* together of the yellow sun and the blue sky, and that he did not try to make them belong *together*. This experience of *belonging* together is reached by dwelling in the phenomenon instead of replacing it with conceptual representatives.

29. Lehrs, *Man or Matter*, p. 123.

30. Ernst Cassirer, *The Problem of Knowledge* (New Haven, Conn.: Yale University Press, 1974), p. 146.

31. Goethe followed the same approach in studying living things in nature. His insight into the growing plant, which he expressed as "All is leaf," is an instance of an encounter with the wholeness of the plant whereby he saw the whole coming into presence in the parts. Goethe did not mean by this that the various organs of the flower—sepals, petals, stamens—grew out of the stem leaves in a material sequence. His perception that all is leaf is an instance of the intuitive perception whereby the particular is seen as a living manifestation of the universal, and hence in the moment of seeing is symbolic of the universal. See Lehrs, *Man or Matter*, chap. 5. See also Henri Bortoft, *The Wholeness of Nature: Goethe's Science of Conscious Participation in Nature* (Hudson, N.Y.: Lindisfarne Press, 1996). The complete text of Goethe's essay "The Metamorphosis of Plants" appears in *Goethe: Scientific Studies*, Douglas Miller, ed. (New York: Suhrkamp, 1988).

32. R. G. Stansfield, "The New Theology? The Case of the Dripping Tap" (paper presented to the British Association for the Advancement of Science, September, 1975).

33. Gay Hendricks and James Fadiman, *Transpersonal Education* (Englewood Cliffs, N.J.: Prentice-Hall, 1976).

34. Ibid.

35. See David Seamon, "Goethe's Approach to the Natural World: Implications for Environmental Theory and Education," in *Humanistic Geography:*

Prospects and Problems, edited by D. Ley and M. Samuels (Chicago: Maaroufa, 1978), pp. 238–50.

36. Wolfgang Schad, *Man and Mammals* (New York: Waldorf Press, 1977). See also Mark Riegner, "Horns, Hooves, Spots and Stripes: Form and Pattern in Mammals," *Orion Nature Quarterly*, vol. 4, no. 4 (1985); also Mark Riegner, "Toward a Holistic Understanding of Place: Reading the Landscape Through its Flora and Fauna," in *Dwelling, Seeing and Designing: Toward a Phenomenological Ecology*, edited by David Seamon (Albany: State University of New York Press, 1994).

37. Martin Heidegger, *Being and Time* (New York: Harper and Row, 1962), p. 58.

38. Hans-Georg Gadamer, *Truth and Method*, 2nd rev. ed. (London: Sheed and Ward, 1989), p. 474.

39. Bortoft, *The Wholeness of Nature* (see note 31).

13

Light and Cognition

Goethean Studies as a Science of the Future

In 1864 the poet Gerard Manley Hopkins, then a very young man, saw a rainbow.[1] In writing of it, Hopkins captured the problem of "emergence" in cognition, an issue central to the kind of understanding that a Goethean science tries to facilitate. Where, asked Hopkins, do we locate a rainbow: in the rain, in the sunlight, in the eye, or in the mind?

> It was a hard thing to undo this knot.
> The rainbow shines but only in the thought
> Of him that looks. Yet not in that alone,
> For who makes rainbows by invention?
> And many standing round a waterfall
> See one bow each, yet not the same to all,
> But each a hand's breadth further than the next.
> The sun on falling waters writes the text
> Which yet is in the eye or in the thought.
> It was a hard thing to undo this knot.[2]

Like a rainbow, phenomena emerge and fill the mind with sights, sometimes sounds, yet how do they arise? What is our part in their production and what is the part played by an external world? More important to Goethean science, is the pattern of emergence immutable, myopic, single-minded; or can it, like a Proteus, assume myriad forms

299

calling forth worlds whose emergent properties reflect connections hidden to other forms of consciousness? Are there ways to reenvision nature and ourselves, and are there cogent reasons for doing so?

Motives for change have arisen within many fields from biology, ecology, atmospheric chemistry, and immunology to my own field of quantum optics, in which compelling new experiments have renewed the challenge made by quantum physics at the turn of the century regarding the strictures of classical forms of thought. By following two threads from recent developments in quantum optics, I hope to strengthen the challenge further and point to characteristics of the novel modes of understanding now required by the facts. Once the need is convincingly demonstrated, the project itself begins of creating the requisite faculties adequate to the understanding of these newly emergent phenomena of science.

The significance of such considerations may seem slight or to be merely so much academic epistemology, but I would argue to the contrary. Thought and, more basic still, the process of thinking are the progenitors of our civilization. The effects of how we think work back on themselves, rigidifying and reinforcing those modalities of thought characteristic of an age and hindering new modalities.

Our manner of thinking has shaped the planet and ourselves and has the power to reshape them once more. The monuments of the past speak of traditions that have sculpted not only our exterior landscape, but also an interior one as well. The textures and patterns of thought in which we now live are the outcome of hard-fought, spiritual battles that established a general mode of discourse, understanding, feeling, and action. While we may be unaware of their history, these traditions shape our habits of thought and understanding—our very seeing. In our own day, spiritual battles and new modes of knowledge are emerging that require fresh patterns of thought and unknown metaphors. These new ways of understanding will one day shape a future landscape.

If we travel to a place like Italy, we always stand within the aura of antiquity. Noble institutions, great artists and thinkers have exchanged the landscape of the wilderness for that of the garden or, better, the protected hillside city, crafted into a work of art. The accomplishments of Dante, Marsilio Ficino, Giotto, Leonardo Da Vinci, Michelangelo, Raphael, and countless others have nourished and defined not only Italian culture but that of the entire West. We are the inheritors of material and cognitive monuments.

OUR COGNITIVE INHERITANCE

> Be praised my Lord, for all thy creatures,
> In the first place for the blessed Brother Sun
> Who gives us the day and enlightens us through you.

He is beautiful and radiant with his great splendor,
Giving witness of you, most Omnipotent One.

Be praised, my Lord, for Sister Moon and the stars
Formed by you so bright, precious, and beautiful.[3]

When in 1225, Saint Francis composed these lines of his *Canticle to the Sun* while in the convent of Saint Damian, he was participant in a long tradition of sacred and mythic knowledge that saw nature as alive and ensouled—that is, as a being. She was still the goddess *Natura* as Bernard Silvestris or Alanus ab Insulis called her at Chartres.[4] Persephone still walked the earth. By the thirteenth century, however, the experience was so attenuated that Nature usually appeared only as a figure within Christian allegory. Her presence there, nonetheless, belies a rich and more intense ancestry that stretches back to Thales' declaration that "All things are full of gods," and beyond.[5]

In the fifteenth century, Marsilio Ficino, student and interpreter of the "divine Plato," was also part of an ancient tradition that he saw as running back through Plato and Pythagoras to Orpheus, Hermes Trismegistus and Zoroaster. Like Saint Francis, he saw God and his multiplicity of angelic beings manifested through light and the radiant celestial bodies of our universe.[6] As the following passage illustrates, Ficino understood that the universe is not a material cosmos in motion but a multiplicity of beings ordered and animated by the Godhead:

> Look at the heaven, please, oh citizen of the celestial fatherland, at the heaven which was made orderly and manifest by God for the purpose of making [clear the multiplicity of beings]. When you look upward, the celestial entities tell you the glory of God through the ray of the stars, like the glances and signs of their eyes, and the firmament announces the works of His hands. But the sun can signify to you God Himself in the greatest degree. The sun will give you the signs; who would dare to call the sun false? So the invisible things of God, that is, the angelic divinities, are seen and understood particularly through the stars, and God's eternal power and divinity through the sun.[7]

Around 1300, shortly after the life of Saint Francis, a novel technical device appeared in medieval Europe that symbolized an incipient change of enormous proportions. This device did not ease the burdens of manual labor, yet it became both literally and metaphorically the machine that grew to regulate the tempo of human life. I refer, of course, to the mechanical clock. There had been time pieces of other sorts for centuries before—sundials, water clocks, fire clocks, sand clocks, and so forth—

but the development of the mechanical clock marks a decisive point in the evolution of the West.[8] I am interested, however, not in the mechanical clock as technology but, rather, in how the clock became an image that shaped the collective imagination and provided a basis for understanding the natural word.

According to historian Lynn White, Jr., the introduction of the clock as part of the iconography of Christian theology occurred shortly after the invention of the clock itself.[9] In the short span of 150 years, the mechanical clock became the invariant attribute of the principal virtue of the fifteenth century—Temperance. Like the clock, the human body and soul require regulation by reason; what was true for the microcosm was true also for the macrocosm. At the end of the fourteenth century in his *Duciel*, Nicole Oresme invoked the escapement feature of a clockwork to explain how God regulated the orbital velocities of the planets. It remained for Galileo to complete the unification of terrestrial and celestial mechanics and thereby provide the basis for the Deist notion of the mechanization of the entirety of God's creation.

With the gradual perfecting of the clock mechanism, life was no longer regulated by the movement of the sun during the day or the stars at night. Men and women were freed from nature and so could order their lives, whether domestic, mercantile, or monastic, by the hours of the mechanical clock. In White's words, "Human life no longer adapts the mechanism to its need; mankind is in some measure shaped by a machine which it adores."[10]

Thus, close on the heels of St. Francis, Ficino and the Italian Renaissance—indeed, almost within their embrace—were the stirrings of another nascent tradition that found fulfillment a century after Ficino's death when the modern world conception was born through Copernicus, René Descartes, and Galileo. Like those thinkers before him, Galileo was also a student of nature who admired its extraordinary order. In it, however, he heard a different voice that spoke the language of mathematics and whose meaning was the principles of mechanics.

Two Traditions

While many threads connected Galileo with the past, both his contemporaries and we recognize in him the founder of modern science that, since its birth 400 years ago, has profoundly changed the world. If the architects and artists of the Renaissance lifted their cities into works of art, we, in turn, have filled them with the technological offspring of the scientific revolution. We realize, therefore, that two traditions and cultures are entwined in the Italian landscape—one that ended in Ficino and another that began in Galileo. I believe that we, in our time, stand at a similar juncture in which the tension between these two cultures may find a resolution so urgently needed.

Our cognitive inheritance is twofold. Our aspirations to be good stewards of the earth, to dress creation with the beautiful work of our own hands, and to recognize within nature the goddess *Natura*, all echo the song of Saint Francis. They are born of a participation in cosmos and an experience of self that reaches to a distant past in which the divine was everywhere immanent and open to us.

The strains of a different song, brilliant and strong, ring out from the technological offspring of the scientific revolution. A clockwork universe excludes human participation except as another component of its vast mechanism. This universe seems without inherent value or meaning. This part of our cognitive inheritance is more recent and more pressing. Both voices still resound, but too often the discord between them leads to misunderstandings and tragedies like Chernobyl or Bopal.

One thinker who clearly heard both voices and the tension between them was the nineteenth-century American writer Ralph Waldo Emerson, patriarch of the Transcendentalist movement.[11] Together with other thinkers on both sides of the Atlantic, he recognized that the old order represented by Ficino and Saint Francis was fast crumbling. The spiritual convictions and values of earlier centuries were being challenged by a newer vision of human beings and nature espoused by the then-flourishing savants of natural science:

> Natural science is the point of interest now, and, I think, is dimming and extinguishing a good deal that was called poetry. These sublime and all-reconciling revelations of nature will exact of poetry a correspondent height and scope, or put an end to it.[12]

As the old forms fell, Emerson held that we were freed to create an original, participatory relation to nature that was not mediated through scripture, prophets and history but could be experienced directly:

> Why should not we have a poetry and philosophy of insight and not of tradition, and a religion by revelation to us and not the history of theirs?... The sun shines today also. There is more wool and flax in the fields. There are new lands, new men, new thoughts.[13]

Emerson saw "the venerable and beautiful traditions" in which his generation was educated "losing their hold on human belief, day by day."[14] As the old forms collapsed, the new possibilities falteringly appeared. The fashioning of a new tradition—a philosophy of contemporary insight—

was the project that Ralph Waldo Emerson, Henry David Thoreau, Amos Bronson Alcott and their collaborators envisioned but left unrealized in their lifetime. The possibility of this new tradition stands before us still, but what might it be?

THE FACTS OF LIGHT

Current motivations for change go beyond the dissatisfactions of nineteenth-century Romantics. At its best, this desire for change is grounded in the scientific facts and powerful moral dilemmas of our modern world. The invention of the mechanical clock is a single instance in the extraordinary technological transformation that dawned with its invention. Since then the industrial revolution and the recent advent of cybernetics have elaborated the clockwork image, expanding its dominion until it appears to encompass all existence. Are there, however, objects whose nature is so radically nonmechanical that they defy all honest attempts to include them in the catalog of machines? I am convinced there are many, but none is so unambiguously nonmechanical as light.

I begin by referring to the old saw regarding the impossibility of creating a classical model of certain quantum phenomena. Recently, the issue has taken on more dramatic proportions with the experimental realizations in several scientific laboratories of what had heretofore been mere thought experiments—only a gleam in the minds of Albert Einstein and Niels Bohr.[15] These developments include John Archibald Wheeler's proposal of a so-called delayed-choice experiment, the Einstein-Podolsky-Rosen experiment, and the phenomena associated with superconductivity.[16] Each of these effects and many others require the concept of "quantum superposition," an idea that defies our traditional clockwork imagination and challenges us to develop new imaginative modalities.

I begin with the specific case of the delayed-choice experiment, an effort in which I collaborated at the Max Planck Institute for Quantum Optics in Garching.[17] This experiment dramatizes the so-called wave-particle duality of light. To understand results of the experiment, we need to establish the criteria for the recognition of particles and waves—that is, how do we know whether we have the one or the other? The standard test for a particle is indivisibility. If we can split the particle, then it might be comprised of other particles or it might be a wave. If, however, the particle is resolutely indivisible, then we can declare it unequivocally to have been a single particle.

The criterion for a wave is the phenomenon of interference. That is, when two wave-trains cross, the disturbance displays very characteristic maxima and minima. Make a slit with two extended fingers and look at a source of light. You will notice alternating light and dark bands in the region between your fingers. This alternation is evidence for the wave nature of light. With these two criteria, indivisibility and interference, we are now ready to interpret experiments that will provide the "definitive" answer to the question regarding the nature of light.

A light source has been invented that claims to produce one "particle" of light at a time. How do I test it? I do so by attempting to divide the particle in half. The apparatus for this test is a half-silvered mirror, which possesses the property of transmitting half the light incident on it and reflecting the remaining half (see fig. 13.1).[18] If there is, in fact, only a single indivisible, "particle" of light, then the mirror will be unable to split the light in two. Rather, the mirror will either transmit the light or reflect it.

The apparatus is completed by placing two light detectors (y and x in the figure) that are of sufficient sensitivity to respond to single "particles" of light. If the "particle" is divisible, then the detectors will fire simultaneously, thereby showing that part of the light was reflected and part transmitted. If, however, only one fires for each particle incident on the half-silvered mirror, then we possessed a single "particle" of light.

Several so-called single-photon sources have been invented and the tests outlined above performed. The results of these experiments confirm that, under special circumstances, one can produce single, indivisible

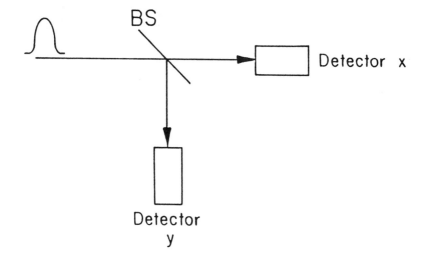

Fig. 13.1. The "Particle Test."

"particles" of light. It is important to stress the experimentally determined *indivisibility* of the "particles" because the paradox hinges on it.

PARTICLES AND WAVES

We now turn to the second aspect of the experiment, namely, interferometry. The principle of an interferometer is very simple. It is a device
designed to divide light into two beams and then to recombine them so as
to show interference effects. Remember interference is proof of the
"wave" nature of light. If we succeed in dividing light into two beams
and, through recombination, to create interference, then we will have
demonstrated that light is a wave.

An interferometer (of the Mach-Zehnder type) is shown in figure
13.2. Light of the usual sort (not the single-particle kind) enters the
interferometer through a half-silvered mirror, is split into two beams and,
after reflection from two fully silvered mirrors, recombines on a second
half-silvered mirror. If one looks on a placard at some distance from the
final mirror, one sees light and dark bands, that is, interference which is
clear evidence for light as a wave.

Now the critical moment. Use the single-particle light source as the
light source for the interferometer. What will happen? Recall that the
success of the interferometer experiment *requires* that the light be divided

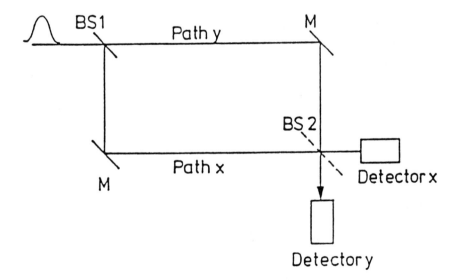

Fig. 13.2. The "Wave Test."

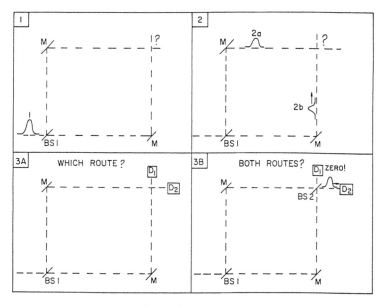

Fig. 13.3. The "Delayed-Choice Experiment."

at the first beam splitter. By contrast, the success of the particle experiment *requires* that the light remain undivided for a single-particle source. These situations are logical opposites. We cannot entertain both ideas at the same time without cognitive dissonance of a rather high order.

We will further heighten the stakes by the following experimental ruse. At first, the experimentalist will set up only part of the experiment, which begins with the final half-silvered mirror missing as in figure 13.3. The attentive reader will recognize an ambiguity in the design. By leaving the final half-silvered mirror out, I have described an apparatus suited to test for single particles of light. By inserting the final half-silvered mirror, the device becomes an interferometer suited to test for the wave nature of light. Simply inserting or removing the final mirror changes the entire intention of the apparatus. Moreover, I am free to insert or remove the final mirror at any time. This situation is what Wheeler termed "delayed-choice."

Allow the single-particle source to emit its particles one at a time into the apparatus and run the experiment in three modes, the first two of which are simply to insert and remove the final half-silvered mirror prior to running the experiment. What happens? With the mirror removed, we find experimentally that half the time one detector fires and half the time the other, but the the two never fire *together*. This is the signature for indivisible "particles of light." Now with the source unchanged, insert the final beam splitter and run the experiment. What do the detectors show? They now display the unambiguous signature of interference. But interference requires the particle to divide at the first half-silvered mirror, which we just showed never to happen with the single-photon source used! Is there some way the particle could, perhaps by "sensing" the intent of the experiment, divide in the latter instance but not in the former? This is a bizarre scenario but one that can be tested by the delayed-choice experiment.

A Logical Impossibility?

In the third mode of running the experiment we *wait* to insert or remove the final half-silvered mirror until *after* the "particle" of light has passed the first half-silvered mirror. In other words, we delay our choice of what experiment to run until the light is deep inside the interferometer. Even in these circumstances, one *still* detects an interference pattern when the final half-silvered mirror is inserted, and no interference without it! What this result implies is that light must be in an ambiguous quantum "superposition" state during the interval from entry into the apparatus until departure through the final half-silvered mirror (or at least until we choose).

For purposes of clarity I will repeat what I take to be the ultimate results of the experiment. If we think classically (by which in this instance I mean mechanically), we confront a situation that requires an indivisible particle of light to travel a single path to a single detector, *and simultaneously* requires it to travel two distinct paths to two detectors. This is a logical impossibility. An entity, whatever it is, cannot both travel along a single trajectory *and* a pair of trajectories at the same time.

The standard conclusion drawn by orthodox quantum mechanics is that one has created a nonclassical, quantum (i.e. nonmechanical) situation termed a superposition state. Invoking such a phase does not, of course, constitute an explanation any more than reference to its somniferous quality explains the effect of a sleeping pill. Such language simply locates that which we do not understand. There does exist, however, a precise mathematical meaning to the phrase, "quantum superposition state." Still, the clarity of the mathematical formalism has not translated into a clear understanding of the physical phenomena themselves. In fact the suggestion is very often advanced that we must forsake understanding in favor of computing. But this loss is to give up too much. There is an important lesson here and a challenge before which we should not shrink.

Understanding appears to require an image, and the inevitable trend is toward the machine. The imagination of a mechanical universe has provided science with a powerful means of understanding a large but finite range of effects. There exist, however, even within the domain of physics, phenomena such as those described above that simply *cannot* be thought of in mechanical terms without spectacular violations of logic or simple common sense. Here enters the arrogance of the tradition. What cannot be imagined mechanically cannot be imagined at all. One can compute and predict on the basis of computation, but one must forego the old pleasures of understanding, or at least modify our traditional sense of what it means to understand.

Nor is the problem with light limited to the wave-particle question. There are other puzzling features of its apparent nature such as the lack of a quantum-mechanically acceptable concept of position.[19] Electrons and similar elementary particles formally possess a clear position variable. This is not the case with light. To ask the simple question "Where?" is far more subtle for light that for matter. But this fact seems consistent with the results of the delayed-choice experiment.

IMAGINING IN NEW WAYS

Such issues are a small matter, some scientists say. After all, consider the extremes to which one must go to find a phenomenon that cannot be embraced within the mechanical universe. We can well afford a few borderland phenomena that fall outside of the mechanical paradigm. I believe, however, that these phenomena are multiplying and, like the few resistant phenomena that ultimately led to the development of quantum mechanics, will ultimately require serious, responsible attention. Many of the solid state electronic devices common today from television to calculator operate because the mechanical paradigm fails. Perhaps the most spectacular failure may involve high-temperature superconductivity.

The single-photon, delayed-choice interferometer ran on one photon at a time. Conceptually you cannot find a cleaner experiment. Its practical consequences, however, are in proportion to the intensity of the light used. Light just never appears as a single photon in nature or in the technical world. With the discovery of superconductivity in 1911 by H. Kammerlingh Onnes, and now the promise of massive technological implementation of the effect, macroscopic quantum effects of a kind apparently similar to the arcane effects of light may literally drive the engines of industry.

The theory of superconductivity requires a cooperative behavior of electrons over distances that, on an atomic scale, are staggeringly large. There again is no classical imagination that can capture the quantum state of a superconductor. Paradoxes and conceptual confusions of the same kind attend any attempt to force the phenomenon into a classical straightjacket.

One can be confident that the pattern will continue to evolve, like a spider weaving its web in ever expanding circles. Just how much of the world and our surroundings are we willing not to understand? Or shall we take up the challenge and begin to imagine in new ways, faltering at first but gradually learning from our mistakes and fashioning other images of nature. How can mathematics capture in its formal net something that our imagination cannot? Should we not follow the lead of our mathematics and create an imaginative faculty of comparable scope and flexibility?

Lynn White, Jr., has traced the origin of the metaphor—"a clockwork universe"—back to the Middle Ages and to the fabrication of the mechanical clock, which effectively freed people's sense of time from the motions of the heavens and fixed it to the rhythms of a physical instrument. Could it be that the technical innovations of quantum mechanics will engender a similar revolution in thought? Will we come to imagine our universe and ourselves differently for the existence of a revolutionary, quantum technology?

GOETHE AS A HARBINGER OF IMAGINATION

If contemporary science points to inadequacies in present-day modes of thinking, we can ask: What will be the shape of the new manner of understanding required by our future? I believe that artists are the harbingers of the future mentality required both by science and by the imperatives of living in our precarious times. For centuries, artists have struggled to create ways of seeing and knowing that often appeared to be at odds with the burgeoning science of our era. I believe that we now truly stand in need, not only as scientists but as a civilization, of the artist's cognitive capacities. In them, when rightly developed, might the two streams of our cognitive inheritance commingle?

Few artists have worked consciously with the ideas suggested here. Goethe is a crucial exception. Although internationally distinguished by his literary career, Goethe's own evaluation of his life's work diverged from both that of his contemporaries and posterity. He felt that his most significant contributions were not to poetry but to science. In the treatment of Goethe's scientific work as illustrated in the articles of this volume, I would have us look not at his impressive contributions to botany, osteology, color science or meteorology but to his distinctive method and objective.

Through an exchange of letters in 1798 with his friend Friedrich von Schiller, Goethe gained clarity about his methodology, which was becoming, as Schiller termed it, a "rational empiricism."[20] Of his process of investigation, Goethe wrote to Schiller that one passed through three stages: (1) *the empirical phenomenon*, which everyone finds in nature, and which is then raised through experiments to the level of (2) *the scientific phenomenon*, by producing it under circumstances and conditions different from those in which it was first observed, and in a sequence that is more or less successful. The final result is (3) *the pure phenomenon*, which now stands before us as the result of all our observations and experiments. The pure phenomenon can never be isolated but appears in a continuous sequence of events. To depict it, the human mind gives definition to the empirically variable, excludes the accidental, sets aside the impure, untangles the complicated, and even discovers the unknown.[21]

It is essential to note that each of the three stages refers to a phenomenon, each later one of a higher order than the earlier, until one finally attains to what Goethe variously termed the "pure" or "archetypal phenomenon." In this mode of inquiry, one does not slip into abstract, mathematical representations of the phenomenon under study, nor is it a "question of causes, but of conditions under which the phenomena appear."[22] In eschewing causes and mathematical conceptions, Goethe distinguishes himself radically from orthodox views of the scientific method and its goals. For Immanuel Kant, as for most thinkers since, science without mathematics is not science at all. Moreover, if one is not searching for causes, then what can be the objective of scientific inquiry?

Goethe's response to the last remark would be to point to the archetypal phenomenon that is for him the endpoint of scientific investigation. He recognizes that many researchers would wish to reach beyond the phenomenon to hypothetical entities or supposed causes but, for him, the archetypal phenomenon represents the point of culmination beyond which one should not go. In that moment, "the human mind can come closest to things in their general state, draw them near, and, so to speak, form an amalgam with them."[23] Or, as he explains elsewhere:

> There is a delicate empiricism which makes itself utterly identical with the object, thereby becoming true theory. But this enhancement of our mental powers belongs to a highly evolved age.[24]

Goethe holds always to experience and to phenomena even when reaching to the theoretical level. In this sense, it is useful to recall the original meaning of "theory," which is derived from the Greek *theoria*, which means "to behold." To understand, one must see, envision, and behold in the mind as well as in the external world. Goethe would ask, are not these two, inner and outer, subject and object, like cause and effect, caught up into a single unity in the phenomenon? By "making itself utterly identical with the object" one's experience becomes true theory:

> The ultimate goal would be: to grasp that everything in the realm of fact is already theory. The blue of the sky shows us the basic law of chromatics. Let us not seek for something behind the phenomena—they themselves are the theory.[25]

As unusual as it may at first seem, the point of all scientific inquiry is to behold a phenomenon as theory. Nor is this goal alien to the history of science but stands behind every scientific discovery. When Sir Issac Newton perceived the orbit of the moon in the falling apple, he saw "fact as theory." He had puzzled long and tenaciously to win from nature his vision of the coherence we now all learn to see after him. Similarly, Galileo, in the cathedral of Pisa watching the swinging chandelier, discovered the isochronous pendulum of a clock.

What is it that allows such theoretical seeing? First of all, we must realize that all our seeing is structured and informed *by us*. We do not have raw sense impressions but, rather, see red, green, blue. We do not see vague entities but particular objects like wood shavings or handheld calculators. What we see, in other words, already possesses a conceptual character. Our observing is always, as N. R. Hanson calls it, "theory-laden."[26]

Out of the practice of science, Goethe saw the possibility for developing new cognitive faculties whose emergence would bring the perception of novel, and hitherto unseen, coherences within nature. Our manner of thinking limits and even forms the very world we experience. Cognitive science has taught us much concerning the hidden forces that shape our individual and culturally shared view of the world. Goethe proposed that, by staying with the phenomena, varying their conditions of appearance, experimenting with them but holding the phenomena always in view, cognitive capacities would arise suited to proper understanding. "Every new object," he wrote, "clearly seen, opens up a new organ of perception in us.[27]

With the new organs so fashioned, understanding arises in what Goethe termed an "*aperçu*," and "such a discovery is infinitely fruitful."[28] Moments such as these—whether had by Newton, Goethe, or any passionately inquiring scientist—are artistic moments. For Emerson, the poet's task was nothing more than this: To walk within nature not as a spy, but as the transcendency of her own being and so to articulate in words what she performs for and within us.[29] Emerson realized the kinship between artistry and the exhilarating moment of scientific discovery when he observed: "And never did any science originate but by a poetic perception."[30]

If we would create the capacities for understanding our future, we must dwell precisely in the tensions, paradoxes, and annoying anomalies of our time. Only thus will we develop the faculties suited to understand the nature of light and, I believe, see the way through our perilous times. We may think with Goethe that such "mental powers belong to a highly evolved age," but I believe that ours is the dawn of that age.

The prerequisites are there: the mandate of orthodox science to develop our imaginative capacities and the dictates of our conscience if we would avoid the technical calamities that threaten our well-being and survival. On nearly every front, we are called to reimagine the world we inhabit. It simply awaits an act of courage for us to begin and patient perseverance for us to succeed in the self-conscious education now in our hands.

Notes

1. An earlier version of this article originally appeared in W. I. Thompson, ed., *Gaia* 2 (Hudson, N.Y.: Lindesfarne Press, 1991), pp. 111–31; the material is used by permission of Lindesfarne Press, Hudson, N.Y. 12534.

2. Gerard Manley Hopkins, *The Note-Books and Papers of Gerard Manley Hopkins*, edited by H. House (London: Oxford University Press, 1918), p. 28.

3. J. Green, *God's Fool: The Life and Times of Francis of Assisi* (San Francisco: Harper and Row, 1985), pp. 256–57.

4. Bernardus Silvestris, *The Cosmographia*, trans. and ed., Winthrop Wetherbee (New York: Columbia University Press, 1973); Alan of Lille, *The Plaint of Nature*, trans. James J. Sheridan (Toronto: Pontifical Institute of Mediaeval Studies, 1980).

5. F. M. Counford, *From Religion to Philosophy: A Study of the Origins of Western Speculation* (New York: Harper and Row, 1957).

6. D. S. Landes, *Revolutions in Time* (Cambridge, Mass.: Belkap Press, 1983).

7. P. O. Kristeller, *The Philosophy of Marsilio Ficino*, trans. V. Conant (Gloucester, Mass.: Peter Smith, 1964), p. 98.

8. Landes, *Revolutions in Time*.

9. L. White, Jr., "Tempermentia and the Virtuousness of Technology," in *Medieval Religion and Technology* (Berkeley: University of California Press, 1978).

10. Ibid., p.198.

11. P. A. Obuchowski, The Relationship of Emerson's Interest in Science to His Thought (Ph.D. diss., Ann Arbor, Mich.: University Microfilms, 1969).

12. R. W. Emerson, *The Letters of Ralph Waldo Emerson*, edited by Ralph L. Rusk, vol. 6 (New York: Columbia University Press, 1939), p. 63.

13. R. W. Emerson, "Nature," in *Nature, Addresses and Lectures* (Boston: Riverside Press, 1985), p. 9.

14. R. W. Emerson, *The Complete Works of Ralph Waldo Emerson*, vol. 10 (Boston: Riverside Press, 1903–1904), pp. 217–18.

15. J. A. Wheeler and W. H. Zurek, eds., *Quantum Theory and Measurement* (Princeton, N.J.: Princeton University Press, 1983).

16. J. A. Wheeler, *Mathematical Foundations of Quantum Theory*, ed. A. R. Marlow (New York: Academic Press, 1978), p. 9.

17. T. Hellmuth, H. Walther, A. Zajonc, and W. Schleich, "Delayed-Choice Experiments in Quantum Interference," *Physics Review A* 35 (March 1987): 2532–41.

18. P. Grangier, G. Roger, and A. Aspect, "Experimental Evidence for a Photon Anti-correlation Effect on a Beam Splitter: A New Light on Single-Photon Interferences, *Europhysics Letters* 1 (February 1986): 173–79.

19. T. D. Newton and E. P. Wigner, "Localized States for Elementary Systems," *Reviews of Modern Physics*, 21 (July 1949): 405.

20. Rudolf Steiner, *A Theory of Knowledge Implicit based on Goethe's World Conception*, trans. Olin Wannamaker (New York: Anthroposophic Press, 1968), p. 119.

21. J. W. von Goethe, "Empirical Observation and Science" (Jan. 15, 1798), in *Goethe: Scientific Studies*, ed. and trans. Douglas Miller (Boston: Suhrkamp Publishers, 1988), pp. 24–25.

22. Ibid., p. 25.

23. Ibid.

24. Ibid., p. 307.

25. Ibid.

26. N. R. Hanson, *Patterns of Discovery. An Inquiry into the Conceptual Foundations of Science* (Cambridge: Cambridge University Press, 1958).

27. Goethe, *Scientific Studies*, p. 39.

28. Goethe, from a letter to Soret, 30 December 1823, quoted by Rike Wankmuller in *Goethes Werke. Hamburger Ausgabe*, 5th ed., vol. 13 (Hamburg: Christian Wegner, 1966), p. 616.

29. Emerson, *The Complete Works*, vol. 3, p. 26.

30. Emerson, *The Complete Works*, vol. 8. p. 365.

CONTRIBUTORS

FREDERICK AMRINE is a professor of German Studies at the University of Michigan, Ann Arbor. He has published extensively on Goethe's scientific works and is co-editor, with Harvey Wheeler and Francis J. Zucker, of *Goethe and the Sciences: A Reappraisal* (1987). His most recent work is the multivolume *Goethe in the History of Science* (New York: Peter Lang, 1996, 1997).

JOCHEM BOCKEMÜHL is a botanist and the director of the research laboratory at the Goetheanum in Dornach, Switzerland. He has written many articles on a Goethean approach to plants and is Editor of *Elemente der Naturwissenschaft*, a journal of Goethean research. He has also edited the books *Toward a Phenomenology of the Etheric World* (1985); *Awakening to Landscape*, (1992); and, with A. Suchantke, *The Metamorphosis of Plants* (1995) He is author of *In Partnership with Nature* (1981).

HENRI BORTOFT is a physicist and teacher. He has written *Goethe's Scientific Consciousness* (1986), which is reprinted, along with new material, in *The Wholeness of Nature: Goethe's Science of Conscious Participation in Nature* (1996).

RONALD H. BRADY is a professor of philosophy at Ramapo State University in New Jersey. He has written numerous articles on Goethean science and evolutionary and biological theory.

ALAN P. COTTRELL was professor of Germanic Languages and Literature at the University of Michigan. His books include *Goethe's Faust: Seven Essays* (1976), and *Goethe's View of Evil and the Search for a New Image of Man in our Time* (1982).

WALTER HEITLER was a professor of theoretical physics at the University of Zurich and one of this century's premier physicists. He made major contributions to the quantum theory of radiation and also developed the important London-Heitler theory of covalent bonding. He was the author of many important articles in the field of quantum physics as well as several book-length studies.

HERBERT HENSEL was a physician and professor of physiology at the University of Marburg in Germany. He was widely regarded as an authority on sensory physiology, about which he wrote several books.

NIGEL HOFFMANN teaches environmental philosophy in the environmental science program at the University of Newcastle, Australia. He is currently continuing his environmental research, using the Goethean method, in a broader ecological study of a water environment near Sydney. He is the editor of *Transforming Art*, a journal.

CRAIG HOLDREGE is a biologist who teaches life sciences at the Hawthorne Valley School in upstate New York. He has written *Genetics and the Manipulation of Life: The Forgotten Factor of Context* (1996).

MARK RIEGNER is an ecologist and professor teaching in the environmental studies program at Prescott College in Prescott, Arizona. His interests include phenomenological approaches to ecology, animal morphology, and landscape. He has published numerous articles on these themes in such journals as the *Golden Blade* and *Orion Nature Quarterly*. He is author of *Long-Legged Wading Birds of the North American Wetlands* (1993).

DAVID SEAMON is a professor of architecture at Kansas State University. Trained as a geographer and environment-behavior researcher, he is interested in a phenomenological approach to place, nature, and environmental experience. He is author of *A Geography of the Lifeworld* (1979); and editor of *Dwelling, Place, and Environment* (1985); and, *Dwelling, Seeing, and Designing* (State University of New York Press, 1993).

JOHN WILKES is a sculptor, teacher, and founder of the Flowforms Research Group at Emerson College in Sussex, England. Since the early 1960s, his efforts have largely been directed toward understanding the movement of water. He has discovered and developed the *Flowform method*—a means to design channels that enable rhythmic movement to be generated in water streaming through them. These Flowforms can work as significant features in landscape and architectural design, and examples are now found throughout the world.

ARTHUR ZAJONC is a professor of physics at Amherst College in Massachusetts. He has lectured widely on quantum physics and has written *Catching the Light: The Entwined History of Light and Mind* (1995); and, with George Greenstein, *The Quantum Challenge: Modern Research on the Foundations of Quantum Mechanics* (1997).

INDEX

Italicized pages refer to figures.

Adams, G., 235, 241, 251n.12
African wild ass. *See* ass, African wild
Alembert, J. d', 15
Amrine, F., 6, 33, 315
animal morphology. *See* morphology, animal
animals: and being-in-world, 229–30; and environment, 216–17; intrinsic organizing principle, 178
antelope, 199–200
Anthroposophy, 10n.1. *See also* Steiner, R.
antlers, 197
aperçu, 26, 98, 312
archetypal plant. *See* plant, archetypal
architecture, 13n.39, 167
Aristotle, 40, 90, 100
art: united with science, 129–30, 166–69, 233, 310–13
artiodactyls, ruminant, 192–95
ass, African wild, 189, *189*
Ast, F., 281
August, Duke K., 21

baboon, 208
Bacon, F., 16, 37
Banks, J., 136, 150
Banksia integrifolia (Coast Banksia), 136, 138, 147–62, *150, 152, 153, 154, 155, 156, 157, 158, 159, 160, 161, 163, 164,* 165, 166
banteng, 202
Barfield, O., 260–61
beaver, 187, 202, *204,* 211n.30
belonging, 8, 165, 166, 292, 297n.28; and architecture, 167
Bergson, H., 287

Bildung, 100, 102, 109
birds: threefold classification, 211n.33
bison, *183,* 193, 202
Blake, W., 17
boar, wild, *191*
Bockemühl, J., 7, 115, 130, 135, 170nn.6,7, 171n.26, 174n.53, 315
Bolk, L., 304
bone, intermaxillary, 22, 62
Bortoft, H., 8, 10n.1, 14n.42, 167, 173n.45, 174n.60, 175n.63, 216, 231n.4, 277, 297n.31, 315
bovids, 197–202
Brady, R., 6, 260, 262, 315
buffalo, water, *203*
Böhme, G., 42

camel, 193, *194, 195*
canines, 181
capybara, 202, 204
Cardamine hirsuta (Pennsylvania bittercrest), 116, *117*
caribou, 197
carnivores, 181, *182, 183*; as rhythmic mammals, 185–88; teeth, 186
Cassier, E., 16
cattle, Scottish highland, 194, *195*
Chartres Cathedral, 301
chevrotain, 193, *194*
Chew, G., 279
clocks, 301–2, 304, 310
Coleridge, S., 20, 85
color: conventional science's understanding, 56–59, 75–80; physiological, *5,* 60; psychological meaning, 78–80; science of, 56–57, 73–74; tension between darkness and light, *5,* 19, 42–43, 79–80

319

colored shadows. *See* shadows,
   colored
Condillac, E., 16
Contribution to Optics, 41
Cottrell, A., 8, 255, 315

Darwin, C., 92, 95, 107, 178, 213,
   214–15. *See also* Neo-Darwinism
deer, 188, 197, *198*
delicate empiricism. *See* empiricism,
   delicate
Descartes, R., 16, *59*, 86, 302
Diderot, D., 15, 17
Dreiseitl, H., *244*
Du Bois-Reymond, E., 73

Eckermann, J., 19, 23
ecology, phenomenological, 166
Einstein, A., 279, 304
Emerson, R., 303–4, 312–13
empiricism, delicate, 2–3, 19, 24–25,
   27, 259, 261, 311
Emrich, W., 266
Encyclopédie, 15–16
Enlightenment, 15–18
exact sensorial imagination. *See*
   imagination, exact sensorial

Feyerabend, P., 32, 48n.2
Fichte, J., 41, 47, 165
Ficino, M., 301, 302
Flowforms, 7, 233; creation of,
   238–41; definition, 233; ecological
   value, 241–47; and hydrological
   cycle, 246–47; Sevenfold Cascade,
   247–48; specific forms, 241–43,
   242, 244, 245; and water
   purification, 246–47; vortical
   meander, 239–40, *240*
Fontenelle, B. de, 15, 16

Gadamer, H., 295, 298n.38
Galileo, 56, 63, 64, 72, 85, 97, 302,
   312
gazelle, 199, *200*
Gebert, H., 41
gemsbok, 199

geometry, projective, 235
giraffe, 196, *196*, 229
Glechoma hederacea (ground ivy),
   116, *117*
gnu, 199
goats, 200, *201*
Goethean method. *See* method,
   Goethean
Goethean science. *See* science,
   Goethean
Goethe: alchemical studies, 21;
   anatomical studies, 22; animal as
   world, 213, 216–17; *Auto-*
   biography, 20; botanical studies, 22,
   92–96, 104–7; and color, 41–44,
   56–61, 87–81, 288–90, 292–93;
   colors of sky, 4, 292; and Enlightenment, 15–18; *Faust*, 255–56,
   256–57, 266, 272–73; and geological studies, 43–44; and Hegel,
   19; and intermaxillary bone, 22, 62;
   Italian travels, 21, 261, 262; and
   language, 33–34; *Legacy*, 270–71;
   literary efforts, 21, 255–56, 258,
   262–66, 269–73; and mathematics,
   38, 57, 76; and meteorology, 44;
   and nature, 19, 64, 213; nature and
   art, 167–69, 233–34; and *Natur-*
   philosophie, 18–19; and Newton,
   42–43, 288–91, 292–93; objective
   thinking, 256–58, 259; organic
   world view, 168, 292–95; and
   osteology, 44, 62; participatory
   thinking, 260–62, 292–95; and
   phenomenology, 1–2, 8–10, 13n.36,
   46, 74, 77–78, 84–88, 98–99, 103,
   130–31, 160–61, 169, 291, 292,
   294–95; and philosophy of science,
   32–36, 42; and plant metamorphosis, 22, 61–64, 104–7, 297n.31;
   as poet, 123, 255–56, 257, 258,
   264–66, 269–73; principle of
   polarity, 4, 5, 179, 208; and Schiller,
   21, 23, 62, 95–96, 97; and scientific
   work, 22–23; and seeing, 9–10,
   126–27, 262–64, 292–95; and self-
   knowledge, 10, 45–46, 257,

258–60, 264, 268–69, 271, 292–95; and sensory experience, 71, 72–73, 259, 262–64, 292–93; stages in understanding nature, 21–23, 131–36, 292–95; theory of perception, 40–42, 72–74; unity of the organism, 216–17; vertebral theory of skull, 23; and Weimar court, 21–22; and wholeness, 229–30
gorilla, 206, *207*
granite, 43, 44
guanaco, 193, *194*

Haekel, E., 92
hand, 180
Hanson, N. R., 32, 33, 49n.6, 312
Hegel, G., 18, 19, 20, 39, 165
Hegge, H., 39
Heidegger, M., 9, 84, 170n.11, 171n.58, 294, 297n.28
Heinemann, F., 12n.36, 130
Heitler, W., 6, 55, 315–16
Helmholtz, H., 73
Hensel, H., 6, 71, 316
Herder, J., 20, 39, 95, 261
hermeneutics, 292, 295
hippopotamus, 191–92, *191, 192*
Hoffmeister, J., 75
Hoffmann, N., 7, 129, 316
hog, wart, 195, *195*
Holbach, P. d', 17
Holdrege, C., 7, 213, 316
holograms, 278–79, 283–84
Hopkins, G. M., 299
horn-bearing ruminants. *See* ruminants, horn-bearing
horns, 193–95, *195*, 200, 214–15
horse, 188, 193, 196, 213, 217–18, 218–19, *220, 221*, 222–24, *225*, 226, 227, 228
Howard, L., 23
human morphology. *See* morphology, human
Humboldt, A. von, 23, 172n.31
Hume, D., 37
Husserl, E., 2, 9, 13n.37, 71, 84, 86

imagination, exact sensorial, 133, 159, 230–31, 291
impala, 199
incisors, 181
Institute for Flow Sciences, 234
intentionality, 13n.37, 86–88
intermaxillary bone. *See* bone, intermaxillary

Jacobi, F., 46
Joiner, A., 243, *245*
Järna, Sweden, 243, 245, *246*

Kammerlingh Onnes, H., 309
Kant, E., 37, 58, 65, 85, 90–91, 103–4, 242–43; *Critique of Judgment*, 90; understanding of organism, 90–91
Keats, J., 17
Kepler, J., 66
Klettenberg, S. von, 21
Klingborg, A., 245
Kuhn, T., 34–36, 45, 84
Kunzea ambigua (tick-bush) 136, 138–47, *139, 140, 141, 142, 143, 144, 145, 148, 149*, 165, 166

La Mettrie, J., 17
Land, E., 50n.20
Lapsana communis (nipplewort), 118–26, *120, 123, 125, 126*
leaf: four activities, 117–19; transformation, 116
leopard, *183*, 186–87
light, 5, 12n.31, 299, 304–8; delayed-choice experiment, 304–8; interferometry experiment, 306–7; wave-particle duality, 304–8
Linnaeus, C., 61, 177–78
lion, 205, *205*, 213, 218, *220, 221*, 222, *225*, 226, 227, 228
lion, sea, 206, *207*
Locke, J., 16

Mach, E., 279
mammals, 177; principle of threefoldness, 179–80; teeth as expression of threefoldness, 181

marmoset, 206, *207*, 208
marten, 205
mathematics, 38, *57–58*, 75, 291
Medawar, P. B., 34, 40
Medicago sativa, 119, *121*
Mephistopheles, 67, 211, 266, 268,
    272
Merleau-Ponty, M., 9, 84
metamorphosis, 36–37, 46, 138, 234;
    leaf, 237, 238
Metamorphosis of Plants, 36, 61, 95
method, Goethean, 2–5, 36–42,
    57–59, 74–77, 130–36, 310–11
method, scientific, 32–36, 40; and
    objectivity, 45
Metz, J. F., 21
molars, 181
monkey, 208
moose, 197, *198*
morphology, animal, 180
mouse, Old World harvest, 182–83,
    183
muskox, 200, *201*, 202
Müller, J., 72

Natura, 301, 303
nature, phenomenology of, 2, 8–10,
    130, 167–69
Naturphilosophie, 18–20, 83
Neo-Darwinism, 214–15
Newton, I., 5, 6, 15, 16, 17, 33, 38,
    41, 42, 48n.2, 55, 56, 66, 288–90,
    292–93, 312
Nordenskiold, E., 83
Novalis, F., 20, 238

Old World harvest mouse. *See* mouse,
    Old World harvest
optics, quantum, 299–300
orangutan, 206
Oresme, N., 302

paca, 202, *204*
Palm, H., 247
Paracelsus, 21
paradigm, scientific, 34–36
Parmenides, 72

Pearson, K., 45
peccary, 190–91, *191*
pecoran, 193, 196–97
phenomenological ecology. *See*
    ecology, phenomenological
phenomenology, 1–2, 8–10, 11n.3,
    13nn.36,37,39, 46, 60, 71, 74, 77,
    84–88, 98–99, 103, 136, 166, 169;
    existential, 9, 13n.39; Goethean,
    233–34, 291, 294–95; of plants,
    129–30; and science, 88–90,
    165–67, 290–92
physics, 56, 279; quantum, 279, 300,
    307–9; quantum superposition state,
    308–9
pinnipeds, 206
plant, archetypal (*Urpflanze*), 4,
    39–40, 61–64, 83, 92–96, 104, 115,
    127, 234, 261, 267; gesture,
    134–35, 165; as theory, 165–66,
    297n.31; transformation, 115–17;
    wholeness of, 297n.31
Plotinus, 20
point, pregnant, 39, 162, 165,
    173n.44, 267
polarity, principle of, 179
Popper, K., 35
Portmann, A., 229
positivism, 34–36, 72
pregnant point. *See* point, pregnant
primary qualities. *See* qualities,
    primary
projective geometry. *See* geometry,
    projective
pronghorn, 200, *201*

qualities, primary, 72–74; science of,
    39; secondary, 72–74, 85
quantum optics. *See* optics, quantum
quantum physics. *See* physics,
    quantum

rainbow, 299
Ranunculus acris (common buttercup),
    93, *94*, 105–6, *107*
reductionism, scientific, 34, 269–70,
    288

Reenpää, Y., 71
Renaissance, 302
rhinoceros, 188, 189–90, *189*, 193–94, *195*
Ribe, N., 43
Riegner, M., 7, 14n.39, 166, 172n.33, 174n.52, 177, 209n.3, 233, 316
Robertson, J. G., 169n.1
rodents, 181–83, *182, 183*; compared with ungulates, 185
Romanticism, 17
ruminant artiodactyls. *See* artiodactyls, ruminant
ruminants, horn- and antler-bearing, 195–97

Saint Francis, 261–62
Sartre, J. P., 84
Schad, W., 7, 178–79, 180–81, 200, 206, 208, 294–95
Schelling, F., 17
Schleiermacher, F., 281
Schwenk, T., 7, 11n.1, 234–35, 238, 243
Schiller, F., 21, 23, 62, 95–96, 97, 310–11
science, Goethean, 2–4, 10n.1, 20–23; compared to conventional science, 56–57, 83–86, 88–90, 288–91; form vs. function, 214–15; stages, 131–36, 310–11
science: hypothetico-deductive method, 34, 39–40, 44–45, 287–90; philosophy of, 32–36, 40–41, 45, 83–84; united with art, 129–30, 166–69
scientific method. *See* method, scientific
Scottish highland cattle. *See* cattle, Scottish highland
sea lion. *See* lion, sea
seal, 206
Seamon, D., 1, 11n.4, 14n.14, 41, 316
secondary qualities. *See* qualities, secondary
seeing, 2–3, 84–88, 127, 271–73, 285–87, 289–95, 299, 310–13

sensation, 71–74
senses, 3, 71, 77–81, 85
shadows, colored, 58
sheep, 200, *201*
Sisymbrian officinale (hedge mustard), 120–21, *122*
Spiegelberg, H., 11n.3, 13nn.36,37
Splechtner, F., 115
Stegmüller, W., 77
Steiner, R., 10n.1, 110n.2, 175n.66, 179, 180, 209n.6, 234
superconductivity, 304, 309–10
Sus babirusa, 213, *214*
Sydney, Australia, 136

tamarin, 208
tapir, 189, *189*, 192
technology, 66–68, 269–70, 301–2, 304, 310, 312–13
Thales, 301
theoria, 311
Theory of Color (Zur Farbenlehre), 5–6, 9, 12nn.25,32, 13n.36, 19, 23, 24, 25, 26, 37–38, 42–43, 46, 55, 60, 61, 63, 67, 75, 78, 271, 289–91
Thomas, N., 248
Thoreau, H., 17–18, 304

ungulates, 180, *182, 183*, 184–85; compared with rodents, 185; nonruminant artiodactyls, 190–92; nonruminants, 188; perissodactyls, 180–90; ruminants, 188; threefold relationships, 202, *203*
Urpflanze. See plant, archetypal
ur-phenomenon (*Ur-Phänomen*), 4, 25–26, 39–40, 41, 44, 59–60, 75–76, 80–81, 290, 291–93, 311; of plant, 4, 39–40, 42, 61–64, 83, 92–96, 104, 115, 127, 165–66, 234, 261, 267, 297n.31

Valerianella locusta (corn salad), 118–19, *118*
vicuna, 193
Voltaire, F., 14

walrus, 206, *207*
wart hog. *See* hog, wart
water, 234; and formative processes,
    238; lemniscate pattern, 239; and
    life processes, 234–35; purification,
    246–47; spiralling patterns, 236,
    238
water buffalo. *See* buffalo, water
weasel, 188, 203–4, *205*
Weizsäcker, C. von, 76
Wells, N., 243, 247
Wheeler, J., 304
White, L., Jr., 302, 310
whole, 8, 13n.35, 165, 168–69,
    173n.45, 226–27, 277, 282–87; as
    active absence, 285–87; arithemetic
    of, 283–84

wholeness, 285–87; authentic,
    291–93; examples of, 226–27,
    277–82; of landscape, 165;
    participating in, 168, 281–87,
    291–93; of plant, 297n.31; in
    science, 287–89, 291–92
Whyte, L. L., 9, 14n.40, 168–69
wild boar. *See* boar, wild
wildebeest, 199, *200*
Wilkes, J., 7–8, 233, 235, 238, 247,
    248, 316

yak, 193, *194*

Zajonc, A., 2, 6, 8, 12n.31, 14, 258,
    316
zebra, 188, 189, 174n.58